Harrier

Harrier

How To Be a Fighter Pilot

COMMANDER PAUL TREMELLING

MICHAEL JOSEPH

PENGUIN MICHAEL JOSEPH

UK | USA | Canada | Ireland | Australia
India | New Zealand | South Africa

Penguin Michael Joseph is part of the Penguin Random House group of companies
whose addresses can be found at global.penguinrandomhouse.com

First published by Penguin Michael Joseph, 2022
001

The views and opinions expressed are those of the author alone and should not be taken to represent
those of Her Majesty's Government, MOD, HM Armed Forces or any government agency.

Set in 13.5/16pt Garamond MT Std
Typeset by Jouve (UK), Milton Keynes
Printed and bound in Great Britain by Clays Ltd, Elcograf S.p.A.

The authorized representative in the EEA is Penguin Random House Ireland,
Morrison Chambers, 32 Nassau Street, Dublin D02 YH68

A CIP catalogue record for this book is available from the British Library

HB ISBN: 978–0–241–55704–4
OM PAPERBACK ISBN: 978–0–241–55705–1

www.greenpenguin.co.uk

Contents

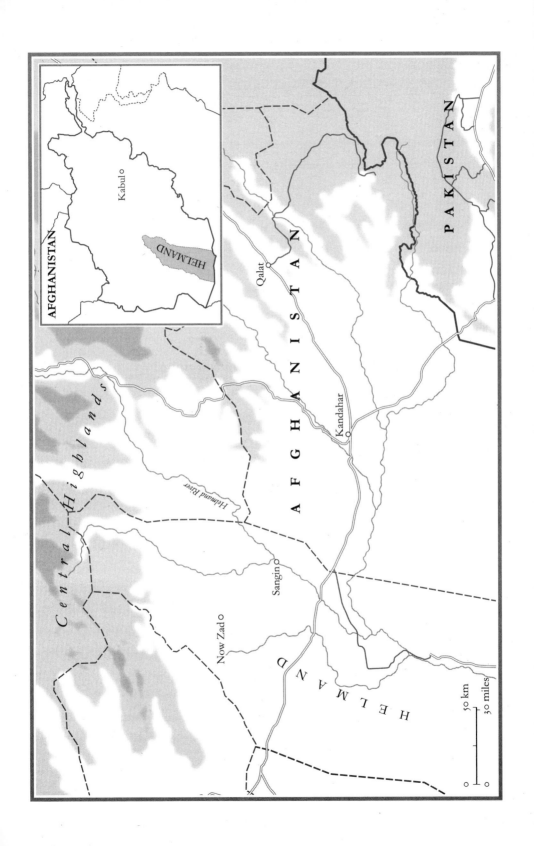

AFGHANISTAN

Kabul

HELMAND

PAKISTAN

Qalat

Kandahar

Central Highlands

Helmand River

Sangin

Now Zad

HELMAND

30 km

30 miles

Prologue: Night Trap

South-west of San Diego, more sober than a judge.

Wrapped in the dark, I was snug in the cockpit of the F/A-18E Super Hornet. Outside the canopy, the engines howled as I had one last check around the cockpit.

Half an hour earlier, the catapult shot that had launched me into the night had been as brutal as ever. By selecting my lights to FULL BRIGHT I had announced that I was ready in all respects for launch from the USS *Carl Vinson*, one of the US Navy's 100,000-ton nuclear-powered aircraft carriers. Pressing my head back against the seat box, I had waited, my eyes fixed ahead on the head-up display but for almost unconscious glances down at the engine instruments. With my left arm locked on the twin throttle levers, I maintained the power throughout the violence of the shot. I'd gathered myself for the end of the stroke and disappeared into the total darkness of the Pacific. From dimly lit ship to absolute void.

For about fifteen minutes I trespassed into the darkness to wait for the 'Blue Air' attacking force to make their move. My job was to act as last line of defence behind another screen of Hornets. And then things went awry at the boat. Two of the four arrestor wires that we required to land on deck had decided not to play. To add to the fun, the low cloud of the marine layer had formed more quickly than usual. We were recalled.

My job now was to know and follow the procedures

and, above all else, to obey the landing signals officer. I trusted him, he trusted me.

Leaving the tactical frequency to say hello to the ship, I got my instructions:

'104, your signal is Marshal.'

'104,' I acknowledged. I made my way to the stack of aircraft waiting to get back on board. I ran through my pre-landing checklist. First up, hook DOWN. The metallic thump told me that the arrestor hook that would, I hoped, catch one of the two remaining wires, was lowered. It was game time.

I told myself that there was nothing I could do about the 3 and 4 wires being missing. All I could do was fly the pattern and let the LSO drop me on the deck at the right point. No point getting too bunched about something you can't control.

Fixing on the ship's tactical air navigation beacon, the TACAN, I entered the hold, occasionally catching glimpses of other jets – all of us allocated to hard heights with 1,000 feet between us. Mainly I saw blackness. The odd star. From somewhere in the darkness below, Marshal was telling me which radial to hold on and from which direction to approach. And with that, I had all I needed to get myself into the right place for one of the more high-end manoeuvres in aviation: the night trap. Trials conducted by the US Navy during the Vietnam War revealed that landing back aboard the carrier at night was more stressful than getting shot at over enemy territory. I could believe it.

I was lucky, though. For whatever reason, I didn't experience 'the fear' that seemed to envelop some of my colleagues. I thought that the night simplified things. I only needed to worry about three things: *meatball*,[1] *line-up* and *angle of attack*. At night they were the only things I could see. Everything else could simply go to the bit of the brain marked Temporarily Irrelevant.

It was a big ship, but the mind plays tricks on you when you're trying to land jets on boats. The challenge was convincing yourself the boat would at some point interrupt your descent through the darkness and prevent you flying into the sea when every instinct was telling you otherwise. It hardly needed saying that in naval aviation even small mistakes could be fatal.

Leaving the holding pattern, I reset my radar altimeter as I passed 5,000 feet.

'Platform,' I confirmed, as I halved my rate of descent and switched on my fuel dumps. I needed to be at max trap weight when I got to the ship. The time to hold on to excess fuel had been and gone.

Timing, fuel, jet were in good order. Engaging both altitude hold and auto throttle, I let the jet do this bit.

I heard a jet ahead of me come back on frequency.

'206, your signal is Bingo!' he was told.

Somewhere out ahead, that boy would be climbing to height, conserving fuel and making for North Island. Bingo meant you were going ashore. I knew the pilot. If he hadn't snagged a wire . . . what hope did I have? Was it the wires, or was it the marine layer that had caused him to miss?

---

1 The 'meatball' or 'ball' is the light signal used by the pilot to land on a conventional carrier.

The anxiety mounted. Just like every one of the 240-plus deck landings before.[2] Just like every weapon event. Just like every intercept.

Following the TACAN, I could see what had to be the ship out in the blackness. A small collection of lights. Where they said she'd be. Where I'd trusted she'd be. I had my approach aids on, and they gave me additional steering cues. Tonight they agreed – I could trust them both.

As I reached the pushover point it was, yet again, time to descend towards the sea. Still out there but still invisible in the blackness. I clicked out the automatics. Time to do some flying.

'104, 0.7 miles, call the ball,'[3] came the instruction.

The ball and datums were bright and clear. The ball was where it needed to be. If you can't be good, be smooth; if you can't be smooth, be high. My left hand established a cadence of small corrections. More power, off a little, reapply.

'104, Rhino ball,[4] 3.8, Tremelling.'

'Roger, ball.' The LSO's voice far gentler than normal. They were working hard but needed me to be as calm as the situation allowed.

About half a mile behind them, strapped to 44,000lbs of metal and fuel, calm was probably the wrong word to

---

2 Although I did quite enjoy my seventy-first.

3 The instruction 'Call the ball' simply meant that I had to confirm I could see the meatball.

4 Codeword for 'I am flying a Super Hornet and can see the ball'. Aircraft type was vital information the ship needed to get the weight setting right for the arrested landing gear wires.

use. The jet was set up for the approach, and I followed my usual pattern of trimming forwards to avoid going slow. With the stick I stayed aligned on the angled landing area as it seemed to move sideways and away.

Meatball, line-up, angle of attack.

It sounds obvious, but the trick was to fly the parameters and assume the few lights you could see were attached to a ship. On this occasion, though, being high wasn't going to work. I had to be good.

'Little power,' Paddles called as I sank by the tiniest of margins. I added a bit of power. My knowledge that I had to snag the first two wires, or follow the procession of boys and girls bingoing, directly opposed my desire to obey. But obey I did: I applied power. On – off – back on. I consciously told myself to ignore the nerves. My field of vision contracted as my pulse rate rose.

In close, I could see the ship. The hulking superstructure. Jets either side of the landing area. I crossed the round down and I was over steel. As I stared at it, the meatball indicated that I was flying 'on and on' all the way to touchdown. My part of the game. The ship went from something I was flying towards to something that surrounded and contained me. Then *bang*. But if proof were needed that I was more tightly wound than usual, it came when the hard impact with the flight deck felt almost benign.

With my left hand I advanced the throttle to military thrust as the jet screamed down the landing area, towards the 60-foot drop to the sea off the front. In theory I should now be attached to the carrier, but if the tailhook had failed to catch one of those two remaining wires I would need full power to fly off the deck again rather than take an unwelcome swim. But in the time it took to sense the wheels hit the deck, and to slam to full power, my heart racing, I was caught. The sudden, massive deceleration was accompanied by the usual physical assault of what amounted to a controlled crash, but also an unusually high dose of in-cockpit euphoria.

I looked for the marshaller, who was giving me 'throttle back'.

'Lights!' came the gentle reminder from Pri Fly. 'Relax, 104, we got you!' The calm and friendly voice reminding me to dim my navigation lights.

I'll forgive myself for having forgotten that small detail.

Exhale.

I was playing with the big boys.

1. Lighting the Touchpaper

Somewhere in Somerset there is a Royal Naval Air Station. It is called either RNAS Yeovilton or Her Majesty's Ship *Heron* – in keeping with the Royal Navy's habit of over-complicating things.[1] The nuance as to why it needed two names was explained to me and others frequently by my father, who was serving there in 1982 as the operations officer.[2] My father had once flown helicopters, but I had no idea what his current job entailed. However, his office was in the air traffic control tower, which meant that occasionally we would go inside the wire and get to see personnel and machines at a far closer range than the public could. We also got to watch Air Day, and the arrivals the day prior, from the tower roof. If you are reading this and once arrived for Yeovilton Air Day in about 1982 in a US Air Force F-15 and decided to stick the jet on its tail, light the blowers and disappear into the wide blue yonder, you made my day and Dad's too. He came barrelling from the door yelling, 'Did you see the F-15?' as if he'd just got Van Halen's signature.

---

1 And staunchly defending the necessity to over-complicate.
2 This was probably a crunchy job for someone who was going places. I suspect a later appointment to Yeovilton as the air training officer was not a crunchy job given to someone no longer on such a gradient.

Rightly so, what a jet. The vortices streaming from the wingtips were sights to behold.

However, in the main my view of the air station was exactly the same as that of the average punter and usually involved being the wrong side of the chainlink, waiting with Mum for Dad to arrive, desperately hoping that whatever was making the jet engine noise would present itself at some point. There was usually a fair bit of heli-copter traffic around. I liked seeing the Junglies.[3] Indeed, my boyhood hero 'Crabbers' was a Junglie and he lived just up the road. His hero status was actually due to him pulling his gear stick out of its mounting and waving it at us on the A303 when he and Dad were having a race to the bar rather than his being a Junglie. It was the jets that my brother and I wanted to see, and, despite lots of noise, close-up sightings weren't common. Those at Yeo-vilton were called Sea Harriers, and I had no connection to them whatsoever. I didn't know that they were new, but I do have a memory of Dad explaining an early Har-rier crash by saying that the pilots were unfamiliar with some of the type's flying characteristics.

I loved my trips to Yeovilton. We lived locally, and it was a matter of great pride to me that I had a connection with the air station. My best friend at primary school was Toby. His father was ex-Fleet Air Arm and a test pilot at Westlands in Yeovil. Toby and I used to fail miserably to hide our jealousy when one of us had a cooler poster

3 The RN Commando Helicopter Force, probably called something different in those days and mainly made up of Wessex 5s, which looked great.

or sticker than the other. Toby's dad even managed to 'out-cool' Crabbers on one occasion by illuminating our house with a searchlight while night flying. It would be fair to say that we were enthusiasts, but very much in the 'I like the look of aeroplanes' sense as opposed to understanding what they actually did.

Until 1982, we only saw the machines. We didn't see the people who flew them and certainly couldn't extrapolate flying to operating.[4] Still, we were seven – so what do you expect? However, if you'd asked me then what I wanted to be, I'd have said that I wanted to be a pilot.

One day in April we went to pick my father up, and everything changed. We used to park just to the west of the Fleet Air Arm Museum in a car park which is still there to this day. This time, things began to stir behind the chainlink fence. The noise was greater than normal. Jets were moving. Sea Harriers with cockpits open, held back by pilots' elbows, began to taxi. From my standpoint, looking south across the airfield, they were moving from right to left, towards what I found out a mere fifteen years later was the approach end threshold of Runway 27. I remember the whine of the Rolls-Royce Pegasus engines and I remember the pitch and volume varying as the pilots appeared to 'run them up'. I now know that they were filling fuel galleries, timing the engine's acceleration and checking that the engine inlet guide vanes[5] were moving in sympathy with RPM increase,

4 Flying is a purely physical act of defeating gravity. Operating is actually using the machine for its intended purpose.
5 These direct the inlet air flow into the compressor at the correct angle.

checking the clockwise movement of the indicator needles on small dials above their right knee. For me this was marvellous, and it wasn't just one or two jets; there were lots. I obviously didn't see the canopies close and wouldn't have been aware that the pilots were removing their pins from their ejection seats as they completed their last sets of checks. I forgot to do that once – but more of that later. I do remember seeing the jets launch from the westerly runway, in pairs. I didn't see them turn for Portsmouth, but their outline and the famous anhedral[6] of the Sea Harrier wing were from then on forever stitched into my grey matter. If you asked me then, and any day of my life from then on, what I wanted to be, I'd have said that I wanted to be a Sea Harrier pilot.

What I didn't find out about until the following morning, at the breakfast table, was that there was a very good reason for the activity we'd seen. My dad described it to Mum as 'Trouble in South America', which is a masterpiece of geographical inaccuracy and understatement. The jets were going to the Falkland Islands. I followed the conflict as best a seven-year-old could in 1982. I kept a scrapbook of all the newspaper clippings I could gather. Somewhat annoyingly, my elder brother did too, and that meant, whenever there was an image that we both wanted, me running across the close to Mrs Pakes, who also read the *Daily Telegraph*, to beg to be allowed to

---

6 Downwards-sloping. I've lived my life using various ways to make remembering things easier. The downwards slope of an anhedral wing looks like an A. The upwards slope of a dihedral wing looks to me like a D on its side.

cut it out of her paper. The coolest picture of the campaign wasn't of a jet, it was of paratroopers festooned with ammunition smiling at the camera after a battle – Goose Green, I seem to recall. I remember writing a story at school about the conflict and how we won – before we had. I clearly remember a friend asking how I knew we were going to win, for which my answer was as intellectual as 'just because'. But winning was very much a soccer score – we'd blown up more aircraft than they had and had therefore won before they could sink all of our ships. No sense of the excitement and horrors of warfare, or any idea of the infantry engagements that actually decided the matter.

If I'm ever asked about why I joined the military I tell that cute but 100 per cent true story. That a touchpaper was lit watching the jets as they left for CORPORATE,[7] the campaign to retake the islands. There is another side, though. Many young people go through the 'drawing jets' stage of liking aeroplanes, and aviation as a whole seems to fascinate people, otherwise museums wouldn't attract anyone – but these people don't join up. I was helped by having a father involved in aviation, but I didn't want to be involved in aviation. I wanted to fly the Sea Harrier. Not mend them, not fulfil any of the countless roles without which they wouldn't leave the ground (or ship), nor fly something else beside them. I wanted to fly the Sea Harrier. And for a couple of reasons that was, in retrospect, not going to be without

7 Couldn't possibly have a related op name for the conflict; that would mean passing up the opportunity to confuse the issue.

its challenges – even without revisiting the point that a seven-year-old has no idea whatsoever what operating a fighter aircraft actually entails. Neither do any children or adolescents. Then again, neither do a lot of grown-up people; most are sensible enough to admit it. Sadly, as I was going to discover the hard way, a vast swathe of the military and indeed military aviators have no idea what it takes to operate a fighter. In fact, it's simpler to say that the fighter pilots do, and that's it.

I wasn't even dissuaded from my Fixed Wing myopia by a rather wonderful gift from Crabbers. He went south and brought us back a belt of fired-out 7.62mm ammunition and an Argentinian helmet. The Argie helmet was a strange thing. It was of the American pattern but was made of some form of fibreglass rather than metal. It also had a bright-red cross on it and 'Aly's' written on the side in marker pen. I hope Aly got home safely. My godfather also went south as the second-in-command of the frigate HMS *Plymouth*, which had a rare old time in San Carlos Water – taking five unexploded bombs inboard. Uncle Iain gave me a picture of HMS *Plymouth* as a gift, taken by a RAF Jaguar on the way home. That picture's pretty cool , but let's be honest, the helmet and 7.62mm are cooler. Given that I was seven, and my closest point of approach to the Falkland Islands could be measured in thousands of miles, it is hard to define exactly what my connection to the conflict was, save for seeing the jets off. But the jet I had made my life's mission to fly was as inextricably bound to the Falklands War as the Spitfire was to the Battle of Britain. As my career unfolded, I began to understand more and more of what the people who went south would have faced. I would make a point, therefore, of taking offence if anyone (and this mainly happened in the US Navy) referred to the islands using the M-word.[8]

There was one further prod.

I have often said to people that the only difference between me walking to the jet at the air show and them watching is that I filled out the form. How many other little boys and girls wanted to do it, could have made it, but simply never applied? I filled out the form, and it wasn't to do with the Falkland Islands, although the Sea Harrier remained the dream. It was a book that I read when I was bored in Taunton, where I went away to boarding school. There wasn't much to do on 'town leave' when we boarders were allowed to venture into town and even less to do if you didn't smoke. So I used to go to WH Smith and read the books. The military history and aviation books. I don't know the precise book I was reading but I can tell you what the precise picture was. A grainy black and white picture of a young mother and two young children. It was captioned 'A family who have been chosen to die wait patiently outside the gas chamber'. That picture is why I went to the careers office – which I was very lucky to have at my school – and filled out my application form to join the Fleet Air Arm. If people could do those sorts of things to other people, I thought I'd have a crack at standing in the way.

8 Rhymes with Lalvinas.

2. Live from the Dit Cauldron

Royal Naval fighter squadrons have always (well – since the advent of radars) enjoyed the services of a fighter controller, or FC. This officer is essentially in charge of pointing you in the direction of the enemy, the little tinkers being quite hard to track down on your own. This is of no great relevance to this book other than it was a fighter controller who once made the astute observation that in the Royal Navy – and the same is true of the wider defence community – we do not converse as other humans do. We simply tell stories. Any attempt at enlightened discussion always ends, usually after only a few seconds, in a descent into storytelling. Each story is linked either directly, tenuously or not at all with the preceding and succeeding one. For reasons lost in time, which a more conscientious author would have at least attempted to identify, the Navy calls these stories dits. We do not tell dits, we spin them. Telling would simply not be enough. The best story ever could be ruined by a poor telling.

Spinning dits comes with a few guidelines. The established dit litany is fairly simple: you must simply state a geographic datum for the dit, followed by the amount of alcohol that had been consumed immediately prior to the events that are about to be explained – as many will come from a unit's downtime. One might, for example, regale one's friends with tales of derring do[1] by starting out with the line 'There we were, in Los Angeles, absolutely ring bolted.' Dits invariably grow a little, potentially for effect, or more likely because the spinner's own memory of the event is slightly skewed, and the scientifically proven fact that there is nothing quite as unreliable as an eyewitness. Other than a Eurofighter Typhoon, but I digress.

The last paragraph contains an interesting implication. The good dits have a massive, sometimes heroic failure in them somewhere. Beware the man who only has 'I'm ace, I am' dits: he is probably not ace in the slightest. The very best dits are spun in a very self-deprecating manner, as to err is human and to talk about oneself is the favourite hobby among aircrew, and stories revolving around military aviation, or booze, and infrequently both together, are bound to have some hefty fallout when things go awry!

There isn't a definitive record of dits, no compendium of military misdemeanour and misadventure.[2] There won't be after this book either – but at least some will be captured.

My story goes something like: 'I wanted to fly the Sea Harrier – so I joined the RN, made it to the Sea Harrier frontline, then went to the Harrier GR9, then flew a tour with the United States Navy and then left having had a hoot and a roar.' The simple narrative is

1 Or derring fuck-up – some of the best dits have some form of totally avoidable calamity at their epicentre.
2 Let's face it, it would take one statute assload of work.

important – but I want to flesh out the 'who we were and what we got up to' bit by way of dits. I started writing them down while sitting in my cabin on a French aircraft carrier. Convinced that there was more to life than simply cocking around in fighter aircraft, or indeed wading through the turgid existence of a staff officer, I decided to write out my entire dit cauldron. There I was, waiting to go to war, delayed by two weeks due to the minor inconvenience of the nuclear reactor needing to be fixed. I had twelve weeks, a memory and a laptop. I was egged on by Patrick Hennessey's excellent tome *The Junior Officers' Reading Club*, to which I reacted with the single-seat fighter community's traditional response to just about anything: 'Fuck it, I could do that.' The writing bit, not the whole being ludicrously fit and brave thing.

I offer you the air warfare instructor's guarantee that I was there for them all. It is nowadays an oft trotted-out line, but the dits may not be 100 per cent accurate, because I may have misremembered them, but what I write is what I think is the truth. Feel free to chip in if you think you have more SA[3] than I. If anything I have written really offends you, then I am prepared to take written complaints from anyone who has a warfare instructor qualification, who has dropped a bomb on Her Majesty's foes and landed a single-engine jet on a deck at night.[4] I'm not one of those people who thinks

---

3 Situational awareness – that priceless commodity which every fighter pilot requires but somehow Milhouse got through an entire career without.

4 I've landed twin-engine jets on the deck at night too, if anyone is counting!

you have to end a discussion in perfect agreement. I have used footnotes[5] where I think something needs explanation or fleshing out. And for fun.

Not all of my opinions have survived, and if any of them, written as they were at the time, seem 'somewhat brusque', it may be a consequence of working my nuts off to get to a frontline that wasn't particularly well understood by its own service, which twice took a hammering in defence cuts, and yet was one of the finest fighting forces that the UK could muster. A loyal gun dog will take as many kicks as its master cares to give it, but they all hurt and they are all remembered.

5 As demonstrated thus.

3. Britannia Royal Naval College

We could always find a way of having a couple.
On occasion, we had a lot more than a couple.

To someone who joined the Royal Navy essentially because of CORPORATE, and the Sea Harrier's performance in that fight, certain things took me a bit by surprise once I had joined up. I'll try to explain.

Joining itself was quite straightforward. I duly filled out the forms after my WH Smith epiphany and completed the Admiralty Interview Board. I was awarded a bursary, which helped towards university. I had wanted a cadetship, which would have meant completing Britannia Royal Naval College then going to university – but I didn't put in a good enough performance at AIB so got second best and did it the other way around. When you ain't good enough, you take it on the chin – 'kill acknowledged'. The RN even gave me a flying scholarship, which I undertook at Bodmin. Leaving school and learning to fly all at once gave me a great sense that there was a wider world out there.

University[1] came and went. I joined BRNC in September 1996 and had some of the greatest instructors the RN could muster, and some others; alongside me were some of the sharpest youths in the country and some

---

1 I studied, in the loosest interpretation of the word, Aeronautics and Astronautics at Southampton.

absolute bin juice. In the July immediately before entry I had completed the 'Bursars[2] Acquaint Course', which was essentially a cheeky head start for those being sponsored through university. It involved a potted first couple of terms at Dartmouth, including ironing, polishing, inspecting, boats, a trip to Dartmoor and a visit to Commando Training Centre Royal Marines, where we got beasted on the infamous lower field. I loved the bursars' course and met great people – a theme that would continue.

BRNC was fine so long as you could stay awake and get your head around the concept that teamwork involved adopting the speed of the slowest ship. If you were fit and wanted to run up the infamous (by Navy standards) Sandquay steps, you would be criticized, because a team player would wait for the unfit. At the same time, if you were appointed as a leader and you asked anyone other than the good fit lads to carry the heavy stuff, you got criticized. If you were on top of your admin and had all your kit squared away for inspection but someone else hadn't, you had to hide yours so that you all looked the same. If you were caught hiding kit, you were punished. Punished for being on top of things! Punishments were menial – things like litter patrols – but it did seem odd to be 'picked up' for being fitter, more organized, just basically better than the lowest common denominator. Weird.

Now luckily there was a raft of good lads on this sea of mediocrity, and they could all be found on the rugby pitch. For whatever reason, my role models among

2 I think that the apostrophe was missing – which is a good thing. They'd have put it in the wrong place.

the great commissioned instructors all played. There were a couple of really decent chief petty officers too – one was called Bob, a physical training instructor, and the other Nick, who taught NBCD.[3] I think Nick might actually have been a corruption of his surname. Nick was the sort of bloke that if you were up against 40 Commando and the other back row contained members of the RN first team, you still didn't worry because you had Goliath at your side. We held our own against everyone other than Brixham, who brought their own Goliath with them. We slayed the Ecole Navale, we held Sandhurst to within a handful of points and we got to play an incredibly rough match against Newton Abbot prison, during which someone stamped so hard on my spine that they chipped a bit of bone off – resulting in a numb right arm for a couple of weeks.

Rugby aside, there were, however, a couple of minor issues beginning to emerge at BRNC. Nothing major, but signs of things to come. My divisional officer had said in his very first meeting with me that the world considered the Fleet Air Arm to be 'up themselves'. Next came my presentation on Sea Harrier ops during COR-PORATE. When I presented the Sea Harrier as the Task Force's 'first and best defence' based upon statistics I'd found in open source, the reviewing officer was quick to remind me that it was 'just a weapon system'. Fair enough. Thought as much. It was almost as if the inner workings of the RN wanted to suppress the Fleet

3 Nuclear, Biological, Chemical and Damage Control. How to deal with the nasty stuff. Put out fires and bung up holes in warships.

Air Arm contribution to the Falklands War and various other crises just as much as I thought they should be celebrated! The amount of aviation fitted into the course can be seen by the fact that during my entire year at Dartmouth we had one Fleet Air Arm day, when helicopters parked on the sports pitches, and we had one visit from some trainee observers.

The next such event was the news delivered by the flight training officer that there was only one Sea Harrier slot for our entry – and we had a bumper entry for aircrew – about thirty of us. This was on the face of it 'not good', even though one of us had to get the one-in-thirty opportunity: 3.3 per cent. The bearer of the news was a typically uninspiring anti-submarine warfare type. Not a bad person and probably very good at his job but without much flair or élan. That wasn't the worrying bit. The worrying bit was that this was the latest in an extraordinarily long line of people who weren't there to help you fulfil your Fixed Wing dreams – they were there to piss on them. Not so much deliberately obstructive but more 'I don't know why you're bothering – it's either unlikely or impossible.'

My own personal issue was that 'dash and panache' were often mistaken at Dartmouth for a cavalier attitude (fair) and arrogance (unfair). Dartmouth was very much the spiritual home of the grey man. I had a great civilian tutor whose name I have long since forgotten. He pulled me aside one day to ask if I had been taking training seriously enough. It struck me as a strange thing to ask! It turns out I'd had a rather odd report written on me. It was term 2. We'd done all the sleep deprivation stuff and the 'logs, planks, barrels' stuff and the aggressive camping on Dartmoor and were now doing leadership exercises based around the river. These were great fun, and with a few of my better buddies always in the same team we were breezing it. That meant we didn't have the spotlight on us and got the fun roles in the exercises.

For one night exercise, I was 'picket boat captain', which meant I had to drive a boat around and do some tasks – easy-peasy. The first was to get a message from a secret agent who was to be found wandering about on the jetty at Dittisham. As secret agents do. No dramas. There was quite a strong ebb tide adding to the river flow, but this was going to be quite straightforward, and the instructions called for us to anchor off and send in a couple of people in our skiff (a small rowing boat). As I approached in the inky blackness, number three in a column of eight or so, I could see a couple of other picket boats dutifully anchoring and letting slip their skiffs in the centre of the river. On the western side, left as I looked at it, of the mainstream were moored all the usual yachts and leisure craft. White hulls standing out in the dark. Behind them was the jetty. It struck me that this was a very laborious way of doing business, so, asking one of the good lads to keep a sharp eye on the echo sounder, I briefed the crew that we weren't going to do any of this low–average skiff nonsense. We were going alongside, using the picket boat itself to penetrate the impenetrable moorings. Our staff member was from a different division, and I didn't know him at all – other than by peculiar coincidence I had seen him at university, as his girlfriend was in the Southampton University sailing club.

'What are we about to do here, Mr Tremelling?' he enquired in that tone that suggests the enquirer and you don't see eye to eye.

'We're sorting this out, sir!' I replied, with 'what could possibly go wrong?' cheerfulness. He enquired about the ebb tide and the safe water under the keel, and I pointed out that I had given one man one job and that was to let me know if I was going to run out of wetness. The picket boats were fun to drive and with a big rudder and twin screws were very manoeuvrable. I went in at a 'smart pace', as to dawdle might lead to a humiliating grounding as the tide raced away. Slower would have been better as I threaded my way between yachts and fishing boats – it would also have been far more boring. We made a fair bit of wash, which was probably 'not very helpful' to the poor souls who were plodding in on skiffs. We made a positive contact with the jetty, port side to.

'OK, let's go, boys!' I called as my boarding team ran off to find the secret agent.

'Are we going to make the vessel fast?' the staff member enquired, using the rather peculiar and contradictory term for tying it up.

'No, sir,' I replied, 'I'll keep it here with power.' Which didn't seem to get the vote of approval I was after. All the time I could hear my human depth gauge counting down the centimetres we had to spare under the keel and I think we got as low as 10 or 20. Exciting and enough to get the heart going, but hardly life-threatening. My secret agent discovery team came running back out of the darkness, which meant it was time to go.

Slamming both engines into reverse for a second or two took us off the jetty. I let full right rudder plus the ebb flow get the nose moving right and away. Then, leading with left engine to take us further to the right, I went to full power on both. A good-spirited slalom through the moored craft took us into the darkness of the centre of the river and past the anchored boats of the other teams. I turned to the crew, 'Dog's bollocks!' exiting my mouth before I could think of anything more suitable.

So it came as a real surprise then that the report my tutor read to me contained the line 'This Lord Flash-heart character would do well to show Naval General Training a little more respect.' As I sit here now, I am justifiably proud of that, but at the time I was incredibly angry and dismayed. All I had done was grip a situation with drive and initiative. The report was odd for no end of reasons. Firstly, the staff officer hadn't been prepared to say these things to my face. Secondly, he'd actually witnessed some pretty special boat handling and quick thinking from me and the A-Team.[4] Thirdly, at about that point, I won the prize for coming top in Naval General Training exams and tests. It was about £50, which was very welcome . . . but more importantly it showed that I was indeed taking the training seriously. I think that night, that officer and that report are probably a useful micro-cosm of the Royal Navy I joined and the Fleet Air Arm I wished to be a part of. My tutor finished the conversa-tion by saying, 'I've never liked that lieutenant – maybe you should be writing reports on him!'

4 If I may say so!

Luckily, following all the basic stuff, we went to sea under the expert eye of Lieutenant Wilkinson, who was a great bloke, knew the Gulf like the back of his hand and had been the navigating officer for a Type 42 destroyer previously. The sort of bloke who told you that life was too short to bull your boots but wanted your nav planning to be perfect – because one mattered and the other really didn't. We loved him, and our time on HMS *Gloucester* bumping around from Haifa to Dubai to Bahrain was a very happy and professionally rewarding one. The icing on the cake was that HMS *Gloucester* had an excellent rugby team, and I managed to convince them to let me play. It's amazing how easy life at sea becomes for a young officer if the chief petty officers are watching out for you after some rough and tumble on the field and a few beers off it.

Despite 'not taking training seriously', I passed out in April 1997 as Best Cadet. I was awarded the Queen's Binoculars.[5] Only side breathers of the General List[6] could win the sword. But the best lesson I learned was from Lieutenant Wilkinson. Know the difference between the important stuff and the triv – and do the important stuff to the best of your ability.

5 These are very expensive Zeiss mariner's binoculars and have been simply superb. I am able to say a little sheepishly that I am not a mariner, but I do like hunting, so I've spray-painted mine camouflage.
6 Ship drivers and supply officers. Two species able to think and act up to, and at, walking pace.

4. Flying Training

*Royal Air Force College Cranwell, Lincolnshire.
Culturally still acceptable to have a drink the
evening prior to flying, but the need to perform
kept that at bay most nights.*

With BRNC behind me, I would next be taking to the air. Flying training was straightforward, starting with the Joint Elementary Flying Training School, JEFTS, at RAF Barkston Heath. The flying scholarship I had been awarded gave me my first thirty hours at Bodmin in Cornwall. I had also done a lot of flying with the Southampton University Air Squadron so knew I could hack the early stages, and the challenge was therefore to do well enough to be streamed to the Fixed Wing pipeline. I even had the great fortune to be reunited with my flying scholarship instructor from Bodmin. Simon was a star and by peculiar coincidence was now employed as a civilian flying instructor at Barkston. Simon and my other instructors wanted to help, Trigger in particular – both he and Simon were brilliant and keen to stretch me in the cockpit (in a mental sense). We flew the yellow Slingsby Firefly, which had the 260 engine and was therefore much more powerful than the other elementary types. At the time JEFTS was used as the selection point for entry into the Sea Harrier pipeline. If you made the grade you went to basic fast jet training at RAF Linton-on-Ouse. Everything was going swimmingly until, at about this point, things went cataclysmically wrong.

Context is everything, and at the time the Navy was losing trainee fast jet aircrew on the Hawk aircraft at RAF Valley, where they simply weren't making the grade. Many had made light work of JEFTS because they had previous flying experience. So had I. It was a theory at the time that people like me were just regurgitating stuff they had seen before and not demonstrating the critical ability to learn fast. This counted against me, and the chief flying instructor decided I ought to go to RAF Shawbury to helicopters rather than into the Fixed Wing pipeline. I tried to argue the toss, but there was no point. I even called the commander in charge of Navy flying training down the road at RAFC Cranwell to protest, but he stuck to the CFI's guns and made it very clear that I was Rotary Wing bound. This made for a very odd evening for me at our course-ending fancy dress celebration (theme: religious fanatics of your choice).[1] I received the news that I had come top in Ground School and best overall. An RAF chap called Neil got the other prize for best flying. Two RN chaps were to be streamed to Fixed Wing, and I was not one of them. Coming top hadn't been enough.

The next day, the CFI told me in my final debrief that he'd seen me on a check ride getting tense when trying to fit an aerobatic sequence into a small gap in the clouds, and that told him I wasn't fit to go Fixed

1 In 1998 this was a lot funnier than it would be now and even border-line acceptable.

Wing. It was a bit weak. If you look hard enough you can find faults. To bring up one specific case of one specific manoeuvre going awry as the reason for fundamentally changing someone's cradle-to-grave trajectory seemed to be clutching at straws. He was a typically uninspiring ASW type with as much oomph as mild cheddar. I didn't mind him marking me down for poor performance – it grated that he was opining about my ability to fulfil a role he knew cock all about. To be fair I knew cock all about it at the time too, and it looked like things were going to stay that way. I couldn't help but feel that my single-minded pursuit of a career as a Sea Harrier pilot had somehow put his nose out of joint. But that should have counted in my favour, not against me.

You know something's wrong when instructors you've never talked to before are stopping you in the corridor to express their surprise and disappointment at you not getting a crack at Fixed Wing. One even went as far as to tell me, 'Get your Fixed Wing crossover application in as quickly as possible.' Then, I am afraid that I let myself down a little. I was leaving the CFI's office on my last day when the secretary that everyone fancied bounced up and announced that I was the only one who hadn't bought a commemorative picture of the Slingsby Fire-fly as a keepsake. Turning to make sure the CFI heard me, I asked, 'Why the fuck would I want to remember this place?' and then left. He might have deserved it, but she certainly didn't.

There were a couple of bright silver linings to the horribly dark cloud of going to Rotary Wing training at RAF Shawbury. The dark cloud was a realization that the dream was in tatters. However, and in no particular order, the silver linings were: Shrewsbury, the joint officers' mess, the Squirrel helicopter, the instructors, the senior course guys, like Baldman and Pi Man, and my tri-service course mates, in particular Screech and Pumba. In fact, there was only one teeny-weeny issue with Shawbury. It wasn't Linton. This wasn't basic fast jet flying training, and I wasn't going Fixed Wing. Apart from that, literally everything was brilliant. Happy hours were great; the sky over Wales always majestic. The flying was brilliant. Who knew that there were so many ways of hurling a helicopter at the ground? We did engine-off landings, confined area landings, mountain flying and winching. We were allowed to fly 30 feet from obstacles[2] so long as we were 100 feet off the ground. We flew so low we had to avoid individual horses. I even found out that when you were flying solo there was nothing stopping you chasing pheasants around.[3] The instructors were, to a man, superb. The squadron bosses truly inspiring. As well as the guys I flew with, there was another enormous Army major who went by either Chewie or Wookie; he was brilliant.

Then there was Lieutenant Commander Nick Clarke. It is not hyperbole, but simple fact, that I owe Nick Clarke everything. The story is quite simple. I did all right at RAF Shawbury. RN types had to complete the basic course on an Army Air Corps Squadron (in civil-maintained helicopters with aircrew from all three

2 Trees, pylons, that sort of thing.
3 This, I accept, was unprofessional.

services plus some civilian instructors) and then the advanced course on 705 Naval Air Squadron (in identical civil-maintained helicopters with aircrew from all three services plus some civilian instructors). I got to the end of 705 and was told by the commandant, an Army Air Corps colonel, that I had scored the highest mark ever awarded at the Defence Helicopter Flying School. I never checked but assume that it's not the sort of thing you make up.[4] Largely irrelevant. What was relevant was that Nick Clarke was CO 705 NAS and he was my examiner for my final check ride, in which I did well. He added to the realism of the scenario by putting on an impression of 'an aircrewman that was trying to help but required thorough and constant briefing', which was really bad. I got lost, I got myself unlost, usual stuff.

Nick's debrief was simple. I'd done well enough to go anywhere so I could choose which frontline helicopter type I went to, and luck was on my side because all three[5] were available. However, Nick wanted to talk me through the pros and cons. The Lynx world was challenging and at the heart of the naval battle; Lynx flights went to small ships in two-man teams. The Sea King 4 and the Junglie world would offer great flying, large team camaraderie and more day-to-day contact with customers such as the Royal Marines. In my opinion ASW would be turbo shit, and anyone that pretended otherwise was on crack. So the choice was Lynx or Junglie.

4 Even if true, it should be noted that DHFS was a relatively new entity, so this was very much an 'in recent years' thing.
5 Lynx, ASW Sea King, Sea King 4 (Junglie).

Nick advised that I should go for Lynx. His reasoning was sound. If you flew Lynx from a frigate or destroyer the bloke writing your reports was going to be a sea-going captain. Therefore, promotion would follow, and the career ladder beckoned. If you flew Junglie, then the bloke writing your reports was likely to be a lieutenant commander.

My slightly cruel view of the Junglies was that most appeared to have wanted to join the Royal Marines but weren't hard enough and now walked around wearing camouflage underpants – arguably I'd fit right in. The choice was hard, and the tribal rugby player in me fancied the Junglie circuit; the competitor in me thought that the Lynx would be harder and therefore better. But neither really mattered to me because I still had one ocean-going, weapons-grade itch to scratch and I sensed that I was at one of life's inflection points. The chat was going well, Nick was giving me sage advice. Had I not wanted to fly Sea Harrier since I was knee high to a grasshopper, I would never have dared do what I did next.

'Which fleet do you think would be able to spring me first for a Fixed Wing crossover?' I asked. This could have gone one of two ways – most likely was he was about to call me a cock and tell me to be grateful for his advice and show some respect for the challenges ahead and get on with them. But he didn't.

'I didn't know that's what you were after, Tremble-thing!' Nick replied. 'Why didn't you go straight from JEFTS?'

I sensed that things might be going my way.

'I'd be very grateful if you could tell me, sir!'

He then lifted up my file, and we sat in silence for a couple of minutes as he read my previous reports.

'Looks to me like you were pretty hard done by,' he said at last and went on to explain that the Navy was critically short of Fixed Wing aircrew so really didn't want to be denying able Fixed Wing volunteers a chance. He went on to say that his next appointment was going to be in the flying training staff world, and he felt that it might need a shake-up.

'Maybe I should call the flying training desk to discuss this,' he mused.

We agreed that I should go to Lynx, and therefore 702 NAS beckoned. Nick was even good enough to tell me that an old colleague of my dad's was on the unit and was looking forward to giving his old mucker's son a hard time. We then got ripped up on champagne[6] in the wonderful officers' mess. But before we wrapped up the debrief, Nick offered: 'Would you like me to make the call to flying training?', the desk that would be his very shortly.

'Yes please, sir,' I replied. Nick was true to his word and on the Monday presented me the most wonderful choice – 702 Naval Air Squadron to start on Lynx the next week or basic fast jet training at RAF Linton-on-Ouse the week after that. The dream was back on.

---

6 Which Nick insisted on calling Charlie . . . which until then I thought was a colloquialism for a more 'frowned-upon' intoxicant.

5. The Fixed Wing Pipeline

No point lying about it, the runs ashore were pretty good, sometimes leading to a baggy head in the morning.

And so it began. Henceforth, my aviation career would always be within the realm of fast jets, Combat Air, fighters and mud-movers.[1] I would have little if anything to do with the other worlds of helicopters and heavies.[2] I have nothing whatsoever against those teams, but they simply weren't for me. The things that the Rotary Wing world in particular achieved in Afghanistan were staggering – but I think the link between Fast Air and anyone else is largely tenuous. Over the next couple of decades, I was very grateful for lifts ashore in helicopters, or lifts home from theatre in heavies and, far more regularly, the gas that you could get from the tanking chaps. But their world and mine had little in common except that we wore flying coveralls.

Years later, this was highlighted very starkly when I came to take the Tristar home from Afghanistan and was chatting to the crew about what we did and what they did. It became clear that they didn't have a clue about how close air support actually worked. No criticism at all: why would they? Equally, I found the amount of activity and number of people required in a multi-crew

1 Those that move mud. Attack aircraft.
2 Multi-engine types such as tankers and trash haulers.

cockpit to descend a few thousand feet absolutely ridiculous. There were four people in the cockpit that day. A doer, a checker, a manual operator of the automatic throttle[3] and some other bloke who sat.[4] For the record, though, if you're flying in the UK and air traffic control ask you to descend to anything above 6,500 feet above mean sea level,[5] can't you just take some power off and lower the nose? These chaps got me home, but everything was turned into an absolute palaver.

The Fixed Wing pipeline by and large was extraordinarily positive, and every person (with three exceptions) I met was straight out of the top drawer. It all started at RAF Henlow, where I met the eleven RAF folk that were going to be on my course; in a broadly representative way we'd lose about half of those en route to the frontline.

The first couple couldn't get up to speed with the Tucano training aircraft – which at the time seemed fast – and so went to heavies. One made it all the way to the Tornado F3 conversion unit before getting chopped, as he was unable to cope with a 2 v 2 engagement – two aircraft on each side trying to kill each other. 2 v 2 isn't easy but still nowhere near the zenith of fighter ops – the limit of the US Red Flag exercises was twelve aircraft all manoeuvring visually with/against each other. One had medical snags. One decided that flying attack aircraft

---

3 You tell me!
4 I can't think of any way of expanding on his duties. He just sat.
5 The Safety Altitude for the whole of the UK, based on Ben Nevis (4,413 feet), rounded up and with 2,000 feet added.

wasn't for him as – spoiler alert – apparently their prime purpose was to kill people.

I do wonder how people like him make it through the door, let alone through any stages of training. Day 1 at BRNC should feature a bayonet drill like you can see infantry recruits doing on YouTube – not because I think that there's a particularly large chance of a RN (or RAF) officer needing a bayonet, but it would clearly and un-equivocally make the point that you've joined the armed forces, and their job, as a whole, is to project violence into the battlespace. If you go to HMS *Excellent*, to the history rooms to the east of the establishment, you will find quite a lot of photographic evidence to suggest that RN training was at some point not dissimilar. Trafalgar and Ladysmith weren't won by standing back.

As it was, this turkey cost a load of people a whole load of time, effort and jet fuel. In fairness there did seem to be a fair number of people in the flying training world who did a good job of not going to the front-line. The caricature of the qualified flying instructor with a silk scarf and new white flying gloves worried about some airborne irrelevance like flying a quarter clover in balance is one I actually subscribe to. I, and many of my warfare/weapons instructor colleagues, would eventually adopt the term 'trimmers' to describe the QFI commu-nity. This came from the good flying practice of flying in trim – all forces balanced so you don't feel them on the control stick – which seemed to be all they cared about at times! Flying in trim is undoubtedly important – for example, when attacking a target, trimming to attack speed will mean that your aircraft is balanced when you release stores,[6] although to be frank, modern-weapon aiming computers don't really care if you are in trim or not. Being trimmed out does reduce forces on the controls so does help with muscle fatigue. By and large, though, there will always be a divide between the fliers and the operators. Yes, I get it, you need to be able to fly aircraft to fight them, but flying is admin, fighting is the reason you're there. There is simply no place on a frontline unit for someone who wants to fly fighters, or mud-movers, but not fight or move mud. To quote the great squadron leader 'Harry the Bastard'[7] from my time on 19 Squadron the Hawk tactical weapons unit, 'If you didn't join the Air Force to kill people and break their stuff, then you can fuck off!' Amen.

If Shawbury was the Sunny Uplands, Linton-on-Ouse was Utopia itself. Great people, great area and a reasonable aircraft in the form of the Tucano, a powerful twin-seat turboprop. The Central Flying School (spiritual home of trimmers, where everyone walks around in silk scarves and pressed white gloves spinning 'how quickly I trimmed the aircraft' dits) technique was explained by their battle cry of Power-Attitude-Trim (although this is reordered when levelling off to Attitude-Power-Trim). In the Tucano you could move the controls and trim simultaneously by holding down the electrical trim switches.

6 Euphemism for weapons. Also called 'shapes' by some air forces. The call of 'Stores!' replaced the historical – and more accurate – statements such as 'Bombs gone!'

7 This was neither his real name, nor his nickname, it was more 'what the students called him' and it was very tongue-in-cheek, as he was a great bloke who we all admired.

I found a lot of flying training was about 'appearing to use the techniques' as opposed to actually using them.

A lot of flying is just the stuff you have to do to get an aeroplane from A to B in all weathers. Things that fall into this bucket would be the obvious ones such as take-off and landing. Take-off is incredibly simple and generally speaking involves applying power, keeping aligned to the operating surface (usually a runway, but not always) and at a certain speed moving the stick aft. Landing, however, can be tricky, depending on the crosswind and how close to the threshold you need to hit terra firma to be sure of being stopped by the time you reach the other end. My friend completely porked this in a Sea Harrier one day. He landed long and fast,[8] did not go around for another go and ended up with an ejection and a parachute ride. Very impressive to those of us watching from the pan a few hundred metres away. The jet was yet to be beaten and was making its way to Dorchester when the River Yeo got in the way and ate it.

So there were potential pitfalls, but a lot of flying can actually be quite dull, in particular instrument flying and radio aids navigation. Instrument flying is the art of not looking out the window, and radio aids nav is about finding your way around using beacons and waypoints, also

---

8 He had too much fuel to hover, as we had nominated Shawbury as our diversion, and the wind was from the south, meaning that we were using the short runway at Yeovilton. Physics dictates that heavier = faster for landing aeroplanes. Short runways are generally unforgiving when it comes to long, fast landings. All these planets aligned, and Steve went for a trip on the Martin-Baker ride. I had landed a few minutes prior so got to watch the whole show!

not looking out of the window. Both are critical activities, but you really would not want to make a career out of them;[9] they are just means to an end. Instrument flying is basically boring hard work. It relies upon your ability to keep your eyes roving around all the necessary instruments to make sure your attitude, heading, speed, vertical speed, location are all where they need to be. Countless aviation accidents have been caused by people not doing this. I didn't like instrument flying, though I was quite good at it. I got the prize for best instrument flying on my course at Linton, but it was the other stuff that I absolutely loved, and of course, if the weather allowed, we would show up at the airfield as fast as we could[10] and then attempt to rip the wings from the aircraft as we bled energy to slow down to land.

The pick of the disciplines we were schooled in were formation flying and low-level nav. I picked up prizes for those two as well. In fact, the others on my course were left with 'best aerobatics', which went to Scott, and 'best officer', to Darren, one of the guys retraining from navigator to pilot. No complaints from me with either of those. Both were great people. Our wonderful station commander addressed the mums and dads at the end of the course and announced, tongue in cheek, that it really pissed him off when the Navy got a clean sweep like that. As you might expect, my parents were very proud. My dad gave me a framed copy of John Magee's *High Flight*,

9 The airline community resolutely refuse to follow this advice!
10 The Tucano had a beeper that told you if you were near the speed limit/doing the job properly.

which to him neatly encapsulated the emotion of military aviation – he's right. Mum's interest probably didn't extend to understanding how one might climb the long, delirious, burning blue, but she seemed to enjoy the day. I got a rose bowl, which has, over the years, become a car keys bowl, and a fabulously large book about every fighter ever made . . . at the time. I got a couple of cups and the like but only for enough time to have a photo taken before they were put back in cabinets. All in all – about time to swap the Tucano for the Hawk.

It was time for jets.

6. RAF Valley

Anglesey, for advanced flying training. Generally well behaved, except when the fog rolled in.

This is a weird time in any aviator's development. Even though the Hawk is a training jet and therefore quite basic and very forgiving, it's still a jet. The transition to jets is a paradox because, although it's the point where you think you might make it, you also realize how much of the mountain there is left to climb.

For my generation it meant attending advanced flying training at RAF Valley on Anglesey, followed by the tactical weapons unit. To me, even the drive to Valley felt strange because it was on that drive that I discovered, deep down, I had harboured some form of assumption that I wouldn't make it that far. But I had. The seemingly endless drive along the north Wales coast wasn't just a geographical shift, it also marked the time that things got serious.

Aircraft hardly ever fly at their top speed. To do so takes a whole load of fuel and probably some form of dive. There are a variety of reasons for choosing particular speeds to fly: for example, to get the best range out of your fuel load or to obey air traffic regulations. One of the reasons for flying at a particular speed is to make the maths easy. Thus in the Tucano we flew around at 240 knots at low level because four miles a minute made sense. The Hawk could fly well beyond 500 knots and could break the sound barrier,[1] but at low level the default speed was 420 knots. Seven miles a minute was going to be our new home.

The powers that be knew Valley was tough. One of our first evolutions was to go to see the padre, who would attempt to calm our nerves. He explained that, as the course got harder, we would begin to struggle if we didn't stay completely focused. To help, he reminded us about limiting the stress of advanced flying training. He gave an example of how not to do it.

'A guy on a previous course even got married when he should have kept his eyes on the course!' he exclaimed, to the delight of my fellow pilots, who knew that I and my beautiful fiancée Fiona were due in front of the altar that June . . .

Of all the things that happened to me at RAF Valley the most important was that I met Fin Monahan, who might just hold the title of 'best person ever created'. Fin was simply excellent at everything (other than drawing runways as you might expect to see them from the cockpit), and to be his primary student on 208 Squadron was a privilege. Fin was great company, had flown the Harrier, was fluent in French, could ski, organized a weekend for us in Snowdonia to, in his words, 'hike and get fucked up', organized a dinner on a steam railway – that sort of person. He left Valley to fly the A-4 on

---

1 My own successful attempt to break the sound barrier in the Hawk resulted in being stuck upside down, stick having no effect in a roll, plummeting earthwards and experiencing a strange aerodynamic effect called 'Cobblestones'. At night. I did achieve Mach 1, though!

exchange with the Royal New Zealand Air Force, and we were to serve together again on one of the Invincible class carriers when I was an air warfare instructor. He was confident and humble in perfect measure. 'Well done, Mr Tremelling, sir!' would come from the back seat when my aerobatics were going OK, and 'I'm watching your head, and it isn't moving enough!' when I wasn't being punctilious with my lookout. He knew what was important and what wasn't. He didn't have to shout – he was one of those people you wanted to do well for. He shared with me one day that he made a point of calling RN lieutenant commanders 'sir' because he knew it annoyed them[2] – and he judged their character by how they reacted.

After one shakedown trip after a short time off, Fin was torn about what grade to give me so went and asked for advice, and we sat in the nav planning room with him saying that the instructors' counsel had ranged from 'Fail' to 'Exceptional'. In the end, he said something like 'It was very good, but I want to keep you motivated – I'll give you a 5.' A 5 (out of 6) was 'Above the Average' – when a good trip earned you a 3, it was not to be sneered at. It was the manner in which he went about it that made an impression. Asking others for input and letting me see him decide. If I left Valley with one wish, it was

---

2 For whatever reason, the Fleet Air Arm doesn't consider lieutenant commanders to be senior, which is great, adds to bonhomie, allows use of first names and reduces the number of salutes you give and receive. The RAF considers squadron leaders, the light-blue equivalent, to be senior – with the reverse effect.

to be like Fin. Good, respected, humble, confident . . .
One day, one day . . .

One thing that happened with Fin comes particularly
to mind. One of the downwind vital actions in the Hawk
was to check that the hydraulic systems were up to pressure, but that the lines to the brakes had no residual
pressure in them. This was vital because if there was
pressure to the brake your tyre would pop when you hit
the ground. It was an instructors' trick to put a boot on
the brake in the back seat to make sure that you were
actually checking and not just paying lip service to it.
Paying lip service to checks was a really bad thing to do.
I had done it on my final handling test in the Tucano,
and the label of complacent was one that I had vowed
to shed. Fin and I were downwind in the left-hand circuit on the southerly runway at one of the local airfields.
As I called out the checks, I looked down to the tray of
hydraulic instruments and called that they were charged
with no residual pressure. As I did so, absolutely simultaneously, I saw one of them begin to rise.

'Check again!' Fin ordered firmly from the back seat.
I verbalized that there was brake pressure. What to say?
That I saw the rise? That I had checked punctiliously
but the pressure rose as I was doing so? I chose to say
nothing. In the debrief, too, I chose to say nothing. Fin
quite rightly rapped my knuckles for lip service to checks.
Why didn't I argue? Well, what's the best that could have
happened? Or the worst? Given that neither of us could
prove the actual sequence of events, arguing would have
been pointless. Worst case, he'd think I was a liar – the
dishonest aviator everyone despised. That wasn't a risk

worth taking – and for what? He wasn't the sort of bloke who'd rush to the squadron OC and proclaim that he had proved Tremelling to be complacent. So I shut up. I took the hit. That's what you have to do sometimes. If you would follow someone through the gates of hell, it seems a little contrary to pick up the timing of a brake application. Good learning point: know when to fight your corner and when to shut the fuck up. Luckily, with a bit of judgement, I'd saved myself from learning that the hard way.

Fin taught me another great lesson about aviation on a land-away to RAF Leeming. We'd debriefed one trip and then briefed for another and walked back out to the aircraft. After completing the walk round, I jumped in the cockpit and began to strap in. At home base I would have got in the jet from a platform and have had an engineer there. As it was a land-away, it was just a case of using the in-built steps. As I sat down, Fin yelled (not in a cross way – we both had helmets on), 'You haven't checked your seat!' I hadn't. Probably because of not being able to do so from a platform. Probably because things were different. Probably because I'd only unstrapped a little time before, and no one had been near the jet. All fundamentally wrong. That ejection seat was my final 'get out of jail' card, and multiple things needed to be checked every single trip with 100 per cent attention to detail. I was totally in the wrong. The lessons? 1) Never miss an opportunity to check something vital. 2) One day, no one will be there to look after you but you.

The last thing I learned from Fin that I care to share was balance. We landed once at RAF Leuchars having had a hoot and a roar at low level. Dropping in at the Amble lighthouse in Northumberland and enjoying thirty minutes or so of the joy that 250 feet[3] and 420 knots bring, I'd made a few small errors with my free navigation and wasn't happy. There was another student in the flight planning room at Leuchars when we arrived. He asked how the trip had gone, and I replied, 'Horrendous.' We then went to a smaller room to debrief. Just Fin and I. When we finished he had one last point.

'I heard you say that trip was horrendous,' he said. 'It wasn't, so don't do yourself down in public.' He was, as ever, unerringly accurate. It's obviously admirable to be self-effacing and modest, but in the aviation world you cannot come across as being needy. Your confidence has to come from within. If you are the sort of person who needs constant slaps on the back then you simply won't get them and will be a pain. If your self-effacement is seen as being a need for praise, then you lose standing. It would be daft to suggest that there was no place for egos in the fast jet world – there are hundreds of them, world-class egos just waiting to be popped and rapidly deflated. As ever, it's a balance. I should have said, 'Things to work on, but overall OK.' Which would have been spot on. There's only so many times you can tell people you're shit before they believe you! Tell them you're great, and they'll think that you're a knob – and

3 Flight at this height was taught in the RAF/RN using the simple measure of 'That looks about right', as at the time no training aircraft had radio altimeters. The other way of explaining the low-level picture was to fly low enough to see cows' legs but not sheeps' legs. I am not lying.

probably think you're shit in any case. Fin walked the correct walk. Confident, but the first to admit a mistake. Not a shred of arrogance. If you can honestly debrief yourself and frankly debrief others, then you may be able to learn at the rate needed to get to the fighter front-line. Good learning point.

Another lesson happened during my first solo, which I fucked up. I had enjoyed my pre-ride with the squadron executive officer – a Jaguar[4] pilot and great bloke. You had to be very carefully supervised for your first go in a jet. That didn't really happen for me. The supervisor asked if I would slip my briefing time so he could have lunch, which got me rushed. I then got a question wrong at the out brief – forgetting to add the 'solo allowance' to my recovery fuel. Rather than simply correct me, the duty authorizer shouted, 'Get off my ops desk!' This was, of course, my fault, in that I should have got it right, but his manner was odd for someone about to send some-one out in a jet for the first time. Having had my timing compressed and having been shouted at, I walked to the aeroplane and got a couple of checks wrong.

This taught me a really key lesson. It doesn't matter in military aviation how you are treated, or how sub-optimal the build-up to an event is. You have to be able to look after yourself. Key skills are compartmentalization – simply concentrating on the task in hand – and my own

---

4 The Jaguar was, for a variety of reasons, a peculiar aircraft, but in my experience the people who operated them were first-class, and their home at RAF Coltishall had a similar feeling of community to the Sea Harrier force.

term of 'temporary focused amnesia', the skill of forgetting something for the period it doesn't matter. If you
have a Horlicks of a brief, or a crap set of checks, or a
poor take-off, you have a choice: sweat about them for
the next hour and let them invade your thinking capacity
and taint the rest of the trip or simply remove them from
your consciousness and move on. Get the rest right, drag
the shit out in the debrief. I had let my interactions with
one slack-arse instructor and one egotist who appeared
to want to shout at students more than prepare them for
their sortie get into my head. If I hadn't stopped the rot
at taxi, then that could have been dangerous.

As it was, it was a lovely sunny day, and I took off from
the north-western surface at Valley. As the gear came up,
I rolled slightly to make sure I was going to pass well
clear of Holyhead and kept the throttle at full power
in the climb to 4,000 feet. I changed radio frequency
to Departures and let them know I was off 'around the
island' and then completed the clockwise tour of Anglesey, staying off the coast by a few miles. This was one
of those trips of sheer joy. Flying a jet in good weather,
completely on my own for the first time. My attempt
at the course speed record was a bonus. Our Kid, our
resident loveable Scally, had the current speed to beat –
which wasn't altogether surprising, as he probably didn't
know the aircraft limits.[5] From 4,000 feet, I unloaded the

---

5 Fin made him retake the aircraft Essential Knowledge Quiz as his
answers were 'too informal'. I remember him being surprised but then
showing us one example where he had written that the fuel pressure
warning meant 'Your FTAP is broke'. FTAP was the fuel tank air

aircraft and bunted at zero g^6 down towards 1,000 feet, and the jet, unencumbered, accelerated very smoothly. Reaching somewhere in excess of 500 knots, and a few knots quicker than Our Kid, I called it a day and set up for my recovery to Valley. From rather inauspicious beginnings the day ended well – I really enjoyed that trip; I learned that it was time to grow up. I still think that both supervisor and authorizer were bells that day, which in itself is a lesson. You can learn a lot by watching bells at work – and promising never to be like them.

I had also sworn to avoid any sign of weakness. At Valley, weakness started to show as some lacked the will (or stubbornness), deep seated in the brain, to see it through. The padre was right. Any doubt or fragility was exposed at Valley. People started withdrawing from the course, and it tended to be put down to some medical issue. I am sure that they all had perfectly valid reasons – sinus problems here, sore necks there. But I observed that other people made it through with the same problems. I remember Our Kid giving a personal masterclass on 'how not to give in no matter what' on two occasions. The first was him coming to me for advice as to whether or not to take himself off the flying programme. I asked what the issue was.

'Well, I had toof ache, and now it's got so bad that I can't really concentrate, and I'm eating by pushing bread

---

pressurization. The question was demanding to know what pressure was indicated by the warning – not that it was 'broke'.

6 The amount of force acting on you, expressed as a multiple of the force gravity exerts. 4 G = four times as much force as one would experience at rest.

down the side of my mouth with a pencil!' came the reply. Now that's fighting spirit. Our Kid also caught conjunctivitis and had diarrhoea in the build-up to our 'wings rides'[7] at the end of the course. I couldn't help laughing as he got into his anti-G trousers.

'Fucking look at me! I've got red eyes, I can't fucking see and I've just fucking shat myself!' will stay with me for a long time. With men like Our Kid on your team you don't lose.

Some other weaknesses occurred. Flying tired is not wise, and you learn from an early age that you have to manage fatigue, but blaming mistakes on fatigue is just weak. One cove came into the crew room one day and, despite looking fresh as a daisy, announced that he was exhausted. I told him that he didn't look exhausted, to which he replied that he had just failed a trip because he'd approached the airfield from the wrong direction, and to have done something like that could only be down to exhaustion. Nope. He fucked up and didn't have the strength of character to admit it. The notion that to mess up must mean something is wrong is not one I have any time for. If you mess up, it's on you, and you hold your hand up.

One last illustration of the point was more imaginative. There was a guy on the course ahead who was doing OK. He had always struck me as being a nice

---

7 The final trip on 208 Squadron, after which we could be called pilots. Weirdly, up to that point everyone asked what you did, but you could never use the term 'pilot' as you had yet to qualify. After that point no one ever asked!

guy but he didn't seem to harbour the natural aggression I would expect from a fighter pilot. One day, my course commander called me into his office to say that a senior student had got worried about his chances of surviving an ejection. The fix was that he was going to be winched out of the cockpit in the hangar while strapped into the ejection seat to check whether or not his legs 'interacted with' the cockpit on the way out. This guy and I were exactly the same size. The course commander invited me to go and be similarly winched. I refused. I'd passed the medical, which included anthropometric measurements. I'm sure that on any given day I could have been shown to 'not quite fit' in a Hawk.[8] I didn't go to the hangar. The other guy did, and it was decided that he should leave the course. He ended up on heavies, I believe, which probably suited him best; like I said – he was a nice bloke. But I learned that if your heart's not in something, and doubt creeps in, it will find a chink in your armour somewhere. Do I believe he was worried about the seat? Yes. Do I, however, believe it was preceded by worries about the course? Yes. The seat issue was the outlet for his other concerns. I don't believe I did anything dangerous by refusing the 'seat lift'. I think I simply stayed focused on seeing the dream through to fruition. Even if, occasionally, you have to eat bread with pencils, go to stores for new long johns or accept that there was a possibility you might one day get kneecapped.

8 I measure 188cm and had a running battle with the ejection seat weight limit.

My next hiccup – partly of my making and partly down to my being a victim of circumstance – occurred in the combat phase on 19(F) Squadron at Valley. The weather had been atrocious, and after a long time on the ground I undertook my first air combat lesson as part of a land-away at RAF Leuchars. I did the second on the way back. The first trip centred on defensive basic fighter manoeuvres or DBFM. In short this was 'what to do if you're losing' and contained all the manoeuvres you could try to use to get back to neutral. Second came offensive BFM, which was 'what to do if you're winning' and contained all the stuff needed to stay in control. The jets passed close by, at high speed, under considerable G, and the majority of your time was spent craning your head backwards to attempt to 'keep tally' on the opposing aircraft. This was high-octane stuff.

On the third trip I stuffed it all up. I was dreadful. At the debrief, Nick, my instructor, adopted a surprisingly positive tone before delivering the good news.

'Don't think I'm a wanker – but I have to fail you.'

'I certainly don't think that!' I told him. 'I'm the only one at fault here.' And that was that. I was a little concerned because, although I had a few reasons for doing poorly, none of them were great, and at the end of the day I had fucked up. I later walked into the course office, and Stinger[9] was reading my file.

'ACM3 went really badly, I'm afraid, Stinger,' I

9 The senior RN officer at RAF Valley, who I would have the immense pleasure of serving under as AWI 801 when he was CO 801. A true great.

said – there's no point sugar-coating things after all. His reply will stay with me for ever.

'Don't worry, mate – you're going to 899[10] whether you like it or not!' he replied with a grin. Of course, it wasn't strictly true. I'd had my chance. I couldn't afford another one, and we both knew it. But Stinger chose encouragement over any other possible motivational technique, and it worked. I flew the 'refly' with instructors called Dan and Tinsel.[11] It went well. After the refly, there was one tonic that really got my course going again: a healthy dose of Snoop.

Snoop hailed from the French Mirage 2000 RDY/RDI air defence force. Snoop was different. If anyone tells you that a fighter pilot is 'aggressive' they probably mean that 'he has character flaws that prevent him succeeding in any other walk of life'. Snoop was the French exchange officer and he was aggressive in the classic sense. Nothing wrong whatsoever with any part of his character – he was a superb bloke. But when he got in the zone he was like an enraged cat. Everyone wanted to win at air combat – but Snoop took this to an amazing, heart-warming, spectacular extreme. The last trip of the 'guns combat phase' was flown 1 v 1, solo, against a staff pilot. I flew against Snoop. He fully kicked my ass from here to kingdom come. His handling was masterful.

---

10 899 NAS: the Sea Harrier headquarters squadron and the grinder one had to get through to make it to the SHAR frontline.

11 Dan was one of those characters that, so long as you showed you 'had something about you', was great to fly with. Tinsel, along with Stinger, was another premier-league human being – and by dint of fate would eventually be my boss too, on Harrier GR9.

Our two jets sat side by side, a mile apart at 16,000 feet, both at 360 knots.

'Outwards turn for combat. Go!' I called. This was my lead. At Valley we were allowed to manoeuvre as we turned outbound, and I wanted to go high, so I opened the throttle wide and turned outwards by 45 degrees. I 'padlocked' Snoop's small Hawk as it went from being a black aircraft to a black outline as we diverged. Hollywood is correct – if you lose sight, you lose the fight.

'Inwards turn for combat. Go!' I shouted, rolling out with my nose low on Snoop to let him know I could see him. 'One tally!'

'Two tally!' came the immediate reply. I was fast so that I could go high, which meant we'd cross at somewhere in the region of 900 knots closure. This was what we called the merge. To get any amount of turn in pre-merge gives you an advantage. It's called a lead turn, and Snoop was a master at it. With Snoop, it was as if he was trying to carve his name across my canopy. His merge technique was outrageous, and he passed over the top of me in a well-developed left turn.

'Fuck me!' I thought – his proximity actually made me duck in the cockpit – and in the subsequent few minutes it didn't seem to matter how I flew the aeroplane or what I did, or how much blood drained from my head, he always ended up behind me, saddled up, in my shorts.

'Guns, guns, guns!' he called, as simulated bullets shredded Hawk and pilot alike.

'Terminate, terminate!' I replied. That was a spanking. He had won. In the debrief he was brilliant – in a school of hard knocks way. He even talked about that specific manoeuvre.

'You think you can beat me?' he asked in his excellent if heavily accented English – as if my grandma had just asked Mike Tyson for an arm wrestle.

'Well, I tried,' I replied lamely, to which I got a weapons-grade Gallic shrug. He didn't have to say anything (he didn't say anything) but he clearly meant 'I simply don't care.' He was excellent at describing what you saw out of the window and what it meant to you in a fight. How to determine whether you were winning or losing based on the ever-changing relationship between the two aircraft. He knew his shit and he kept it simple. Snoop finished off – I assume he could see I was quite glum – by saying this wonderful line: 'Paul, cheer up, you are not shit. You are just average,' which from that great man was quite a thing! I took something away from that trip with Snoop. Winning is sometimes irrelevant. Sometimes winning is everything. In the first, you should obviously try your hardest but not get too wound up if it doesn't go your way. In the second, you needed to kick like fuck and never, ever accept defeat.

This new and exciting way of learning did have a downside, as my attempts to replicate Snoop's fighting spirit were taken as flagrant disregard for training rules by some instructors. However, I was progressing and soon got to the end of the course – for which the finale was a simulated strike through Scotland.

Dunc Mason[12] and I planned and flew a fabulous trip through the Highlands. We launched from Valley into a gloopy cloud layer that went from the deck to the firmament. About thirty minutes later, we broke out over Scotland, just to the south of Arran, with the entire country basking in the sunshine, laid before us like a map. Another staff pilot was ahead and was going to try to stop us in 'the bounce aircraft'. Eyes hunting for the bounce, we entered low level in battle, 1 mile abreast. 450 knots, 250 feet – every fibre in my body enjoying the spectacle of flying in the Scottish terrain, the thrill of the chase and the added piquancy of being hunted. Where possible, we stuck to the valleys, constantly monitoring time and fuel – neither of which was in plentiful supply after our transit. I tried not to look too much at the map, and every second or so I was checking that there was 'no bastard Hawk' settling into Dunc's six o'clock. We used well-practised techniques to keep us in battle formation[13] and simulated attacks on Cruachan, a power station on the north shore of Loch Awe and a bridge further to the north-east. Thirty or so minutes later, we were done, and I finished the course a sweaty heap in an immersion suit taking my jet into RAF Leuchars to refuel. As I checked nothing had fallen off the jet, Dunc came bounding up from his jet, beaming from ear to ear. Gripping my hand, he said, 'Well done, mate, great job.'

---

12 Yet another grade-A human from the single-seat workshop of grade-A humans.

13 Line abreast at about a mile, able to cover the airspace behind the other aircraft – also known as their 'six o'clock'.

Snoop saw me at the Visiting Aircraft Section and said something truly profound like 'You have finished! You don't have to do any more of this mud-moving shit.'[14]

On hearing that the trip had gone well, 'Harry the Bastard' said, 'Well, I guess we had better send you to Sea Harrier, then.' And with that, advanced flying training was over. It was time to go yet again from the top of one mountain to the foot of another. And this next one was big. It was to be my Everest: 899 and the Sea Harrier beckoned.

14 Not strictly true, given the Sea Harrier's multi-role capability.

7. The Sea Harrier: A Short History

The story of the Sea Harrier is pretty simple: engineering genius and warfighting success. It manifestly wasn't a one-trick pony that had, by sheer good fortune, had the opportunity to demonstrate its single trick at war in the South Atlantic in 1982.

The engineering feat was incredible and owed nothing to luck. I thought that the innovative use of the Pegasus to provide lift was remarkable. The jets themselves, able to contribute meaningfully to all sorts of conflicts, environments and basing options, actually fitted the British psyche very well – given our propensity to get involved in tussles that belie our status as owners of a small windswept rock in the North Atlantic.

Neither was the calibre of the men who flew the FRS Mk 1 and the GR 3 in the Falklands campaign anything to do with good fortune. As the FRS Mk 1 was relatively new, many had flown Phantom and Buccaneer and no doubt some harboured thoughts that they'd rather be back in those magnificent beasts.

By contrast the Sea Harrier that the boys took to the Falkland Islands was actually an incredibly simple machine that happened to have nozzles. Armed with two AIM-9L missiles and two 30mm cannon, when tasked air-to-air, the RN and RAF pilots of 800, 801 and 809 Naval Air squadrons won the air war. An amazing effort with a score of something like 23-0.[1] But where the FRS Mk 1 filled a small chunk of a dark Buccaneer- and Phantom-shaped hole, the FA2 that replaced it in the mid-1990s got us back in the game. The FA2 put a lot of things right with its superb integrated Blue Vixen radar and AMRAAM,[2] when others were still carting older and less capable weapons such as Sparrow and Sky Slug[3] around. By using 190-gallon drop tanks to replace the 100-gallon ones used in the Falklands, we got 1,400lbs more gas – or approximately 140 miles more at height.[4]

In October 1998, Joint Force 2000 was announced, which seemed to make eminent sense – even if it did promise to rip the Sea Harrier from its spiritual home at Yeovilton. JF2000 promised a carrier-borne mailed fist in the form of RAF GR7 strike aircraft operating with a sweep or escort of AMRAAM-firing FA2s. Very sens- ible and very potent. Arguably the best combination the UK was able to construct at the time.[5] This didn't change much for me, other than to create a lot more uncertainty

---

1 I've seen this figure quoted as 23, 28 and 32 to nil. Whichever is cor- rect, it was a proper kicking.

2 Advanced medium-range air-to-air missile – at the time, and still, the best all-round air-to-air weapon around.

3 Don't look it up – it's actually called Sky Flash. Flash was never more inappropriately used.

4 Still not enough, to be honest.

5 At the time the F3 had no AMRAAM capability to speak of. In time successive upgrades would give the RAF fighter better missiles, a means to support them in flight and a Link-16 capability. Tornado GR4 fans will argue the point about the platform's efficacy compared to Harrier GR7/9.

about where to buy a house, as I'd be doing 899 in Somerset, but in the future Rutland beckoned. JF 2000 made sense as we waited for the FA 2's replacement, the Joint Strike Fighter,[6] then slated for an in-service date of 2012. X-32 and X-35 prototypes were flying when I was at Valley.

What also made partial sense was that we would remain in the Royal Navy but we would be subsumed into No. 3 Group Royal Air Force, which would be commanded by a Royal Naval officer. This meant that we would be treated a bit like an RAF squadron from an exercise programme, operating rules and wartime command and control point of view, but we would still embark in the carriers when the Royal Navy needed us and would maintain our Royal Navy careers.

While I was in flying training, the Sea Harrier and Harrier contributed to operations in the Balkans, Sierra Leone and Iraq between the major hostilities. In comparison to the Falklands War, these probably escaped much public attention.

Any aircraft's capability engenders debate, usually in the manner one would play Top Trumps. However, air warfare is not fought by kids using cards. It's fought by warriors in a high-octane world with a myriad of facets that change in each and every fight and enhance and nullify advantages in ways that armchair warriors will

6 Which was going to be either the F-32 or F-35 at the time, with both being in X-aeroplane prototype stage. Called the Lightning in UK service, the aircraft was actually going to achieve an operational capability in 2018.

never consider. All the nuances of air combat added up to make the Sea Harrier a very potent platform. In its FA2 guise it wasn't necessarily the best in the world, of which there can be only one per generation,[7] but it would certainly give most air forces and naval air forces from around the world a far bloodier nose than other systems.

Yet my suspicion was that because we spent time bobbing around on ships we didn't necessarily demonstrate how good we were often enough to the right people. Our capability always took the allied air forces of Europe and beyond by surprise when we showed up. Sadly I think this ignorance of both our performance and potential extended to the MOD and politicians as well. It seemed that in most minds the best fighter of the day had to be de facto whatever the RAF were using, and the RN fighter was merely a plucky little metaphor for the Fleet Air Arm.

However, for me, when faced with a challenge such as 899 NAS, it was probably best to focus on the task in hand. To fly the Sea Harrier until it was shown the door in 2012, whether or not we were moving to RAF Cottesmore and sister station RAF Wittering, was why I had joined, and I'd now made it as far as 899 Naval Air Squadron, where I would finally get to meet the FA2.

---

7 In my generation this was the F-15C. Full stop. Not open for debate. Until the F-22 joined the debate and won.

8. 899 Naval Air Squadron and Sea Harrier First Impressions

RNAS Yeovilton — sober but wishing that there was a nerve-steadying tot on hand.

899 NAS was the Sea Harrier headquarters squadron[1] and by reputation the school of hard knocks. The unit was based on the south side of the airfield at Yeovilton, and I would go through the course there with two great friends. The first was Jim, who I had been through Dartmouth and JEFTS with. He had got one of the Fixed Wing places that I had failed to achieve and should have been ahead of me had it not been for him having ejected from a Harrier T8 while (not) learning to hover. Jim's back had healed, and he had returned to the course. My other course mate was TJ of the USMC. Another of life's greats. TJ bought himself a flyfishing ticket for the River Yeo just in time for foot and mouth to put the countryside out of bounds. When the restrictions were lifted, TJ went to prepare his rods at about the same time as Steve was lobbing an FA2 into the River Yeo, which apparently reduced the downstream fish stocks somewhat.

Fiona and I had taken the plunge and bought a house

---

1 In the RAF this would have been called the operational conversion unit.

in Somerset, as the move to Cottesmore seemed some way off, and we didn't fancy the communal living offered by the married quarters at the airfield's western end.

On day one, Jim, TJ and I were sat in our smart uniforms in one of the student offices. 899 ran two courses at once, three students on each, so we were in the junior course office while the senior team were in theirs. TJ was a seasoned campaigner and was obviously aware that 899 had something of a reputation.

'Is this place as bad as they say it is?' he asked. Then in walked Tats. A pocket battleship, air warfare instructor and inked-in starter on any world XV run-ashore team.[2] Tats took a swill of his coffee and spat it out theatrically straight onto the office floor.

'Morning, Fucks!' he announced, and with that was gone. It was all true! I had been told at Valley by Tinsel that you had to think of 'getting to the frontline despite 899'.

However, it quickly became apparent that the staff were, almost to a man, simply there to help. The flinty edge was there to make sure they didn't lower standards and passed only worthy blokes on to their mates in the frontline units. The Sea Harrier force was simply too small to carry deadweight. When I had visited 899 as a sub-lieutenant, they appeared to be actively trying to 'chop'[3] two pilots (which they managed) in a manner

2 Runs ashore, as the RN terms piss-ups, aren't limited to fifteen, but it's a good starting point.
3 Commonly accepted verb for removing from the flying pipelines.

that suggested they were trying to exacerbate the front-line's manning problem, not solve it!

Perhaps unsurprisingly 899 was spilt into four distinct packages. After all, it was a new jet, so one needed to convert to it. To add to that, it could take off and land vertically.[4] The Harrier, instead of a single jet pipe, has four nozzles that look like hairdryers on the side of the aircraft. They operate in unison[5] and are joined to the nozzle lever by big bicycle chains. The pilot could move the nozzles and therefore the thrust that came out of them – this was termed Vectored Thrust. Nozzles that move presented an opportunity – well, many opportunities – to embarrass and/or kill oneself. If the first two elements of the course were about flying, the remaining two were about fighting. The Harrier was a warplane, not a trainer, and at last things were going to progress past theoretical and become actual![6] Lastly, it had a very potent radar. Mastering the aircraft would fall into phases collectively termed Operational Flying Training. Convex, or Conversion Exercise, came first, then came the rest of Operational Flying Training 1 – doing all the stuff you'd done in other jets but in the Sea Harrier – for example, instrument flying, formation and

4 Which led some bright spark to coin the phrase 'jump jet' which I personally refuse to use. Apart from just then.
5 If you ever see a Harrier whose nozzles are no longer working in unison you are guaranteed to see a crash.
6 And for those of you thinking something like 'Well, the Hawk is a warplane', you can obviously think what you like. My advice would be: 'Please don't . . . '

low-level navigation. Then there was 'the hard bit'.[7] OFT 2 contained the air combat manoeuvring phase, the radar phase and the operational phase at the end. The radar phase was, by reputation, the hardest bit, and where most people were expected to fail or at least struggle.

Convex was all about the thrills and spills of trying to harness this new beast and the new regime of vertical/short take-off and landing or VSTOL. In the main, things centred around the elegantly simple addition of the nozzle lever alongside the throttle to the pilot's left, with which you set the angle of the nozzles depending on where you wish your thrust to act for a given manoeuvre.

I went solo on my third trip. I had some helpful advice from the squadron senior pilot as I left to go to the jet.

'Don't come back if you crash!' he said with a smile. I saw TJ on the stairs.

'Don't fuck it up!' he added. Well, I didn't crash, but it would be fair to say I did fuck it up.

Pushed into my seat as I accelerated down the runway, I joined the ranks of people who have had the joy of being thrust along in a single-seat jet by the howling Rolls-Royce Pegasus. Most things about the Harrier were impressive, but its speed out of the blocks was breathtaking. A little rearwards stick at 100 knots, and I was off the ground.

Once upstairs, though, things began to unravel. I configured the jet for the first landing and as I hit terra firma kept the aircraft straight with the rudder. I snatched the

7 I actually did better on OFT 2.

throttle back to idle, then attempted to use the engine to slow down with runway disappearing behind me as I careered westwards. I needed to swivel the nozzles forwards before applying retarding thrust but couldn't get them past straight down. Seven thousand feet of runway sounds a lot until you are going down it at 140 knots and haven't been taught how to take off again. All our take-offs had to be from a standing start when we were beginners. My left hand jammed the nozzle lever repeatedly back against the hover stop, but to move the nozzles forwards I had to lift the lever over that stop to the braking stop. I was lifting it, but not enough.[8] Four thousand feet to go, still not slowing down. Three thousand feet to go, desperately needing forward nozzle, I simply failed to lift the nozzle lever over that small piece of metal to get to the braking stop. The runway ran out.[9] I was left with no option but to jam on the toe brakes, well above the normal application speed. I taxied off the end of the runway.

'Yeovil 44, request intentions?' came the polite request from air traffic.

'Yeovil 44, I'm struggling with the nozzles, suggest I return to dispersal,' I replied, dejectedly.

'Yeovil 44, this is Tower, your supervisor agrees.' I taxied back, crushed. My woeful inability to cope with

---

8 In the new-build fighter the stop was a tiny bit bigger than in the well-worn trainer.

9 Some runways catch jets in a big net called a barrier. A barrier engagement in the FA2 was prohibited, as the net was likely to snag on parts of the jet and bring the top wire through the canopy at head height like some form of 100-knot garotte.

the smallest of differences between T8 and FA2 led to having to refly my first solo. Unbearable humiliation!

After that, most things went well,[10] as we explored the Harrier's unique abilities in ever greater depth.

It's fair to say that, for a vertical take-off, exuberance and excitement at going flying were replaced by trepidation. As I sat in the FA2 on Charlie Pad for my first solo vertical take-off and hover, I experienced 'disco leg', as my nerves found their way out into my right leg. Still, fuck all I could do about it at that stage, I thought, so might as well put the metaphorical gumshield in and lift to the 80-foot hover. The cadence of the VTO is awesome.

I set the power to 55 per cent and checked my engine instruments. All good. I snatched the nozzles to 50, checked that I had duct pressure,[11] and then moved them again smartly to the hover stop. My left hand moved from nozzle lever to throttle. SLAM. One heartbeat later and the Pegasus was at full power. With a healthy dose of noise and vibration the jet lifted crisply through ground effect. This is the reason why I hate the term 'jump jet'. It doesn't jump. It bludgeons physics into submission.

Snatching back a bit of power, I stopped my ascent, and a small reapplication caught me at hover height. Done. Flying a Harrier in the hover. I held my position. Throttle controlled height, stick controlled where I went, rudders which way I faced. My orders were simple. First

---

10 If we gloss over a short take-off strip at RAF Wittering, where I slammed to full power with nozzles still at 50 degrees. Cue hurtling down the short strip in a wheelbarrow simulation before I realized my error.
11 The ducts are the high-pressure pipes with which you control the jet at low speed.

off, I sat on my column of air and deafened the surroundings a bit before coming down. Next, I repeated
the VTO, included a 360-degree pedal turn, then landed.
On the last one, I launched and then shifted position to
land on a different spot. All actually pretty straightforward, although my right leg was still shaking as I taxied
back in. In fact, the only downside of learning to fly the
Sea Harrier in the hover was having to down a 'Hover
Pot' of beer in the bar.

By the end of Convex we had been introduced to the
Harrier's complete repertoire, including the mini circuit,
which was forbidden in the RAF at the time following an
accident. The process called for you to take a Sea Harrier
in the hover and to fly an oval pattern at hover height, a
couple of hundred yards long and about half that wide.
I'm not totally convinced that it had any utility, but it was
a good way of keeping your VSTOL up to scratch.[12]

As with all things in military aviation, new types,
characteristics and procedures gave rise to new ways
of killing yourself, and in the Harrier a phenomenon
called intake momentum drag (IMD)[13] was top of the
pile. Early Harrier pilots found out the hard way, and it
remained true forty years later that if you flew a Sea Harrier in the 30–120 knot speed band, with side slip on (i.e.

12 Its primary value was probably to maintain a skill that the RAF did
not possess.
13 All intakes experience intake momentum drag when pushed through
the air, but most aircraft experiencing asymmetric IMD operate at speeds
where any side effect is overcome by the vertical stabilizer or fin . . . or
are on the ground.

not going truly forwards), with a raised angle of attack,[14] you may well very violently flip over. If it happens, you have fractions of a second to get out of the problem. Removal of any of the three conditions means removal of the problem. Hence, it doesn't happen in the hover because you are below the speed band (unless the wind exceeds 30 knots). For this reason, we learned and slavishly abided by the rules governing the 'IMD triangle' or, as some termed it, 'the triangle of death'. The IMD triangle was the reason that we flew mini circuits below 30 knots. Other Harrier-isms included the strange effect of 'control reversal', which happened if you went backwards too quickly. Not really wanting to have to figure out how controls worked in reverse, I simply never went backwards at anything other than a crawl.

Even sitting on the ground, the Harrier was a beast. When you start a Hawk there's a point where the engine stops getting noisier and things become smooth. That didn't happen with the Harrier. The Harrier sat there snarling. This was partly to do with jet efflux playing on the tailplane, which shook the stick, and partly to do with the Pegasus just wanting to unleash 21,000 lbs of thrust . . . which was 'quite a lot'. We would set 10-degree nozzle after start to get the jet blast off the tailplane. Whereas some jets like the Tornado or F-16 would surprise you by how little of the airframe volume was taken up with engine, the Harrier was the opposite. It was a fuselage shrink-wrapped around a Pegasus with

14 The angle between your wing and the airflow over it. Also called Alpha.

aerodynamic surfaces added as an afterthought. It was a product of function over fashion and it gave rise to an ability unique to the Harrier. As well as using the nozzles to vector thrust for take-off and landing, we were taught to VIFF, or vector in forward flight, a manoeuvre not used in the Falkands War to the best of my knowledge but regarded as something akin to witchcraft at the time. By VIFFing, you gain advantage in combat.

High above Somerset, I had completed my pre-aerobatics checks, which amounted to 'high enough, not in a stupid place like over a town, aircraft set up correctly'. I simulated defending against a hostile aircraft – telling the instructor what I was imagining.[15]

'OK, aircraft in my left 9 o'clock, appears to be nose on . . . chaff, flare!' I called, simulating release of counter-measures as I simultaneously turned hard left towards the imaginary fighter to give him a really tough closure and angle problem, at the same time reducing power and bringing the nozzles to 60 degrees, tightening the turn and getting my efflux away from his IR-seeking weapons and reducing it at the same time.

'Bandit looks as if he's going to fly through!' I said – no need to repeat the three telltale signs of high crossing rate, right behind me, in planform.[16]

15 This sounds a little lame. It's not.
16 Just imagine someone running towards you on your left-hand side, trying to shoot you but missing – then being unable to change direction and continuing to run really fast just behind your chair. They would appear on your right-hand side, looking away from you. If you could turn very quickly to the right, you'd be able to shoot them in the back. In fighter terms that's called prosecuting a fly-through.

'Fly through!' I shouted. Now to stop myself going the way he was, which means he should have overtaken somewhere on my right-hand side.

Reselecting full power, I nozzled out, feeling the aircraft buck slightly as I did. I snapped to wings level and snatched the stick back to start going up and in so doing reduce my forward travel. The imaginary fighter was overtaking me on the right, it was a race to an imaginary wall, and the prize for getting there first was a Side-winder[17] right up the ass. Now for the party trick. Rolling right where we should have been canopy to canopy,[18] I pulled in nozzle, all the way to the braking stop. No jet in Christendom could match this, and he was going to fly right out in front of me . . . until my aircraft flicked so violently, departing from controlled flight, that my senses genuinely couldn't keep up with events. From 'possibly sounds quite lame but good fun combat against an imaginary foe' to jet tumbling through the sky happened in a heartbeat.

A departure in the Harrier is far more violent than a spin in any other aircraft, and because the aircraft was actually tumbling the movement was completely alien. I knew what to do, but whereas in the past it was easy to believe that an aircraft would stop spinning if I opposed yaw with rudder, as I went through my drills I genuinely wasn't sure that I was going to be able to recover.

17 The fabulous American missile, in its AIM-9L guise a great contributor to victory in the South Atlantic.
18 In certain highly accurate films this allows you to gesticulate rudely to an adversary.

Whatever happens in these situations, you stick to your drills. I was rattled by the ferocity of the movement but I knew that I had to do as I'd been taught and ride it out. The Harrier cartwheeled through space. I focused on my altitude and keeping the tailplane and rudders neutral. Alternatively hanging in my straps and then being forced down into my seat, I watched as precious thousands of feet, all that stood between me and the pre-briefed ejection altitude, rapidly wound down. As my pulse raced and the anxiety built, I did have one thing upon which to rely. Total trust in the experienced QFI in the back seat and the knowledge that by selecting idle I had preserved the engine for whatever was to come.

'This is a Level 9 departure!' came his grading of our predicament. His tone as calm as a news reader. I stayed silent as, on cue, the T8 settled out of the departure, nose low, and I allowed flying speed to build before I added power and entered a gentle climb for the next exercise. I was a little shaken but knew from the crew-room banter that departures were just something you had to get used to as you learned the ropes.

'How do we get to Level 10?' I asked.

'Ah, for that we have to surge the engine too!'

The VIFF is probably one of the most misunderstood concepts in aviation in that it buys you far less than some people assume but used correctly could be a very handy trick to have up your sleeve. There were various ways of using it, but the two I liked the most were the braking stop barrel roll and the nozzle flop. The former involved deploying forward nozzle when you and an adversary were at the beginning of what would ordinarily be a rolling fight. If the enemy jet was about to 'fly through' behind you and you slammed the nozzles forwards while flying a barrel roll around his flight path, you would fly him out the front as you slowed down at an unnatural pace. Being in front of a fighter that is trying to kill you is not a great place to be. The nozzle flop was handy if you were very slow, and therefore the consequent lack of Bernoullis[19] over the wings was making control tricky. If your adversary chose to run to either exit the fight or reposition, there wasn't much you could do about it in, say, a Hawk. At low speed there was simply not enough air going over the wings to allow you to bring your nose to bear on a jet accelerating away. You had no choice but to wait until your speed had built up a little. In the Harrier, you rolled on your back and gave it a bootful of rudder. A momentary unload with the stick followed by 60 nozzle, and your nose sliced down straight onto the bastard.

VIFFing or not, air combat manoeuvring[20] takes it out of you physically and mentally. A combination of high-speed, high-G, three-dimensional chess in an unscripted rollercoaster might come close. Two in a day is tiring. To finish the ACM phase at 899, I flew three

19 Mr Bernoulli invented lift – or was at least the first to explain it – but forgot to patent it, so it's there for everyone to use.
20 ACM, sometimes simply called 'combat'. This was also called air combat training or ACT. At some point we started calling it basic fighter manoeuvres or BFM. If you were against a different aircraft type it was termed 'dissimilar'. So you would ACM or BFM with your mates and DACT or DBFM with other folk. All the same thing.

ACM trips in one day. That evening, I think I sat and looked at the wall.

The truth was, though, even with VIFF, the Sea Harrier wasn't really a match in the visual arena, or dogfight, for most modern US or Russian fighters from an aerodynamic and power point of view. It was a 1950s design. However, being a fighter pilot is about finding a way to win. We could turn tightly, fly slowly and we had a very potent sting in the tail – or more accurately a sting in the nose. The Blue Vixen radar fitted to the FA2 was superb, both beyond visual range and within visual range, combat in fighters being broken up very basically into what you can see and what you can't.

The ingredients of a successful intercept boil down to: being in the right bit of sky, looking in the right bit of sky, using weapons at the right time and keeping a constant assessment going of how you're doing. In manoeuvres which would have got WW1 infantrymen shot for cowardice it was now quite all right to turn away from the enemy if things weren't going your way and turn back again once you'd convinced yourself they were looking better. There was obviously a limit to this, as there's no way you can defend something by continually running away. The point, as ever, was judgement. There will be times on an intercept where it's better to be running and alive, and there will be times when you simply have to put the gumshield in and face the enemy.

In the constant pursuit of tactics and counter-tactics the romantic notion of the silk-scarf-wearing fighter pilot smoothly using his flying controls to bring guns to bear had gradually been replaced by the cold, hard science of modern warfare, laden with radars, missiles, counter-measures, data links and communications that pretty much made up a brand-new language. This is one of the many reasons why I don't think there should ever be talk about a 'best fighter pilot' – because best probably means 'most likely to win', and that changes with platform, weapon, context – you name it. There are so many variables that it doesn't actually even stand up to scrutiny as a concept.

Your job on intercepts could be to engage, visually identify or – good fun but ridiculous – identify and engage if hostile. Ridiculous in the 'who else is it going to be?' sense. I never really struggled with the overall theory of intercepts, as a lot relied upon simple geometry made slightly harder by speed and the enemy. I found that I could usually keep a fairly decent picture in my head of where the other players were – particularly as when they were anywhere near your nose the Blue Vixen would invariably find them, so long as you kept your side of the bargain and asked it to look in the right place. To finish the radar phase we got sucked into some $4 + 4 + 4$ v 4[21] mayhem. Four of us sweeping for four French Super Etendards and four Jaguars versus four Tornado F3s. To say that I was a 'little confused' probably doesn't do the sortie justice. In the early part of the fight all I

---

21 The easiest way of describing an air-to-air engagement is merely to add up the number of people playing on both sides and display it like a sum. You versus someone else would be a 1 v 1. Two pairs butting heads would be 2 v 2. Defending against a fourship of muds with a pair in escort would be a 2 v 2 + 4. A small push at Red Flag is probably something like a 4 + 4 v 4 + 4 + 4 + 4 + 4 + 8.

could find were airliners. I lost sight of Tats, and had the classic Battle of Britain experience of the sky being full of jets one second and none the next. Oh dear. Then I got lucky.

An observer in an Airborne Early Warning Sea King gave me the information that there was a hostile aircraft bearing 020 from me at 20 miles and he was heading south-west, towards the friendly muds behind us. What a stroke of luck. Rather than have to admit I'd lost my leader, I pushed the throttle forwards to full power and racked the aircraft round to the north. 150 degrees of bank plus 4 G got me turning and descending from 30,000 feet. I wanted to lose 10,000 feet to get down towards where I expected the F3s to be operating. I immediately saw a track build on my screen and designated it, selecting AMRAAM with my right thumb. However, I didn't know it was the F3, I just thought it was.

Without confirmation from the Sea King I couldn't be sure it was the hostile. I needed to be sure – there's no margin at all for error. Nothing for it, I had to identify the contact visually – a task we call a VID.

I saw the light-grey fighter just as he snuck out of my radar scan, outlined beautifully against the Bristol Channel. That meant I now had a VID, as it was definitely an F3, but I had no radar lock.

This was a problem.

Dishonest aviators are despised for one particular party trick: claiming kills they can't substantiate. To guard against this, we had had it beaten into us that we didn't just 'point and shoot' with our weapons but needed solid radar tracks and video evidence that each shot would have worked. This was going to be my first ever multi-squadron debrief, and I was simply not going to fuck it up. No problem, I brought up Sidewinder and selected my favourite radar mode. The Blue Vixen immediately attached itself to a nice big stable track. The only issue was that I could immediately tell it wasn't my target. It was higher and further away, and the HUD was giving me no radar symbology over the F3 I was actually looking at. Then beyond the first fighter I caught sight of another F3 to which my Sidewinder was locked and howling in delight. Fantastic. I simulated a shot at the newcomer while manoeuvring to get a shot off on the original leaker,[22] who got one too.

'Fox 2[23] double, splash two F3s,'[24] I called on the radio.

As ever, it was better to be lucky than good, but that made it no less sweet.

Following a couple of weeks' leave,[25] we were due to fly a BITS (back in the saddle) hop with an instructor in the T8 twin-seater. I was sitting in our office with

---

22 Untargeted baddy.

23 Fox is a codeword for a missile shot. Fox 1 for the largely worthless semi-active shot of yesteryear which required a fighter to illuminate the target with radar; Fox 2 for heat seeker; Fox 3 for an active shot – whereby the weapon at some point would find its own way to the target aircraft.

24 Before anyone gets upitty, this is not evidence that I was better than those crews, or that the Sea Harrier was better than the F3. It is simply what happened in that instance. For the record, though – I was, and it was!

25 I'd never had a long leave period during a flying course before – this felt weird.

TJ when my instructor walked in and said (verbatim), 'Er, right, you and me for a BITS ride. Out, up, PAR, nicky-nacky-noo. Out, SRA, nicky-nacky-noo.'[26] He then walked out.

'Tell me that wasn't your brief!' exclaimed TJ who was still getting used to various things British.

'You know what, mate, I think it was!' I replied. And it was. I coped, so you could say that the brief was sufficient, but it felt a little sparse for a new-to-type pilot coming back off leave! In the 899 school of hard knocks, you roll with the punches.

It didn't always go my way. I failed a couple of trips on 899. I didn't do well enough on the twelfth trip of the radar syllabus, a complex (at the time!) 1 v 2 sortie involving taking simulated AMRAAM shots before flowing in for simulated Sidewinder shots. Because the simulator was offline for the entirety of our radar course, I'd missed the opportunity to practise and was therefore entitled to have another go. I passed the difficult bit only to make a mess of the vertical landing at the end.

In so doing I had not completed the VSTOL manoeuvre of the day. There was an instructors' coven, and

26 What that actually meant was 'Let's launch to the west and go upstairs to about 7,000 feet for some aerobatics and VIFF before calling for a radar letdown for a Precision Approach Radar back into the field. We'll roll to the visual circuit and we'll do the heavyweight circuits, such as Fixed Power Slow Land and Fixed Nozzle Slow Land. Then we'll depart the field for a second time and position for a Surveillance Radar Approach, again roll to the visual, before doing some lightweight landings and take-offs, each requiring its own technique. Do you have any questions?'

it was rightly judged that I needed a VSTOL refresher. Still, it turned out that we were actually due a mid-course VSTOL check that had somehow been left out as the staff prioritized our progress with the radar.

I failed the VSTOL sortie in a single second taxiing to the short runway at Yeovilton. To confirm that I was checking critical controls, the instructor took control of the flaps and prevented them from lowering. I should have followed the usual 'Limitation, Operation, Indication' cadence of: be in limits – do it – check it has happened. I obviously didn't check my flap had lowered. Flap is critical for take-off in the Sea Harrier. Rather than say, 'Mate – you've not checked your flap,' the instructor let me get on with it! We didn't really launch, we just kept accelerating along the short runway with no indication whatsoever of getting airborne. First time I deflected the nozzles absolutely nothing happened. No sprightly take-off. No shuddering exit from ground effect. Nothing. We just kept accelerating and we were already past the runway intersection; there was no hope of stopping. I ran the nozzles out and hauled them back in as we got to the far threshold. Fuck me! We were airborne but only just – and so fast . . . I got the gear up just in time to avoid going through the 250-knot limit. From there we went to Boscombe Down for some practice approaches, and when I configured for the first I noticed that the flap hadn't travelled. Shit. It was only as we taxied back in at Yeovilton that the instructor said that I'd failed for taking off with no flap. I was so cross with myself. Fucking idiot Tremelling had fallen for the oldest trick in the book.

However, as luck would have it, as we climbed out of

the jet Steve careered off the end of the runway. With an almighty bang he ejected and, from where I was standing, flew in a majestic arc over the Fleet Air Arm church and landed like a sack of crap beneath a fully developed parachute somewhere near the runway threshold. The same one I'd scorched off about an hour ago. Not something you see every day and obviously no way of telling that he was OK until we got back inside and someone let us know that all was well. 'Well' being a relative term.

I was told that the instructors had decided that the flying programme would go ahead. But if you had actually witnessed the ejection you might not fly again that day. So, prior to us being told that we were done for the day, there was some sort of market research going on to find out which students had seen what. I said that I had seen Steve's impressive trajectory; however, I would like to fly but with the caveat that I probably wouldn't be able to as I'd just porked my VSTOL check ride. When I was asked how, and I explained my flapless launch, this second instructor's eyes popped out on stalks.

'You fucking what?' he said. 'You actually got airborne with no flap?'[27]

Still (rightly) beating myself up, I repeated the story and was given a 'Leave this with me.'

This second instructor – I am led to believe – went straight to the squadron boss to tell him what had happened, and the instructor from my VSTOL ride was called in for a bit of 'rug shuffling'. The facts of the case

27 In the 'that's ludicrously dangerous' sense, not in the 'that should be impossible – well done you' sense.

were simple. I had failed the trip. I had failed to check a critical control surface. What should have happened is that the instructor should have stopped me, explained my error and maybe even failed the trip then and there. What should not have happened was a flapless launch, with 99 per cent power set on a short runway. Unbeknownst to me, I had just completed the most dangerous manoeuvre I would ever fly in the Harrier![28] When I sat down for the VSTOL check refly with a completely different instructor, he started off by pointing to the centre of his forehead and saying: 'So, Tremors, you can probably see that I do not have a penis growing out of my head, so I can promise you that what happened last time won't happen again!' My incompetence and unacceptable lack of attention to detail appeared to have been dwarfed by the achievement of taking off at all.

And so it came to pass: following bewildering ground school, 'just behind the aeroplane' VSTOL, high-octane ACM and the mental gymnastics of the radar phase, we found ourselves on the North Sea Air Combat Manoeuvring Instrumentation Range fighting F-16 and Mirage 2000 jets[29] before one last trip at Yeovilton. The 899 final handling test. The last hurdle in a twin-seat T8. Mine involved a low-level strike, a collection of VIFF manoeuvres, a diversion into St Mawgan and a simulated emergency to bring me back to Yeovilton for a

---

28 As in the manoeuvre itself was inherently dangerous, not the dangerous execution of a fundamentally safer trick.
29 We warmed up with a bit of seal clubbing against Jaguars. Good fun, but not what we needed in the work-up to playing with the 'big boys'.

fixed-power approach. I finished the test with a vertical landing on Charlie Pad. TJ later said he was watching and, using a lamppost as a reference, could tell that the VL was perfect. As I taxied in, the squadron boss asked me from the back seat how it felt to be a Sea Harrier pilot.

'Fucking brilliant,' I replied.[30]

I had always maintained that the dreaded chop could come at any point, right up to the final test. Fiona had had a bit more faith in me and ordered a special edition Sea Harrier watch for me as a present for making it to the end. If I'd had that confidence, it would probably have made the whole experience far more enjoyable!

I would go to 800 Naval Air Squadron, one of only two frontline units. Our jets wore red tail flashes and were emblazoned with the cross swords of our squadron badge. The weapons pointed upwards, denoting a fighter unit. In many ways I sensed that I had made it and could now consider myself a fighter pilot. In other ways, yet again, I realized how much I had left to learn. We would operate from home, from other airfields worldwide and from the Invincible class aircraft carriers. The extraordinary was going to become my everyday.

Jim and I went together to 800, whilst TJ went to 801 NAS, our sister squadron and one with which we had an intense if friendly rivalry. Apparently it hadn't been friendly following the Falklands War, when relationships

---

30 I really wish I hadn't accepted the whisky in the debrief, though — that stuff was gopping. However, to wear that Sea Harrier patch on my coverall sleeve I'd have necked an ocean of it.

between the two had been poisonous. Both were about a one-minute walk from 899. We inhabited either side of a horseshoe-shaped building, which I customized by denting with my car on my first morning. Maybe I was too excited. The office layout meant that we could see into 801 NAS, which made it perfect for crank calls to their phones and irresponsible mass printing when we learned the addresses of their printers. In the air things sometimes got a little out of hand. In one of my first 800 vs 801 grudge matches an 801 pilot had soaked up simulated shots but was still making a pain of himself. My leader broke with our usually immaculate radio discipline.

'You're dead, Benny, now fuck off!'

Our squadron motto was 'Nunquam Non Paratus' or 'Never Unprepared' . . . the local wags claiming it actually meant 'Never Knowingly Seen Off'.

It was going to take a little while, however, before Jim and I genuinely felt prepared for all eventualities.

9. Flying the Sea Harrier

RNAS Yeovilton, Somerset. Broadly speaking sober.

My first week on the frontline saw me walking to the jet for a pretty tough trip. We were supporting an exercise in the north of Scotland and would ordinarily be doing this from a carrier that was actually bobbing around somewhere off the Hebrides. This time, completely dependent on tanker aircraft, we were going to do it from Yeovilton. The weather was poor, which meant that we were probably going to be in thick cloud for most of the next four hours, while we alternated between air-to-air action and air refuelling. I conducted the walk-round checks, gloved hand moving from aerial to aerodynamic service – checking for movement, checking locks had been removed. Using both hands, I made sure that there was no play in any of the four nozzles and that the reaction controls were working as advertised. I cast my eyes over the bulbous nose of the aeroplane, searching for cracks, dents, anything out of place. This was the single-seat game, and whilst the plane crew would follow me around, it was my life on the line if I missed anything.

We weren't carrying live weapons, but hidden in the gun pods beneath the fuselage were the pieces of kit that pretended to be AMRAAM missiles. These would allow me to simulate shots with that fantastic weapon. If you could get the AMRAAM up high prior to launch then it performed brilliantly. The FA2 loved high altitude, and we would regularly place our combat air patrol (CAP) above 30,000 feet and could climb higher still if need be. This extra height, even though we launched at sub-sonic speed, gave an AMRAAM fired from a Sea Harrier longer legs than one fired from a supersonic interceptor, for example an RAF Tornado F3, at lower launch altitudes. A point lost on everyone from the general public to Air Warfare Centre (AWC).

Once in the cockpit I punched in my navigational way-points, pressed the start button and moved the throttle forwards to idle. Behind me, the engine sprang to life. I moved the radar switch above the display to ON. That thing was crucial – better to get it started soonest, just in case it was sulking and needed a reboot.

'Satan, tell off,' came from lead. We didn't 'check in' in the Royal Navy, we 'told off'.

'Two,' I replied.

'Three.'

'Four.' The staccato radio calls from the other jets telling everyone we were ready to go. Some forces would add some words to show that they were ready, not us. If there was one thing we took pride in, it was our communications. All by the book. Not a single wasted syllable.

We would launch as two pairs. Me on the leader's wing, slamming to full power when he nodded his head. As we accelerated along the runway, the next head nod called for 50 nozzle, which I pulled in with my left hand. My hand leaped from nozzle lever back to the throttle for a small nudge of power to keep me in a tidy formation. Back to the nozzle lever, I slowly moved the nozzles aft, trying to match the leader's as they moved backwards. Hand back to throttle to catch a small over-take. The famed 'Harrier Juggle'. Another head nod from leader, and I felt for the gear switch with my left hand. Not taking my eyes from the aeroplane a couple of feet to my left, I punched the gear up and moved the flap switch from FULL to MID.

My job now was simple. Stay in formation. Using hun-dreds, maybe thousands, of control inputs to stay in a box of sky just off my leader's wingtip. Occasionally changing hands on the stick to free up my right hand for radio changes.

'London, good morning,' called my leader, Satan 1, as we climbed away from Yeovilton. 'Satan's with you, looking for flight level 330 and direct track Stornoway when able,' he continued, opening the chat that would last all the way to Scotland and back. Forty-five minutes later, we drew up alongside a wonderful old VC10 as it waited for us above the Highlands. These converted airliners served as tankers, with hoses trailing from each wing. We pulled up on the right side. I made sure I could see the head of the guy in the cockpit. If I could see his head, he could see me.

'Satan 2, clear contact right.'

'Satan 2,' I replied. I had already established the wait-ing position just aft of the basket, the funnel-like mesh at the end of the hose into which I had to plug my jet's refuelling probe. Pushing the throttle forwards, I felt the healthy surge of power as the jet moved, probe head-ing straight for the basket in front of it. Impact. In the wrong place. My probe hit the basket in the four o'clock position. The bow wave caused by my aircraft had shifted the basket away from me, and I hadn't compensated. The probe rested momentarily on the drogue lip and then barged past it, sending a wave up the hose. The trick now was to be calm.

'Small amount of power off. Get away from the basket as it sorts itself out,' I thought. 'Get back in the waiting position.' I knew that, to my left, lead would not only have the capacity to keep tanking but would also be monitoring my technique. Looking out for the new kid. Many more misses and I'd still be stabbing at the basket when 3 and 4 showed up. Forwards again, this time with a satisfying clunk, and the hose slackened as my probe made contact. Pushing the jet towards the tanker, I saw the small lights on the hose unit bolted to the VC10 wing turn from amber to green – fuel flow. I was tanking, like a grown-up.

I found the tanking stressful. Having to maintain position on the tanker, keeping the hose in the right place, particularly in cloud and through turns, wasn't an enjoyable five minutes for me. Tanking complete, and having gathered the rear pair with us, it was time to play.

There was more cloud than open sky, but fortunately we found a small break in the weather to conduct our weapons checks. I locked lead up with my radar, checked that all my weapons worked and tested my chaff and flares.

'Candles sweet,' came the terse call from lead, telling me that he'd seen my flares deploy. We checked our radars before once more being enveloped by cloud. Although fighting the enemy was our task today, my main focus would be on not flying into the leader.

We checked in with the controller, some poor soul on a destroyer being flung around by the sea state we couldn't see through the murk. My job: be in the right place, radar looking at the right bit of sky, using perfect communications. Our first task was to get on CAP – our allotted combat air patrol station. Lead was flying a six-minute race track, with me on his wing and Satan 3 and 4 three minutes behind us. This way, one pair was always pointing up threat. In places like Scotland, where inbound raids could terrain mask behind the mountains, it was common for us to see the enemy before the surface fleet did. Sometimes we even outdid the AEW Sea King.

Ordinarily each pair would patrol at the same altitude, flying CAP in battle formation, or combat spread,[1] as the USAF would call it, but given the cloud I sat 1,000 feet above my leader and took comfort in every radar sweep that showed me his jet, a mile or so in front and slightly to the side. At high altitude I knew that I had to be careful about keeping my speed up around 0.8 Mach,[2] or the aircraft would descend, particularly in the turn. I tried to be as gentle as possible in the turns. No pretty contrails today, just dense grey cloud.

The fight therefore fell into five separate pieces. The

1 'Battle', 'combat spread', call it what you will, is a formation where two jets sit parallel at a range that allows them to keep a visual lookout behind and below each other, being far enough away to be separate and close enough to help. About a mile line abreast.
2 80 per cent of the speed of sound.

CAP allowed us to gain as much situational awareness as possible. In this phase the priority was good formation and sound radar handling, and the trick was to listen hard and talk by exception.

'Satans commit, single group, bullseye 050 at 60,'[3] came the directive from our fighter controller.

We'd entered the second stage. The enemy had crossed the line where action became inevitable.

'Satans,' replied lead. We didn't need to say any more. We began the intercept. Behind us, 3 and 4 would be doing exactly the same. They were our insurance policy. If we screwed it up, we'd leave it to them and reset behind them. I pushed the throttle lever forwards, my radar searching ahead, left thumb slewing the radar, left fore and index fingers moving the scanner up and down, left thumb changing range scale, left thumb keying the main radio into life.

'Satan 2, same, bullseye 045 at 55,' I called as two blobs formed on my radar screen, lines out the front showing that they were headed for the friendly fleet. On my HUD symbology my aircraft was now telling me how far they were away, how likely the AMRAAM was to kill them. All the things I needed to know.

Lead's job was now quite hard, in that he was running the intercept, but I was the one who could see the enemy. This all changed when we got ready to shoot, which we did at different ranges, depending on who we

---

3 'Satans, we want you to target some specific enemy. They are all close together, so we can refer to them as a single group. They are currently 050 degrees at 60 miles from a point we agreed upon to make this easier.'

were fighting. Shooting the right people at the right time was the third stage.

'Satan 1, Fox 3.' It was time to let the AMRAAMs go.

'Satan 2, Fox 3,' I called as I got ready for the fourth and hardest stage, supporting your shots. Very dynamic manoeuvring of the aircraft while keeping the enemy in the scan and knowing where lead was. We turned away as far as we dared. By keeping the enemy away from our nose, but still in the radar scan, we were giving the weapon as much time as possible to do our jobs for us. Why flow into a visual fight if the AMRAAM can sort things out at range? As I turned away from the threat and descended following the leader, I was crashing a fighter down through thousands of feet, while not flying into lead, at the same time staying in a tactical formation on him – and supporting the shot which was the reason for being there in the first place.

Tense seconds followed, but it looked like the threat fighters were going to walk into our shots – maybe without even knowing we were there. The aircraft equipment counted down the seconds until the simulated weapons would have impacted.

'Satan 2, time out, kill,' I declared, trying to sound firm rather than triumphant, which was viewed dimly.

'Satans, splash single group, Satans resuming CAP,' called lead, before we ran through our post-intercept checklists to make sure we knew where everyone was and how much fuel we had. This was our fifth stage – the reorganization. It would soon be time to go back to the tanker before coming back into the exercise and repeating it all over again as the raids continued to build.

It really didn't matter how cold I had the cockpit conditioning, this was a day for a very sweaty immersion suit.

After our second refuel and our second brave attempt at defending the fleet, it was time to go home.

This was exactly what I'd signed up for, with one glaring omission. We hadn't been to the boat[4] yet.

4 Yes, it's actually a ship. If you are one of those folks who take offence at people calling ships boats, you might want to relax a little (or possibly stop reading). I enjoyed boat operations, sitting on the back of the roof, watching the front going up and down, while people inhabited the floors below.

10. An Introduction to Naval Aviation

RNAS Yeovilton, Somerset.
Not a drop had passed my lips.

Naval aviation is a thing of beauty to behold when aircrew, deck crew, Flyco[1] and the operations team are all acting in unison. However, when I was on the frontline, you might have formed the opinion that the RN wasn't particularly air minded. Hold that thought, as we'll come back to it. First, though, landing on a boat.

I was almost introduced to naval aviation proper on Monday 11 February 2002. I was one of four 800 Naval Air Squadron pilots due to embark that day at the beginning of our period as the designated 'on watch squadron'. The weather was dreadful. So dreadful that the crosswind limit for getting the boat out through the hole in the wall in Portsmouth had been exceeded, and the wind wasn't going to abate. This small bit of news took hours to reach us, however. To pass the time while we waited, we watched the 'VSTOL Horror Video'. Why would you have more than one video on a squadron? It's a compilation of an earlier generation of Harrier pilots crashing, burning and dying as they got to grips

1 Like an air traffic control tower bolted to the carrier's bridge, just with very low SA and far more shouting than you would expect.

with VSTOL flight. Strange aerodynamic effects, burning water pumps, you name it. If you can kill yourself doing it in a Harrier then it's on the Horror Video. It was a really useful tool for bringing inexperienced but over-confident pilots down a peg or two when they needed a reminder that VSTOL was deadly. Very sobering. Particularly if you are the Fucking New Guy (FNG) on a squadron about to do your first deck landing.

We went the next day, or at least the others did. I got about as far as Bournemouth and was sent home. Descending through thick cloud all the way down to the minimum of 200 feet, my far more experienced colleagues had 'only just got in'.[2] There was no hope for me. When I got home, I had to telephone the ship and ask, 'Please, sir, can I bring the last jet on tomorrow?' Given the palaver it took to call the ship, which had to be done via Whitehall, it amazes me sometimes that we ever got an air group to the Falklands. Anyway, I was told that I should embark on the Wednesday. That would have worked had the aeroplane not broken. I was finally going to do my first deck landing somewhere off Plymouth on Thursday 14 February 2002.

The weather was glorious, the sea looked a little lumpy. For my first go I was given someone to follow, and Matty was launched to come and find me. 'Hey, Tremors, mate,

2 When a fast jet pilot tells you he 'only just got in', what he actually means is 'I breached minima by a smallish margin that we really don't need to discuss, and everything came good in the end.' Arguably unprofessional. Arguably the height of mission-focused risk management.

where are you?' he boomed in his cheerful Australian accent over the R/T.

'I'm 080 at 18 miles, mate, orbiting at 4,000 feet.' I should have given him a terse 'as briefed' because I was exactly where I was supposed to be . . . but whilst comm brevity is laudable, being a knob isn't, and as the FNG your main aim in life was to be embraced by your unit, not rejected by it! Now, getting on board a ship in a VSTOL fighter does involve some complexity, but at its very heart is the elegantly simple problem of getting to the ship at the right time, with the right fuel load, to make an approach in good order.

Getting to the ship – that bit was easy, because I had to sit just off Matty's wing in a position called Arrow, until we got to the boat, when I would move into close formation. Fuel load was the next issue and to be frank would be an issue for every single minute of my career flying in and out of fleets, to and from ships. Ships are not like airfields. They have other things to worry about than the recovery of aircraft, and this is managed by all parts becoming a well-oiled machine. Key to us playing our part was timing. We were expected, unless briefed otherwise, to launch on time and recover on time, and if you weren't within about five seconds then something was wrong. For launch you did exactly what the deck team told you – so that was out of your hands. Recovery, how-ever, was well and truly 'in your hands'. We strived to nail our landing times, known as Charlie times, to within five seconds. If you were outside fifteen seconds, the skipper used to have words. That would be utterly humiliating.

In the Sea Harrier you could dump the contents of your wing and drop tanks through vents in the wings. You couldn't dump the contents of the internal fuel tanks, which contained 2,200lbs of fuel – which was therefore the minimum you could 'dump down to' using the jettison facility. We used to want to arrive at the ship and be able to hover (naturally!), which was loadout dependent: more stuff being carried = less fuel in the hover. Simple. If it was possible, we carried a bit more than the bare minimum, as it might allow a more comfortable ride to a diversion or give you a cup of fuel in case of some sort of faff – but never enough that would compromise hover performance. It always seemed to boil down to needing to be through the slot[3] with about 1,200lbs of fuel, sometimes plus whatever the atmospherics of the day and your load out would allow – rarely would this make more than 400lbs difference. We therefore had quite a small window to aim for. But we knew our load at the slot, and we knew our fuel burn, as we always set the throttles at 70lbs per minute for recovery – or 700lbs every ten minutes. That meant that if you dumped everything above 2,200lbs and had done it by eleven minutes to go, then eight and a half minutes later you'd have 1,600lbs.

This could be refined by dumping fuel a couple of minutes early if need be or by increasing the fuel burn by using airbrake or nozzle. We dumped fuel on most trips. Over land you had to be above 5,000 feet to dump – which meant that none got to the ground. Over the sea you could dump wherever you wanted. Probably

3 Overhead the boat at 600 feet, 2.5 minutes to Charlie.

environmentally reprehensible to not only jettison fossil fuel but to do so directly into the ocean. The alternative was to dump a whole fighter that couldn't hover, so on balance not the worst outcome. The extreme of fuel management was what to do if you ran out.

There are two ways in which you could run out of fuel. The first was to simply use up all your fuel – a challenge we shared with all aviators and something drummed into you from the start as being unacceptable. I'm sure most folk agree. The other way a naval aviator can run out is to go below the fuel you need to make it to your Charlie time. At any point in the sortie, if you got to the figure that matched the amount of fuel you needed to make your Charlie time, you were termed 'Lamb'. If you were Lamb you were tactically useless – but you wouldn't crash or suffer the humiliation of asking for an earlier Charlie time.[4] On everyone's knee board was written a 'Lamb Ladder' which was simply a set of figures that was the minimum fuel at any given point in the sortie to make the planned Charlie time. It would say something pretty simple like 'C[harlie]-10 = 2,100, C-20 = 2,800, C-30 = 3,500', etc., and you looked at it about every two seconds, and every third look you had a panic attack that you'd messed up before realizing all was well! Of course, it was easier if you made the references to Charlie times into 'actual times' – which wasn't possible if you'd arranged a Flexi Charlie. What he giveth with one hand he will find a way of taking somehow!

---

4 In all my time flying around ships, I only witnessed one case of someone having to plead for an early Charlie.

So timing was straightforward, and fuel was too, so long as you were disciplined. How about being in good order? We did checks to take the jet from being poised for warfighting to being ready for 'flying about'. We then did pre-descent checks. These were all vital as they stopped you descending into problematic things like hills. They were also followed by the downwind checks or 'vital actions', which, as the name suggests, were adjudged just as vital by whoever had named them.

On that February morning, Matty took care of timing, and as we neared the ship I snuggled up into close Echelon.[5] As the old adage goes, 'better to die than look bad at the boat'. Checking and rechecking that I wasn't about to completely pork the fuel, I switched my dumps on at twelve minutes to go, pushing both switches forwards with my right hand while taking my left hand off the throttle to control the stick. I tried to contain my mounting anxiety as the ship went from 'distant thing of interest in the sea' to 'relatively close thing I was about to land on'. It didn't seem to get any bigger.

Matty led us through the slot with me tucked in close on his starboard side. He waited for fifteen seconds, gave me the finger and broke to the left. I started my stopwatch and maintained heading. Now I was well and truly on my own. 'Red 5, 20 knots,'[6] came the wind call from

---

5 In close and slightly swept – a bit like the Red Arrows but a little bit closer and in a decent paint scheme.

6 Measured in degrees from the ship's heading. Red is on the port side, green on the starboard. Red winds meant no interference from the

the landing signals officer. I kept lined up on the Devon coast and fifteen seconds after Matty had gone I broke left, starting the vital actions straight away in the 60-degree banked turn.

A touch of airbrake brought my speed below 300 knots.

Speed below 300 – flap full.

Speed below 250 – gear down.

Still turning, I threw on a handful of throttle to fix the correct angle of attack. I allowed myself one quick look out to see the ship at about seven o'clock. I held the turn.

Check STO stop clear.

Combat switch OFF.

Nav lights, landing light, strobe light all correct. Rolling out astern of Matty, I checked spacing on the ship, which was now in the ten o'clock on a reciprocal heading. Still not big. Moving. The spacing looked about right.

Pressures all correct. Brake pressure up and down in sympathy with a pump of the toe brakes. No residual.

Four green indicators told me that the gear was down and locked.

Then I tested my water system. Water primed – in manual. Slam full power. Check water flow light. Manual OFF. Select LAND.[7] I watched Matty com-

---

superstructure – but you wanted them as fine to the bow as possible. Red 5 was perfect.

7 The manual check showed that water would flow – in LAND the system needed rpm and jet pipe temperature limits to be tripped so you could quickly check the system and then select LAND knowing it was working.

mence his turn to land as I completed the rest of the checklist.[8]

Harness tight and locked. Toes clear of the brakes.

I looked out to see the boat was at about my eight o'clock. It was time to go.

Selecting 20 nozzle, I set a descending turn.

Nozzle 40, more power. With a quick glance out, I tightened the turn a bit to run in from 175 degrees off the port bow.

Rolling out of the turn, I pulled in more nozzle. Fuck me, the ship was moving, the whole deck appearing to rear up to face me.

I snatched the nozzle to the hover stop. Matty's jet was already alongside, kicking up spray as I approached the back of the ship. I used stick and forward trim to catch the 'buck' as the jet tried to rear up from the high nozzle setting.

Down through 100 knots – I made the absolutely critical check that I had enough power margin to hover. I was good.

'Maybe a bit fast, though,' I thought. 'Time to use nozzle nudge.' By holding the airbrake aft I gained 10 degrees of more nozzle[9] and therefore a little reverse thrust. I needed a bit more power. Then, as I got very close to the ship and released nozzle nudge, I went a little high. I was trying to come up the port side at a 'fast walking pace'; however, it felt a little slow.

8 For the avoidance of doubt, you learn these actions from a checklist but have to perform all drills from memory.
9 A wonderful feature not included in the Harrier 2.

'Hellcat 2, you are slow,' came the confirmation from the landing signals officer.[10] Fuck, aspirations of making a flawless approach were rapidly replaced by hopes of a 'broadly speaking safe approach'! Obviously shouldn't have taken that nozzle nudge.

As I drove up the port side, arresting my descent with power, I ended up hovering, there or thereabouts, alongside a ship. A real live ship. A real live person in a yellow jacket was waving for me to land on 4 Spot. Real live people were in Flyco watching.

It was still no bigger.

At Yeovilton, landing off the pad was embarrassing. Here it was unthinkable. Now the trick was a stable hover. I identified the white line painted athwartships that I had to land on. My bum line, so called because you run your bum along it as you transition over the deck. I kept Flyco level with the horizon. I knew that if the heads of the real live people in Flyco appeared on the horizon to me, mine would to them. You could overthink this whole situation. The ship was going one way, the tide another, the wind another – there was a complex vector diagram at play. The simple answer was to pretend the ship was an aeroplane and fly in formation on it, close enough that you didn't see water between you and it.

As soon as I was settled, I inched across the deck. With a nudge of power I tilted the lift vector to move me across. Over the tramlines, a touch of left stick brought me to a positive stop. Now in a hover again, this time with a dirty great superstructure to the right. Not too

10 Callsign 'Paddles' – one of your mates keeping you alive.

close, but close enough. The squadron ops officer was standing on goofers.[11] Not quite touching distance, but closer to my wing than I'd ever seen a pedestrian before. There's a balance to be struck between nailing the steady hover over the deck and 'just landing the damn thing'. I went for the latter. Power off, power back on.[12] No real time to think. I came positively down through ground effect.[13] Thump – not a teeth-chattering collision but firm. I chopped the throttle immediately to avoid the dreaded power bounce and stamped on the brakes – I was down.

Not even the remotest hint of a celebration just yet. Landing on a postage stamp is one thing, staying on it quite another. Time to stick to the drills then look up. There was a yellow-coat beckoning me on – desperate to get me off the hotspot. On the deck you do exactly as you're told. Moving the nozzles to 10 degrees, I released the brakes and taxied up the deck. The yellow-coat gave me a hard turn to port and indicated that they were going to wash the compressor. Simple process – fire freshwater down the Pegasus intake and clean the salt off everything. I was then directed to sit with my hands on my head, the yellow-coat doing the same with his. If his hands were on his head, mine had to be. This was the simplest (and 100 per cent effective) way of ensuring that wandering aircrew hands didn't do anything that would endanger

11 The open part of the superstructure from which one could watch the deck ops. A goofer was a spectator; to goof was to spectate.
12 Power back on gave a steady, unaccelerated descent.
13 Forgive the misnomer.

people working close to the aeroplane. Eventually he let me know that I was all chained up and with two fingers up directed me to replace my seat and canopy pins. Seat and canopy safety pins in. Job done, I gave the two-finger gesture back, and he gave a cut-throat signal. I pulled the throttle back past idle and all the way back to CUT OFF. I'd done it. Landed a Sea Harrier on one of Her Majesty's turd barges.

Fuck me.

11. The Day We Were Told That the End Was Nigh

A fortnight later. RNAS Yeovilton.
Slightly shabby as it was a no-fly day.

Two weeks to the day after my first deck landing, we were called to the station briefing hall at Yeovilton. It was 28 February 2002, and the sky was genuinely about to fall down on us. Sir John Day, commander-in-chief of Strike Command, had come to Yeovilton to give us some news that, to paraphrase, wasn't great. We were going to go out of service early. We weren't going to take our jets to Cottesmore. The Sea Harrier was going to be on the scrap pile by 2006, and its replacement wasn't expected in service until 2012.[1]

We were, in the main, naval aviators flying naval fighters but had been placed within the RAF structure as a result of a reorganization. Hence it was an RAF officer who delivered this bitter pill.

As I sat and listened to the usual and expected pleasantries about defence financials and pride in one's achievements, and those of the community, I felt the seething anger inside of me that would sadly repeat itself over my career. Not so much the life-changing decision

1 'Expected to enter' and 'actually enter' separated, in the end, by a mere six years!

that some unseen person had made on my behalf, rather my complete impotence in affecting it.

As a recently qualified pilot I had no idea what it all meant to me. We were already scheduled to move to Cottesmore. That would still happen but without our beloved Sea Jet. With its demise, we would now have to retrain on the RAF's Harrier GR7, which would waste a significant part of a career and mean going to the bottom of the pile again. The great idea of fighters and muds working together in a joint force had become a questionable idea of flying off CVS with just muds.[2] What it meant downstream for someone who didn't really have a downstream plan, beyond a wish to keep flying jets onto and from ships,[3] wasn't immediately clear.

Others could see exactly, however. We got back to the squadron building quickly after the brief. My senior pilot, maybe, just maybe, the finest fighter pilot who has ever walked this earth and slipped those surly bonds, was in the operations room.

'What does it mean for you, Splot?'[4] I asked, thinking that I would get an eloquent reply about diminished chances of squadron command. In response Splot reached for his squadron name badge, Velcroed to his

2 My assessment is based upon the broadly accepted premise that, as people don't like being bombed, they tend to obstruct bombers. Usually with fighters and SAMs. The FA2 could deal very nicely with one of those.

3 This did become clear in time. Answer: you can't keep flying to and from ships if your jets are required elsewhere – for example, Afghanistan.

4 Fleet Air Arm corruption of Senior Pilot. Quaint if unimaginative.

left chest where the RAF would wear their wings. He ripped it off.

'I'll show you what it means to me!' he announced, throwing his squadron badge on the floor. 'It means this!' And he started stamping on it with increasing vehemence.

Time to leave! Glad I asked.

By coincidence, a formation of RAF Harriers arrived that day as their pilots, squadron bosses, had been invited to a dinner. As I helped one with his bags, he smiled and said, 'You can have the bag, but you can't have the jet just yet!'

I genuinely hadn't considered that the RAF community would have to find space for us and would be subjected to some turbulence. But we were the ones losing our jet, our role and our career time, and who would move across the country and into someone else's command structure. It felt a bit like having your teeth booted out and a medic complaining that they had it just as bad as you'd got blood on their rubber gloves. I bit my tongue, just as well, as sharing my thoughts at that slightly heightened moment with a senior officer wouldn't have been a great way of teeing up my transition to a weapon system which in time I would love as much as the Sea Harrier.

For now, though, I resolved to make the very best of the Sea Jet's twilight. After all, we only had two options. The first was to blub into our beer about a decision we couldn't affect. The other was to be the very best we could at everything we did and pray for hostilities. There was still a chance we would deploy, and there was plenty to learn about my trade and flying from the sea base that would stand me in good stead whatever the future held.

The Harrier GR7 and the new aircraft would both go to sea, and therefore it was imperative that a core of us kept those precious maritime strike skills alive. This would be tough, though, with fewer jets.

We knew that flying to and from ships is a great example of teamwork based on very high-end but perishable skills. Across the whole team, not just the aircrew. It was very efficient when the team worked. One reason we knew that we would have to remain focused on deck operations was that even when there were enough jets for frequent embarked periods things still went wrong – sometimes very quickly. Read on . . .

12. The Day That the Boat Tried Its Hardest to Shake Us Off

The Mull of Kintyre. Sober, following a disastrous attempt at a run ashore in Largs.

Deck landings are fairly obviously what set maritime pilots apart from their land-based brethren. Deck landings could be made harder by three things. The weather, the complexity of the mission that you had just flown, as we all have a limit to how long we can keep doing high-end stuff, and the boat. The boat had ways of making your life harder, the simplest of which was to make the landing itself tough.

We had been ashore in Prestwick because the ship was broken. We had launched on one final 'out from Prestwick then back to the boat' mission with me leading. Two of the three of us had previously practised ARH (aircraft recovery heading). This is when the ship is on a designated flying course, but you aren't going to land on DFC – you're going to do something else. Not something you want to try in a conventional aeroplane – unless you are the proud possessor of a white headband with a red rising sun on the front. It allowed us to land across the deck or aft facing. Best not to overthink it. Use the ARH and 'make shit happen' when presented with a boat at an unusual angle. Both cross-deck and aft-facing were straightforward but weird. The most entertaining was to land cross-deck on 1 Spot, which meant that you landed vertically at the foot of the ramp, pointing your nose at the folk on the bridge. It felt like you were scratching your radome down the superstructure, and the trick therefore was to override the temptation to be too far back. Too far back being 'off the ship' on the port side. Overshooting really wasn't an option. The other place you could go was 'centre deck aft' – right at the back, which was a far bigger area, no ship drivers to entertain or crash into, but equally no close-at-hand references to tell how you were doing, so it was easier to land without being purely vertical. I once watched my cabin mate Jim land centre deck aft and 'bunny hop' forwards on touchdown, which was a little uncomfortable.

We were recovering to the boat which had left Glen Mallon and was on the eastern side of the Mull of Kintyre – offshore by about a mile, heading south but with a westerly DFC nominated. Westerly made sense because the wind was indeed from the west. Only westerly would mean heading straight for the Mull and going aground, which the ship's team seemed to have missed. They did turn onto the westerly course for us to land, which we set up for. No sooner had we started our approaches than the ship's team noticed the large piece of real estate right in front of them and made an emergency turn as they realized their mistake. We had no fuel to go to a diversion, and the ship was now doing a manoeuvre which would shake off any Fixed Wing aircraft – other than a Harrier. The ship would be at right angles to our approach. We could land on – but would do so facing across the ship. We had no fuel to go to a diversion, and the ship was actively trying to throw us off!

'Oh, bit of emergency break-away action!' transmitted number 3, followed by a wonderful call from Flyco.

'Venoms, I can give you 1 Spot cross-deck and centre deck aft!'

'Flyco, we'll take it,' I replied, '2, take another spin for spacing, I'll go to the front, 3 to the back, 2 to the front.' There – all sorted in one call.

Three cross-deck landings and a few heartbeats later, we'd made it. Luckily we were in the only type of jet in the world that could cope! Quite how the boat team had failed to notice the well-advertised bit of mountainous Scottish real estate I will never know. Quick thinking by the Flyco team and our unique capability saved the day.

13. The Day the Boat Simply Wasn't There

Western Mediterranean. Perfectly legal to fly but enjoying the nights in the wardroom once flying was done.

Another technique the boat can use to raise the pulse rate is to simply not be where they said they would be. Well, the day was a very murky one in the Mediterranean (which almost, but not completely, removed the fallback plan of 'find Mum[1] by accident') and a very hot one, which meant we were coming back with enough fuel to slot, fly one circuit and land. Full stop. Any more and we'd have been unable to hover. We were practising EMCON 50 – or 'emission control out to 50 miles'. The RN is actually pretty good at EMCON[2] with all systems turned off so that the enemy fleet couldn't find us. The one rule of the game, and therefore the only thing to remember, was that we were forbidden from talking

---

1 Our affectionate nickname for the boat.
2 The premise being that if someone wants to find you with a radar, well, they have to get one of their pings onto you and then receive the pong. If they just want to know where you are and you're transmitting on navigational aids, radars, voice nets, tactical data links, etc., then they just need to listen, and as all that stuff will simply be carrying on far further than a two-way radar pulse, you will make the enemy's life very easy by using them. The answer? Turn it all off. It is – and I am not being facetious – a great idea.

on radios or transmitting on our radar sets within 50 nautical miles of where we thought Mum was. This meant that we all needed to be on our game, and all of the things that we were usually able to check, confirm, have another look at using any form of emission (EM) radiation were no longer 'checkable'. Small things like 'Where, actually, is the ship?'

We were actually doing a sweep west to east down the Mediterranean and had pre-mission tanked, which gave us more gas and Mum more time to go and hide somewhere.

When the tactical fun ended and the admin of going home started, things went awry. We had no way of knowing, though, because we were working EMCON 50. I just know that when we got to the place Mum had said she was . . . she wasn't. There was simply empty sea, and the weather was really gloopy. This was serious and was every naval aviator's nightmare. Nothing to land on but sea. I had, however, noticed a big merchantman in the gloop as we descended about 30 miles out to the north-east.

'Any ideas?' asked our intrepid leader.

'Satan 2, there's a big merchantman to the north-east – we could try to land on that?' I replied.

'Satans, zip lip!' came an abrupt order – it was the ship! They were going to enforce EMCON. By transmitting. Which is just about the worst thing you could have done. Logically speaking it was now a case of 'What you Fixed Wing idiots have done is risk giving my position away. I have decided to actually give my position away to let you know.'

'You're not at the recovery position. Where are you?' replied lead, his voice rising with the stress of the situation.

'Satans, zip lip, EMCON 50,' came the reply.

'Fuck me, this one's going to take some explaining!' I thought. 'Not only are we going to lose three jets and have three sore backs, but we're going to do so in EMCON, when the ship has broken radio silence to tell us to be radio silent!'

We were now settled into a slow flight to the north-east, and Jim and I were told to take trail. Whatever was about to happen would need space, and ordinarily patience, but that was going to fly in the face of our other necessity – getting onto the deck (any deck!) quickly. We had been planning to be back at Mum with the minimum fuel for a visual join, 1,200lbs. We were now engaged in a search for a ship below that.

This was horrible, there was simply nothing we could do now but hope that the merchant vessel had space to land on. That's when we got our lucky break. Purely by chance, as lead was staring to the north-east to try to see the ship I was talking about, and I was doing the same having suggested it, Jim glanced out to the north-west and saw Mum! Right on the edge of perception, as grey warship melded into grey gloop.

'Tally Mum!' Jim called excitedly. 'Left ten o'clock, maybe about 8 miles!' The small inaccuracy not mattering at this stage.

Our job now was to 'just land on'. We didn't have the fuel to piss about or fly any of the usual patterns.

'I'm going in first. Take spacing on me!' came from

lead. We simply arrived in a clatter of bits down Mum's port side in order and made appropriately hurried approaches to land on, not waiting for yellow coats to show us the spots. There comes a point when you simply have to get the job done, and 'precise' becomes the natural predator of 'good enough'.

When we debriefed that one we hung back to see what the ship's team would say. Nothing. Not a thing. So at last the leader, who was an air warfare instructor, snapped.

'Guys, the recovery, we almost lost three jets because you gave us the wrong position!'

It turned out that the recovery position was out by 20 miles,[3] plotted incorrectly on their chart. The reply that came just about summed it up:

'What do you want, boys? An apology?'

It would have been nice.

---

3 Can you imagine them getting this wrong for anything other than Fixed Wing ops? 'Good morning, officer of the watch, where are we?' 'Portsmouth, sir.' 'Portsmouth? Isn't that Sandbanks I see? Is that not Brownsea Island? That's Poole, you dozy prick.' 'Actually it's Portsmouth, sir.' 'No it isn't.' 'Yes it is, sir, it's Portsmouth accurate to within 30 miles.' 'Get off my fucking bridge!'

14. The Day I Went and No One Followed

Bay of Biscay. Lumpy seas. We'd had a glass or two the night before, but nothing of note.

The bow seemed to describe a flat oval before it came crashing down, sending a large chunk of the Atlantic airborne and decorating most of the deck with spray. The jet lurched uncomfortably on its undercarriage. Yes, it was chained to the deck, but that didn't stop it moving. I was used to rain on the canopy – but salt water was a new treat. Crystallized salt gave the glass a speckled look, and the rag that the team were trying to get it off with seemed to make things worse, not better. This was Biscay, a region of the North Atlantic separating Brittany from northern Spain that was famous for stormy weather and upwelling that caused fog. The deck was heaving as the ship turned into the wind to launch us. I was the leader, I'd be going first. Instead of rushing to the aircraft, we had left lots of time. Time was important as it meant you could 'bubble up'. We had been through the usual post-brief fandango of changing into immersion suits in a locker space that was far too small. After picking up my helmet and life jacket, I made my way to the flight deck. Helmet on and visor down, I walked across the sodden flight deck to the equally sodden plane crew, leaning backwards into the wind, which threatened to knock me over and whisk my maps and all the cards I needed for the mission off the deck and into the sea.

Watching the deck from inside the cockpit was anything but settling. We had limits for a deck launch, but they still meant that the bow and stern could rise and fall through 30 feet or more. However – and I've never got to the bottom of this – the heave as witnessed on a fighter's HUD always looked bigger. Nor was the bow movement of the Invincible class uniform. The bow would sometimes move up and down rhythmically and at other times seemed to stay high, move horizontally and then crash down – this is what it was doing today.

I was still relatively new so was walking a tightrope between having faith in my supervisors and wanting to pipe up. I didn't want to be the first to start crying about deck movement, but in aviation you simply have to 'call things out' if they appear awry. If it looks and smells like a pig, it's probably a pig. But if no one else has noticed it, should you be the one to pipe up? What if they have noticed it and it's just 'what we do round here'? In that case you aren't going to get a pat on the back for being sharp, you're going to get a smack round the chops for being a drip. Plus, limits are there to test you, and yes there was a deck motion limit, but would a 4-degree pitch actually stop you in wartime? I hope not. Could you launch in worse? Yes. Would getting back be tricky? Yes. Impossible? Probably not. As leader, though, this time, I thought it was worth actually bringing it up.

'Flyco – this is Satan 1. My HUD is showing that we're outside limits.' (This wasn't marginal, she was 'dancing'.)

'Satan 1, Flyco. We're happy.'

Sea Harrier FRS1s are refuelled and rearmed on deck on HMS *Hermes* after the first bombing raid on Port Stanley airfield.

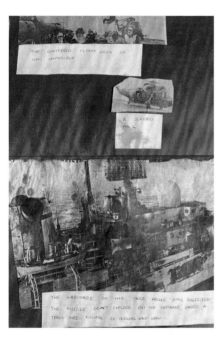

A shot of my Falklands scrapbook. Over the years I have perfected my use of scissors. The captions appear to have been copied from the donor newspaper.

My brother's scrapbook. Mark had primacy for the cuttings. The image of HMS *Arrow* putting herself in harm's way to aid HMS *Sheffield* is truly inspirational.

Initial sea training. HMS *Gloucester*. Arabian Gulf. Under the command of the excellent Lieutenant Wilkinson, we had a roar from Haifa to Karachi.

A Squirrel as used at the Defence Helicopter Flying School, RAF Shawbury. Great aeroplane, great fun and amazing people – just not quite what we were after.

Escorting HRH The Queen having been awarded Best Cadet. Her Majesty didn't slow in pace as she approached – which meant my sword salute got uncomfortably close to her handbag. She's actually asking me about the Commonwealth officers on parade.

My mother took a short break from photographing the back of someone else's head to take this one of Sub Lt Tremelling shortly after passing out of BRNC.

My two course mates through 899 NAS. Actually taken later when goofing on HMS *Ark Royal*. About five minutes after this shot was taken, a young pilot messed up his nozzles and plummeted seaward, disappearing from view below the flight deck.

The T8. Different seats, kit and switches to the FA2, but all we had! Flying 722/ZB604 when I was an instructor, my nozzles jammed straight down when fast and heavy on the runway. Couldn't fly, couldn't stop. From the back seat my Royal Marine passenger added to the excitement: 'Are we bailing out Boss?'!

The FA2 stick top. All the switches necessary to use all radar and weapons modes, trim the aircraft, employ all the weaponry and do other things such as use the autopilot, fix the nav kit and steer on the ground. Oh, and run the recce camera.

Just as I had finished mucking up my mid-course VSTOL check, Steve plonked his jet in the River Yeo. A decent reminder to all of us of the dangers of fast jet aviation. If someone that good could have an off day . . . what hope for the likes of me?

How it always began. In this case, me going off the front of *Ark* carrying a live 1000lb bomb and eight practice weapons. The answer to the perennial question 'How do we make Sundays in the North Sea more interesting?'

Myself in the nearest Sea Harrier. If getting a VSTOL jet onto a boat wasn't fraught enough, the fact that your mates were behind you running out of fuel, water and tracking juice focussed the mind somewhat.

My first cross-deck landing. This skill came in very handy the day that the boat turned through 90 degrees as we approached to land off the Mull of Kintyre. (Chapter 12)

Landing serenely at dusk. Not serene in the cockpit as we all got bunched up alongside and Wings made me go around for a second attempt. Here running out of fuel and being unhelpfully criticized for dawdling.

How JFH was supposed to work. Sea Jets and GR7/9 muds working in tandem off the boat. Here in Magic Carpet 05 off Oman.

Taken by the senior pilot using the F-95 recce camera. JFH at play. 800 NAS FA2s prepare to sweep for 1(F) Sqn GRs as we all top off pre-mission. I am on the right hose.

The unambiguous result of seeing if it's possible to get a photo with a Sea Harrier balancing on your head whilst appearing to be unaware of its presence. Answer: No.

World famous anhedral, and the probably not world famous but simply excellent Blue Vixen. Torrejon 2003. Me leading out the first mission against the Spanish F-18s.

Spanish Harriers refuelling from a KC-130. By day. No picture exists of my night tanking from a Spanish KC-130 as a) there was no light whatsoever and b) I didn't have a spare pixel of capacity left. It was the hardest thing I ever did in an aeroplane.

Downtime. With Swampy, scourge of the F3s (Chapter 16), ashore in rig in the Mediterranean, which probably seemed like a great idea at the time.

With the boss immediately after landing off Ibiza. Goon suits now very sweaty having been worn from a cold UK. Cdr Stone was my guardian angel through my emergency at Red Flag. (Chapter 15)

Walking back to the air con with Craig after our fabulous mission in Red Flag. We got under the F-15C Eagle Wall and had a rare old time. (Chapter 15)

It usually looked bad, but this was ridiculous, and yet occasionally you just have to put the bit between your teeth and crack on. Not so much 'my next stunt is considered impossible', more 'you know what? – I think we can get away with this.'

Beneath a filthy sky and behind the rain being whipped down the flight deck, the traffic lights went from fixed amber to fixed green, and the flight deck officer raised his flag. I did my own private last-chance checks, including confirming my visor was down, and with my left hand – eyes never leaving the HUD – selected my landing light ON to show I had 'accepted the launch'.[1] In the RN, your order to fly was an order to fly, in the RAF it was more of a suggestion.[2]

Oh my giddy aunt. The heave was enormous. Up the deck went – pause – crash down, creating a whole cloud of spray that whipped down the deck and plastered the cockpit in salt water – up again, crash down.

Oh well – this'll make for a good dit.

Up again, and as the bow crashed seawards, I went for it. I knew that if I waited until the bow was moving down through the far horizon to slam to full power, by the time I got to the ramp, it should be going up.

Slamming to full power, I felt the force of the Pegasus behind me. IGVs and RPM moved on dials above my

1 We changed the order of this to the far more sensible use of the landing light to signal 'My jet is ready' prior to green lights and flags later on. I think it was Paul who came up with that elegantly simple masterstroke.
2 Not just banter – in the RAF the decision to take off rested with the aircraft captain, who has to be a pilot. In the Royal Navy the decision to launch was made by the ship's commanding officer.

right knee. Power overcame inertia as I started to skid[3] forwards. I released my toe brakes – staying straight with the live nosewheel steering. I hit the ramp and snatched in nozzle as I left the ship. Moments later she was accelerating. I like fellow Harrier pilot Jerry Pook's description of an engine 'screaming defiance' at the waves.[4] I nozzled out, brought up the flap to MID and selected GEAR UP. I called the air traffic team sitting in the operations room, five decks down.

'Good morning, Homer, Satan 1 outbound.'

'Satan 1, Homer, good morning, be advised you will be single ship – the launch has been cancelled, deck out of limits.'

Of all the fucking, shitting . . . seriously, what, you are fucking kidding me? Really? I could have told you that! In fact, I think I did! Ah feck.

Two things to do now.

1. Work out how best to spend seventy-five minutes on your own over the Atlantic.
2. Spend seventy-five minutes worrying about the deck landing at the end. Anyone can select full power and launch, it's the recovery that's the tricky bit, and the chances of Mum finding anything flatter in the next hour? Cock all. Good thing I'd got one or two of these under my belt.

---

3 A chap called Mark holds the record for the longest skid, which went on for the entire length of the flight deck and led to popped tyres.
4 He was talking about the helo crew that came to pick him up after surface-to-air fire left him with an irrecoverable fuel leak.

I couldn't think of anything better to do than to practise approaches to the carrier for my own training and
that of the ship's team – whilst unsuccessfully trying to
forget there was one hell of a deck landing to come at
the end of it.

15. Red Flag Control Restriction

*In the Red Flag exercise
areas of Nevada, stone-cold sober.*

Red Flag was conceived to remedy the shortcomings of the USAF aircrew in the Vietnam War. It is the world's premier air exercise, involves huge numbers of aircraft and acts as a bit of a yardstick for aircrew. There are those who have done Red Flag, and those who haven't.[1] Despite the Sea Harrier being destined for early retirement, we were still able to take part in world-class events such as this.

What a rare old exercise Red Flag is. Everyone's heard of it and everyone wants a crack. It's the ultimate experience, other than going to war itself, and slightly more intense at times. Seventy or more aeroplanes going up against the clock, the weather, an array of surface-to-air missiles (SAMs) and stacks of fighters. You had a better than even chance of messing something up, and a 100 per cent chance of it being picked to pieces in front of hundreds of aircrew in glorious technicolour in the Red Flag building with its world-class facilities. It was simply a box you had to tick. Oh, and it's based out of Nellis AFB, and Nellis is in Las Vegas.

The Red Flag areas are huge. The supposed border runs north to south in the eastern part of the area. Every

---

1 I was lucky enough to do it twice. Once in the Sea Harrier and once in the F/A-18E Super Hornet.

day the goodies went to the east of this line, ganged up and then headed west towards us, the baddies, US F-16s in full-up Soviet paint schemes and us. We were there to provide Red Air.[2] Now, in the air defence environment you make things hard for your enemy any way you can. This can be having aircraft in different places, at different ranges, at different heights and in different formations, going different ways. Everything you did to confuse the enemy would make their jobs harder, and if you made it hard enough, then they would make a mistake. I think it was Napoleon who said that the winner is the bloke who makes the least mistakes. He was right.

The rarest time we ever had was as the result of a very simple plan. Craig and I would take the most southerly station at low level. The Migs (F-16 aggressors) and the other two Ivans (Sea Jets) would clutter the picture up to the north at various altitudes, all of them at least 20,000 feet higher than us. Being careful not to stray anywhere near the Container,[3] lest we be sent home, we crept up on the start line, able to see most of the inbound raid in the east on radar and some of it visually as the ground controlled intercept (GCI) called 'Fight's on! Fight's on!' A fighter pilot cannot hear the words 'fight's on' without hairs standing on end.

---

2 Statement of the obvious but actual enemy fighters don't join in one's training events. That means allied fighters have to take turns in providing realistic opposition for each other. Friendly forces are referred to as Blue Air, opponents as Red Air.

3 American terminology for the area surrounding Groom Lake, Area 51, home of alien autopsies. If you flew into it, you went home. Full stop. End of story.

'Ivan 1, target group BRA[4] 030 at 30,' came our instruction. As we were simulating a 'dumb' threat, we did exactly as we were told. We were being snapped to targets to our north-east, where we knew that the Eagle wall would be in all its majesty. Eight F-15s. The best, most formidable and beautiful fighters in the world in perfect line abreast. Their contrails telling all the baddies in the world that their day had come, and it was coming at us supersonic, above 30,000 feet. Daily these boys and girls carved a massive channel of safe airspace out for the guys behind them. The tactic only had one weakness, and that's that it had to work. Because they flew in line abreast with no one behind them, if someone got through, then they had an immediate leaker. And today they had two. We got under the net. Was it the terrain? Was it the look down?[5] Were we just lucky? Had some young wingman not covered his allotted piece of sky? I don't know, but I do know what it feels like to watch the eight contrails of impending doom sweep overhead. It was clear that we were untargeted.

'Ivan 1, naked.' I transmitted that nothing was giving my RWR anything to worry about.

'Ivan 2, naked,' replied Craig. As I rammed the throttle forwards, I could feel the aggression burning through me, willing the Sea Jet out of the desert and into the

---

4 Bearing range altitude. Far simpler than Bullseye. A simple statement of where the target was from you. In this case, bearing 030 degrees at 30 miles. The downside of the simplicity was that, unless you were me, this made no sense whatsoever!

5 As I mentioned, radars love looking up or across, they hate looking down. It's a long story, but essentially the earth confuses them.

fight. Our left thumbs steered the radar beams, index and middle finger bringing the scanner up to where the fighters would be, left thumb using two more buttons to get the range scale right. Using the fabulous close-in search patterns of the radar, we quickly found our opponents. Right hand sorting out the weapons.

The Blue mud-movers, who the sweep was supposed to protect, were used to finding the enemy either far away or dead (or both); I can only imagine the confusion in the cockpits. Who was spiking[6] them? Where were the bandits? What the hell was going on? The Eagles had pushed, and that surely meant they were in the clear.

On my radar screen I saw the lovely big white square in the middle of the scope – a good lock – which we only really used when simulating someone else, as the AMRAAM didn't need us to lock a target up to work. The tail pointing directly at me meant he was on my nose and coming straight down the snot locker.

'Fox 1!'[7] I called with throttle wide open. Craig was splitting to north, having also simulated a shot, and he disappeared off in my left nine o'clock 'Tally F-16s!' he shouted. 'Splash the southern of six, Fox 1, splash the southern of five!' That sounded exciting.

My weapon timed out, and I could see the dead man held perfectly in the radar cross in the HUD. It was no F-16; it was a Canadian Hornet, a CF-18.

'Fox 1 kill, F-18 bullseye 200 for 23!' I called. 'Targeting

6 Illuminating with air-to-air fire control radars.
7 Semi-active missile shot. Not something we could do for real but we could simulate when Red Air.

his number 2,' I added, as I visually acquired his wingman, high and right, as I looked at it. Working my hands-on throttle and stick controls, I quickly achieved another firing solution.

'Fox 1,' I called again, and a few seconds later, 'Fox 1 kill, F-18 bullseye 198 for 24,' on the main radio, then 'Where are you, Craig?' on the second radio, which only we could hear.

Bloody hell, this was absolutely top-drawer high-octane stuff, and we had yet to be even targeted. We joined quickly, for there was more trade on hand, and the Blue formations were in a bit of disarray. The Eagles were still pushing west, as were the remnants of Craig's F-16s. The CF-18s had gone back east, and another group was trying to press west, just to our north, with no protection at all. Taking up the targeting, we struggled for radar locks and simply followed the GCI bogey dope.[8]

'Ivan 1 Section, target single group, north at 10 miles,' came the edict from our controller. It soon became clear why our radars were suffering; we'd found the Trons – EA-6Bs, big fat USMC electronic warfare aircraft, huge things, with perhaps the world's finest geekery stacked up inside them, considered absolutely vital for any strike. Up the front to jam and potentially destroy air defences with their kit and missiles. No wonder the radar hadn't got the measure of them – these guys were a flying e-nightmare. In we went. It would be a job for 'heaters and guns' – heat-seeking weapons and, if that didn't work, good old-fashioned cannon.

8 Voice cueing from the guy on the ground.

'Fox 2,' I called as I simulated release of a 'heat-seeker' IR weapon, quickly mirrored by Craig.

'Fox 2.'

Like the cavalry at Waterloo, completely drunk on its own success, we closed to make sure. Guns live on the weaponry panel, above the left knee, and I had a floating gun sight in the HUD. With my right forefinger I made the trigger live and then pulled it rearwards as the Tron filled my gunsight. 'Guns, guns, guns, kill two Trons, heading west, bullseye 245 for 25,' I called. We, gentlemen, are now officially a big deal.

And then it was time for the showdown. We'd done our bit for the motherland and now it was time to pay the price. We faced up east, and to be frank the calls we were getting from GCI were no longer particularly helpful, as we were surrounded by Blue Air fighters at multiple altitudes. The Eagles were coming back from the west, the rest had marshalled, and this time they meant business. The CF-18s were sniffing for blood to avenge their loss, the F-16s out to avenge their two dead, and the Eagle wall furious at missing us. We were also very keen not to ruin our good work by breaking any training rules. Getting kills is great, but merging outside your sanctuary makes you look a complete cock in the debrief.

Still, we had time to take a few more with us. Eyes on my radar screen, I achieved another track on a fighter to my front. Craig had obviously done the same.

'Locked,' we shouted, in perfect unison.

'Fox 1!' I called quickly, followed by Craig, as we both managed to get off one last shot. I counted down the seconds, maintaining the lock to give a valid simulation for the other side. These last two turned out to be F-16s as well. In reality we weren't there to kill them, or to die; our only job was to simulate the threat as best as we and our machines could, and for a Fox 1 that means the Blue Vixen in Single Target Track, spitting out wiggly-amps into their warning systems and supporting the weapon until simulated impact.

'Time out kill, bullseye 250, 22,' I called. Craig timed his out seconds later. And then we became the pin cushions. Simulated weapons flew in from all points of the compass. Our Sky Guardian threat-warners screamed under an assault of volts, amps, ergs, therms, watts, calories . . . you name it!

'Ivan 1 and 2, multiple kills called on you!' came the confirmation from GCI that the Sky Guardians weren't lying. Every fighter of the free world was raining them in. Every fighter, that is, other than the four F-16, two CF-18 and two EA6-Bs we'd splashed. Staying in our sanctuaries, we turned to the west. There was never going to be time to get all the way back to the western edge of the play pen, regenerate[9] and recommit before it was all over. We sauntered gaily west, knowing that we'd had a good day and that, so long as there were no surprises at the debrief, we were going to look pretty damn good.

The funny thing about this is that it was the first Thursday of Flag. Which meant that any other air force

9 Magically come back to life to rejoin the fight. Depending on how many fighters were available compared to the threat required, this was sometimes necessary.

in the world would have met the Eagle wall three times already and had its airfields and air defence system pulverized. Not many nations in the world are going to be standing after three whole days of attention from Uncle Sam, so you have to take our escapade with at least a modicum of salt. Still, we'd been given a 042+[10] fit to simulate, and we'd killed eight jets. The debrief went our way, the USN exchange guy on the CF-18 squadron coming over to congratulate us on a job well done. He then asked in incredulity if he'd heard right and we were going out of service! One of those laugh-or-cry moments!

Red Flag was excellent. High drama in the skies above Nevada with nights spent wondering how exactly the Voodoo Lounge made drinks smoke.

Another day, another great Red Flag mission in the clear blue skies of Nevada. I was on combat air patrol (CAP) – the fancy way of saying 'fly in circles and wait for trade'. My station was over a dry lakebed in the northwest of the ranges. It was called Bear Paw, because it looked like a bear with a paw 10 miles across had left a footprint there, white with salt. I was low, between mountains; Blue Air were going to struggle to see me. As ever, I sat watching both my radar screen and Sky Guardian, while completing 'airborne task number one' – not flying into the ground. I could see the enemy formations

---

10 Coded load for a fighter, active weapons, semi-active, heat-seeking, gun. So we had no Adder, but we did have 4 AA-10C Alamo 'Long Burns' and 2 AA-12 Archer each. Plus the cannon . . . never leave home without one.

until they were almost overhead, the Blue Vixen able to look 70 degrees up. But the Sky Guardian remained clear. Keeping a tight race track at 420 knots, 250 feet, as per the UK standard, I craned my neck to watch the contrails of the Eagle wall go over the top, followed shortly by another: this time they had a wall of F-16s as well, wonderful jets that pretty much the entire world had bought for tuppence while we poured pound after pound into the problem called the Tornado F3.[11]

To the east of me there were mountains running north to south, and across them, on the deck, with telltale soot coming from its four engines, was a Hercules, a C-130, better prey than any fighter. Potentially filled with Special Forces en route to a drop off.

I called GCI: 'Ivan 4, engaging C-130, BRA 120, 5 miles!'

'Ivan 4, clear your own flight path, clear engage,' came back the reply. I was a bit low for GCI to be able to ensure I was clear of everyone, so as per the rules I was completely responsible for clearing my own flight path. With Blue Air within 10 miles, I was out of my sanctuary. With neck swivelling, eyes darting to see either threats or more targets, I hauled the jet round to face the C-130. With my right thumb, I commanded a radar search and hawked the radar screen to see the radar lock on. Four

11 I actually felt for the F3 community. Trading in F-4 Phantoms for the F3 seemed odd. Having to perpetuate the amazing Fighter Command legacy with the F3 was quite a tall order. As the jet matured with data link and new weapons, it increased markedly in capability. However, it was never going to be fit to spike the drinks of the F-14, F-15, F-16, etc., which anyone sensible bought. Some will disagree.

miles, target on my nose, and me approaching from his one o'clock, same level. My right thumb moved right a fraction and flicked up the cover on the weapon release button before pressing it down and holding it there. 'Fox 1, C-130, BRA, 120, 4.' Pause, two, three. (The weapon would cover the distance at about two seconds per mile.) 'Time out, C-130.'

Now, if it had been a fighter, then that would have been game over, even though in the real world one missile can never be absolutely guaranteed to account for one fighter, the average is more like two. In these exercises to kill a heavy you had to fire more. Now the C-130 knew he was in trouble, he was probably on the Blue net shouting for help. He turned to the south-west and began to weave. The hard bit now for a fighter was to stay behind him. A skilful crew could have you out the front and harmless in no time at all. Luckily, I had had a few goes at this with the UK heavies and wasn't going to pass up this opportunity. My left hand moved momentarily from the throttle to drop full flap. Using slow speed and mimicking his weaving, I was able to maintain separation behind him while the radar didn't let him go for a picosecond.

'Fox 1, C-130, running south-west.' And as before: 'Time out C-130.'

It must have been hard work in that cockpit, trying to establish where I was with reference to their tail and trying to throw me off. Now, was it two Fox 1s I needed? If only I'd listened!

'Fox 1, C-130.'

Maybe it was four . . . oh well.

'Fox 1, C-130.'

That was four weapons! It must be dead by now. A
Sea Jet had splashed an Argentine C-130 in the Falklands
War. 801 NAS boss Sharkey Ward had put a Sidewinder
AIM-9L into one of its engines and then gunned its tail
to shreds. I had to have killed the damn thing with four
Fox 1s. I began to climb, telling GCI that I was climbing
into the Red sanctuary and heading south-west, inevitably to face the Blue fighters as they came back east. I
was glad to be leaving the Blue Air sanctuary – it's a very
unnerving experience being out of your safe level for any
length of time. Of course, the world is not without its
bullshitters who will claim to have complete situational
awareness at all times. There are probably a few Jedis
around that can actually do it. I am not one of those,
and although I wasn't bad at keeping myself up with the
plot, a human brain can only take so much.

So, no safety infringements, and a big fat Herky bird
on the kill list. Excellent.

Excellent ended pretty quickly. Excellent became bad,
and bad quickly became turbo poo. I probably owe the
state of my spine to my decision to ease up from the
chase when I did. As I headed south-west, just as I settled
into a gentle climb, my stick jammed. Jammed absolutely
solid. Oh crap. The aeroplane was flying itself; luckily it
was going up, and the wings were level. That meant that
I had at least a little time to play with. Had it been going
down or one wing low, then I would have had no choice
but to eject, and Martin Baker would have needed to
rush out a new tie, and I would at the very least have a
few sore spots.

I told my leader, the CO, Commander Paul Stone, test pilot to the gentry, on this occasion, and we quickly talked through some possibilities as he tried to find me to join up. The Sea Jet had a little-known history of completely untraceable control restrictions, from notchiness in the controls to what I had, controls that simply didn't work any more. The usual suspects were the autopilot and the q-feel. The autopilot was suspected of joining in when it shouldn't, the q-feel was supposed to give you feedback on the controls to simulate the aerodynamic loads on the controls, which the hydraulics reduced to nil. The only other source could possibly have been the reaction controls that controlled the jet in the VSTOL regime – but they shouldn't even be charged without some nozzle down. The result of our diagnostic work was that even with everything definitely switched off, the stick was still jammed. Then came the saving realization. It was only jammed in pitch. With both hands, I could actually move the aileron to keep the wings level or roll from side to side, and I still had a rudder that worked. Now we were in business. It also meant that I could avoid Area 51, which I had, by sad misfortune, been pointing at when the excitement had started. We were going to infringe some US-only airspace, but not the Container, that big box of forbidden airspace around Area 51. So provided I lived to tell the tale, we were looking at a smacked wrist rather than immediate extradition.

As an aircraft speeds up, the nose will rise as the lift of the wing acts forwards of the centre of gravity; conversely the nose will drop with a deceleration. So theoretically one can make do without a stick. In a

Harrier you can go one better. Hauling in a handful of nozzle brings your thrust vector forward of the centre of gravity as well, so you pitch up – the basis for the much-misunderstood VIFF. So I had two ways of getting the nose up and one of getting it down. Left and right were going to be pretty tiring, but at least from now on it should be possible to land. It was a pretty serious emergency, though, so I still tightened the straps and confirmed that my visors were down, because if things went much worse I'd be ejecting. However, once I'd established a safe and (vaguely) level flight path going south down the west face of Area 51, I thought that I probably had the measure of the jet.

The problems facing us were largely administrative, as the boss joined me in battle port, level with me on my left-hand side. To us this was now a PAN, a second-grade emergency for which I needed priority but not much else. To the Americans it was an 'in-flight emergency'. To us it was a 'control restriction', to them a 'primary flying control malfunction'. It took me three goes at explaining that I was PAN, with a control restriction, before Mig 1, an absolute hero called Mole with real kills to his name, stepped in.

'He's got an IFE with a primary flying control malfunction, you morons!' came the most un-American transmission I have ever heard.

'IFE acknowledged,' came the immediate reply. 'Ivan, request intentions?'

'Ivan 4, I'm going to attempt a landing at Indian Springs.' It was always going to be an attempt rather than a certainty.

All sorted out, I left the areas at the south-west corner and started a ginger left-hand turn and settled myself going east to divert to Indian Springs, which was half-way home. The sooner a lame duck is on the ground the better, especially as this could be a hydraulic snag or might be heat-related. Both have a tendency to end somewhat badly. My intention was to fly south of Indian Springs' main runway and then to enter a sweeping left-hand turn from height to bring me onto a long final approach. This gave me loads of time to get the nose where I wanted it with the nozzle, power and speed combo available. I'd turned left once, so another should work – I didn't fancy seeing if I'd have the same amount of luck turning right.

Now sometimes fate can be a bit of a cock. Sometimes he just wants one more go at you, one last cut, to see if he can get you past the one thousand it reputedly takes to kill you. On this day, fate should have buggered off, but he had one last card, and it was actually quite a good one.

Every day an airliner goes to and from Groom Lake, taking geeks to talk to the aliens they have there in big fridges. Little-known fact, but by no means a secret. We weren't told about this. We weren't told that – due to my control restriction and the fact that I was therefore porpoising a couple of thousand feet – we were moving up and down through its cruising level. We certainly weren't told that it was on a perfect collision course with us. It was heading due south as we headed due east; it was in our left ten o'clock, and we were both headed for the same bit of sky.

The boss didn't see it – he was watching his young pup meander up and down, wondering whether or not he was about to get the awesome experience of actually watching an ejection from close range. I was on the right, the airliner was on the left. I must have been 'head in' for some reason, for as I looked up I saw the airliner.

'Fuck me!'

It looked to me like it was going to give the boss a fairly close shave. It looked like it and I were going to meet. This would mean failing in 'airborne task number two' – not flying into other aeroplanes. Both hands grasped the stick, and with all the force a 14 (or so)-stone Cornishman can muster, I heaved back – and bugger me if it didn't snap back into my groin. The jet reared up, momentarily freed from having the stick central, before a split second later the control restriction decided that it was in fact stronger than me and took over again. But it was enough. The jet went up at about 20 degrees, well away from the airliner. The boss still hadn't seen the 737 and thought that my cobra heralded the end of my sortie. He was going to get his ejection! What to say in these situations? 'Get out, Tremors'? 'Eject, eject, eject'? No. What my CO transmitted, for everyone in the Western hemisphere to hear was 'Oh-oh! Here we go!' Fabulous.

My jet and I didn't give him the satisfaction. I didn't eject. The landing was hard work, but I got the poorly Sea Jet down in one piece. The CO of Indian Springs was an amazing gentleman who took pity on this Third World aviator, with a broken aeroplane, with no cash and leather gloves. With a free dinner and Nomex gloves, I was driven back to Vegas by the down bird team, one of whom sadly died in a car crash when we got back to Yeo-vilton. The team at Indian Springs were superb, as was the boss when I met him next. At the debrief, the C-130 crew had asked how they could escape from a 'hovering' Harrier. The boss had nodded sagely, then explained that it was impossible, in that position they were always going to die[12] . . . before walking off grinning. Of course they could have denied me a shot opportunity by man-oeuvring aggressively . . . but sounding like a ninja never hurts.

12 I was nowhere near hovering. I had full flap down and was below 300 knots but not much slower. If you tried hovering at that height, at that temperature, in that fit, you would have, quite simply, crashed in the most humiliating way possible. Actually, the second most humiliating. First place goes to crashing a fully serviceable Harrier T12 into the main runway at Akrotiri.

16. The Cruel World of Air Defence

*We were at RAF Coningsby. I think we
were all sober, but I do remember Special Boy
throwing up out of the minibus window on
the perimeter track – so maybe we weren't.*

The art of defending airspace against baddies is quite
complex; indeed there are some of us who have devoted
large parts of our lives to understanding it.[1] Armed with
a Sea Harrier, you and the fleet's other weapons and sen-
sors could make a fair old fist of defending relatively
large chunks of air. Without one, well, you had better
hope that luck was on your side, particularly if all that
separated you from a watery grave was luck, and your
ship's own weapon systems. It would, of course, not
start off watery. It would start with a deafening bang and
probably involve choking smoke, darkness, white-hot
metal, confusion and pain. The water would probably
come as blessed relief.

Defending airspace at its very simplest level is about
waiting for the enemy, setting off to get him when he does
something you don't like, killing him or scaring him away,
then finally getting ready to do it again. So long as you
could keep all the relevant criteria in your head, as well
as the ranges you could shoot, and the ranges at which

---

1 Most of us would have devoted larger portions had successive defence
cuts not made it impossible.

he could kill you, at various heights, then you were fine. Obviously, you had to react appropriately to any threats, maintain formation integrity, keep and analyse the picture in your head, work the radar and talk concisely as well. I suppose that we might to this add the ability to handle the flying controls, and the HOTAS,[2] stay at your pre-defined level, or climb to give the weapon a better chance of flying in the thinner air. You probably have to add intercept geometry to the mandatory tasks as well. I have omitted the obvious, such as being able to take off from a carrier and find it again, prior to landing, and to do the landing itself. But so long as you could do those things, then flying a fighter was a piece of old breeze. It was a minor inconvenience that you had to do it at night and in shit weather as well, but we got paid and everything.

What is my point? Good question. The point is that the environment is demanding. And that there is someone who is working as hard as you for all the same reasons. The baddy. The absolute joy of air defence is that you fight against fighter pilots, people with about the same ability as you with an aeroplane that would have weak points and strong points compared to yours. If you knew all of your own criteria, and understood all of his,

2 Hands On Throttle And Stick. HOTAS has always confused me as a term. Not in the grammatical sense but in the sense that it has a title which, therefore, suggests someone thought of it and coined it as an acronym. It is so blindingly obviously how a cockpit should be designed – it's a bit like having an acronym for Being Able To See Out (or BATSO as it would be called). Can you imagine anyone saying, 'My jet's better because I've got BATSO technology on my side'?

then you could make it count in the fight. To kill someone in a fighter you have to create a kill chain, a logical
sequence of events from hearing about an incoming raid
to watching your radar screen as your AMRAAM shat-
ters cockpit and pilot alike. If you can construct your kill
chain, but prevent him from making one on you, then
you will win and survive while he dies – hopefully before
he starts a fire on board your boat that evaporates the
beer and melts your camera.

What does this have to do with Coningsby? Well, Coningsby was home to the Tornado F3 qualified weapon
instructor (QWI) course. This was the weirdest environment I had ever seen. These guys took no prisoners,
ate their young in public and were pretty damn unpleas-
ant to each other. Bravo, on the one hand, because they
were growing killers, and the need to be nice is not one
recognized in mortal combat. But fuck me, these guys
had got a little out of hand. I think we could have all
accepted them if they flew the F-15, 16 or 18 and were
therefore true knights of the sky. But they didn't; they
flew the twin-seat F3 and they weren't really knights of
anything.

One day, we were asked to be Red Air. If you were
Red Air, you did whatever the Blue Air leader had asked
of you. You were his or her tool with which to achieve
their training aims. They would dictate what tactics you
were free to use and what missile you were to simulate. We were again simulating the pretty basic Soviet
AA-10A. This is a fairly short-range weapon, but one
that would give the Blue Air Tornado F3s a bit to think
about as they were simulating the Sky Slug, sorry Sky

Flash, which outsticked it, but not by as much as other weapons. Other than that, we could do what we wanted but we had to stick as two pairs. We were going out into the North Sea for the fight. The range there was fully instrumented, so the whole fight was displayed on big screens at Coningsby, and guys could watch the fights in real time if they fancied it.

For this mission our 'safe' was in the southern bit. The Blue Air couldn't come in or shoot into the safe. This was a very real scenario in a period that included policing actions such as those over or next to Iraq. The eight F3s – four from Coningsby, four from Leuchars – would be in the north. They would be CAPing, we would commit at them. We were told that the fight would start at 1205, when we crossed the 'imaginary border'.

So off we went. Four fighters in neat formation out over the cold grey of the North Sea. The layman would be amazed at some of the mock battles that took, and take, place over that expanse of water. Our 4 v 8 was fairly simple compared to the carnage that could develop. Swampy, who joined the squadron shortly before me, was leading for this mission. He checked us in with the range control, then our own Freddie and with Blue Air leader, on this occasion Horseman 1.[3]

'Horseman, good afternoon, Satan are as fragged and ready to play.' Ever the gentleman, Swampy let them know that there were as many of us as there should have been, and we were happy to get going. The F3s

3 We are all fiercely proud of our callsigns. The more warlike the better. Satan is an 800 NAS callsign and is easily the coolest in the world.

marshalled in the north. It quickly became apparent that they were using a very strange tactic. Well, strange to us. There were eight of them in two CAPs, split east/west. This was normal. They were operating as two fours, probably with a demarcation line between them, which was also normal. But they were flying race tracks in perfect synchronization. This was, to us, unheard of. All eight of them would fly towards us on the 'hot leg', and then all eight would turn cold.[4] This flew in the face of everything we would have done in the same position. We would have kept half hot and half cold. We would then have come at the enemy as two formations, one behind the other. Defence in depth, as we called it, worked well. The guys up the front caused the carnage, and the guys down the back swept up the pieces. Any bloke up the front who lost the picture or felt threatened could turn around, get out of trouble and fall in behind the sweepers. But this lot seemed like they were going to come at us as one big unruly mob. This probably made sense in this specific scenario. They slightly outsticked us, so they were going to smack us with everything they had all at once, proving yet again that quantity has a quality all of its own. We were going to get monstered, and the fight would last only the time it took to meet in the middle of the range. Most fights start with the sides 40 miles apart. They would be flying at about 0.9 Mach; we would be at the Sea Jet's realistic top speed of 0.8 Mach (technically we could get to 0.88 Mach but that happened in dives, not commits). With closure of 17 nautical miles

4 Hot being towards the enemy, cold being away from the enemy.

per minute and the first shots coming off the rails at about 14 miles, this fight would last about one minute and fifty seconds.

The time for the fight approached. Like a bright beam of sunshine, an epiphany beyond belief, our leader had an idea, and it was a good one.

'Right, boys, they're CAPing on the lead timings,' he noted. He had twigged how well choreographed this fight was. Fighters flew CAPs on time. CAP orbits were six minutes long, and the formation leader and his section went through the CAP datum, the point where they stopped flying towards the enemy and turned cold, at specific times. This would be on the hour, six past, twelve past, eighteen past and so on. His subordinate would be three minutes behind him. In this way, any fighter from any NATO country could join a CAP and operate with his allies.

It all became clear.

'If we push at 1205, they'll be one minute out from the CAP station – they'll commit straight away.' Swampy described what was going to happen. They were CAPing on the lead timings. That meant that when we pressed across the border at 1205 they would be on the hot leg. One minute later, already on the attack track, they would pass through the datum at 1206, by which time we would have fulfilled their 'commit criteria', so they wouldn't turn cold, they'd come at us. All eight from two CAPs. We'd die shortly after that. But what if we didn't fulfil this criteria? That was what Swampy was thinking.

'Right, fellas, let's just stay in the safe!' called Swampy. Genius!

So we stayed in our orbit and listened to the picture. Sure enough, Freddie told us what we knew must happen, they committed. At 1206, eight F3s came thundering down the North Sea towards us, the baddies.

'Satans, picture. Two groups, azimuth 20, hot, hostile, western group bullseye 330 at 15.' Yep, here they come. However, the baddies were orbiting lazily in the safe. In the safe. We were safe. We were the wrong side of the border; they couldn't shoot us. And as the seconds ate up the miles between us, this obviously occurred to the Blue Air: they had committed too early, shot their bolt, as it were. And, left with no alternative, they did what they had to do. They turned around and ran, attempting to reset. But crucially their leader had let them down. If he'd realized early enough what we were up to and hauled arse back to CAP, it wouldn't have mattered, but he didn't see what was actually happening. Like countless fighter pilots he saw what he wanted to, believing the pre-assembled picture in his head, the choreographed one, not the one that was unfolding before him. They left aborting far, far too late. But Swampy was on his game, as was Freddie.

'Satans, Freddie, all groups now cold, centroid BRA north at 15.' Freddie found it easier just to tell us where the middle of the group of fighters was, all of them running away not so bravely.

'Satans, commit!' called Swampy. Off we go. Hunting time! Timed to perfection, we left the safe. The F3s did the sensible thing and kept going north.

But then came the weirdest thing. One of them tried. One of them left the other seven, who were doing the right thing. One of them had a go at attacking us! Good lad, daft lad, targeted lad, dead lad. We each simulated a shot and each registered a kill. How we chortled. Our plan had been good, but this bloke had just pretty much killed himself. The F3s then said that they had to go home. They had launched without drop tanks, and therefore very low fuel loads, as they assumed they would always punch them off in a real fight, thereby getting more performance out of the jet, with less drag and higher speed and G limits. This was fine, and their call, but it did mean that you usually only got one run against them. Most other fighters would give you three or four good training events.

So back home we went. Cock-a-hoop. Absolutely chuffed to bits that we'd fucked up their plan with a bit of guile. We'd been set up to be slaughtered, but the hunted had become the hunter. There was an overt and understandable hostility between us and the F3. Not on an individual basis, as we all had many friends in each community. But they were the RAF's fighter jocks, top of the tree in a tree made solely for fighter pilots. We were the Royal Navy's bastard stepchildren, least-appreciated weapon system in the admiral's list of weapon systems, the bottom of the liquid leaching out of the very bottom of the pile. They were invested in, we weren't. So the rivalry was intense. We both loved getting one over the other, and this had been great. A pre-planned bit of Sea Jet seal clubbing had been fucked up, and we'd blown the living shit out of the guy who'd been stupid enough to argue about it.

But then the mood changed. We got a call from their

staff, the instructors. Before we came to the debrief, could we please ensure all our shots were valid? What? We had four valid shots on the guy, of course they were valid, and the instrumented range would show it! But this guy wanted us to go through the time-consuming task of running the shots on a computer program just to check that all four AA-10As would have actually killed him. A bit pissed off, we did what we were asked, not really understanding why they couldn't take our professional opinion, or that of the computerized range. In the debrief it became clear. This plan had been one of the student's last chances. He wasn't doing well on the course, and his eight-ship death squad thing had been his last attempt to impress the instructors. His was the only aircraft to try to fight, he was the only one to die, and with that coffin placed around his aircraft on the debrief screen a similar one fell on his career as an air defence instructor.

God, we felt awful. We thought it was funny in the air, and in the crew room, and as we watched our cassettes of the flight. We thought we'd taken the edge off someone's day, not ruined the poor fucker's life! We enjoy knocking the community, the jet, not the individuals, and certainly not the poor bastard students. If he ever reads this, and he recognizes the story, from late 2002, I am genuinely and absolutely sorry. It really does torture me that for that one officer his life could have been unimaginably different if we'd simply pushed over the border at 1205.

17. Downtime: The Edinburgh Three

We were off Leuchars, and we were drunk.

Friday and Saturday nights at sea have the potential to be great fun. No flying the next day, and the mice will play. Good-quality drinking, high-quality banter and occasionally some top-drawer violence[1] can make a suitable outlet for an air group following a week's maritime military aviation. There is one minor stumbling block in all this. The surface fleet, given that there is no way you can die doing their job (unless you forget to keep living through another game of 'I spy' on the bridge), don't understand the need to unwind.

I feel I must add some context. Just about every air force in the world observes some form of Happy Hour at the end of the week. It allows you some release and helps build camaraderie. So, before you judge us too harshly, I want you to note that I have witnessed RAF Happy Hours that got out of hand, USAF and USN beer calls and parties that were brilliant but outrageous, and even had the wonderful experience of carrying an RN surface fleet commander to bed one night after he'd 'overcooked it' somewhat. USMC boys let loose in our bar were sights to behold. That probably sets the context for what was acceptable then.

---

1 Mess rugby. A bit like rugby, but with no rules, fluid team composition, a notional ball and a whole load of rotary targets to have a crack at.

What may surprise you is the lengths others will go to to ensure that the aviators don't enjoy themselves. For example, we were once told by a senior officer[2] that we weren't allowed to buy bottles of wine. The USAF exchange officer on the GR7 was with us and immediately saw a hole in the edict. 'Here,' he enquired politely of a steward, 'you know I'm not allowed to buy a bottle of wine?'

'Yes, sir.'

'Can I buy a pint of wine?'

'Yes, sir, we've only been told to not sell bottles.'

'Seven pints of wine, please.' Our hero's work was done.

In one party, just in case someone tried to meddle late on, we decided to stockpile throughout the entire evening. Every round would include one for the ammo dump or, as we termed it, 'The Alamo'.[3] This is where we would make our final stand. Three of us then decided to visit the bridge, which was a monumentally stupid thing to do. The bridge at night is the epitome of professionalism, and we really weren't going to fit in. We realized our mistake pretty quickly and beat a hasty retreat, but you can't get away with stuff like that. Luckily, in the morning the ship's leaders thought a damn good (world-class, as it turns out) bollocking was in order rather than summary trial.

2 The irony being he was the one I carried to bed!

3 Named after the American location of a famous last stand, not the Russian missile, the Charlie and later variants of which can be rather fruity little tinkers.

They had the last laugh. We were denied leave. We were kept on board while the rest of the ship got leave in Edinburgh. Edinburgh! One of the finest runs ashore in the world. They won. Kill acknowledged.

18. Northern QRA

RAF Leuchars. On the doorstep of St Andrews and Edinburgh. Attempting to stay out of the immediately available runs ashore would have been a bit like the challenge faced by King Canute.

Our assumption and our prime motivator was that, despite the news of early retirement, we would still deploy if hostilities did break out. We certainly weren't told anything different by the Royal Navy leadership. As the Sea Harrier's untimely demise drew closer, we began to sense that its swansong would not include any warfighting deployments. No senior officer told us this, but it appeared that the Establishment had decided that a quiet exit was better than one last hurrah. This was incredibly frustrating. Until the final day of the Sea Harrier we could still have contributed in any of our roles, and we fantasized about highly unlikely opportunities to demonstrate our capability to senior officers, civil servants and MPs alike. This led to the distressing but unavoidable conclusion that it simply didn't matter how well I performed on any given sortie, we were still going out of service and we would not see combat in the Sea Harrier. We were cricketers doomed to spend an entire tour in the nets.

It came to pass that the Tornado F3 would go to Gulf War 2 – and the Sea Harrier would stay behind. We hadn't gone with our boat, which was sent east full of helos to play a major part in the amphibious invasion of the Al-Faw peninsula. This was gutting for a variety of reasons, foremost among which was that we had had two of the three anthrax jabs, so had probably collected all the side effects and none of the protection. But we did get the chance to complete the most important job in the UK – quick reaction alert in defence of the homeland. The plan was simple. Go to Leuchars and take over Northern QRA from the Tornado F3.

We spent lots of time doing aircraft recognition training and looking at what our rules of engagement would be. We quickly surmised that we would need to take a couple of different warloads and settled on the leader taking cannon and 2 AMRAAMs, with the wingman taking cannon and four Sidewinders. That focused the mind, but we were essentially bunched about a couple of things, and they were all to do with whether or not we could get the jets airborne quickly enough. There were a couple of ways we could fuck this up: 1) by not being personally ready and able; and 2) by the jet simply refusing to get its navigation and attitude systems ready because it couldn't 'see' satellites from within the confines of a hardened aircraft shelter. As ever, practice was key. We practised being in the crew room with our immersion suits rolled down to waist level and rushing to aeroplanes to see how quickly we could take off. I think we had ten minutes, which was easily enough, especially if we had made the jets ready in all respects.

We weren't allowed to tell anyone where we were going and what we were doing there. We flew up to Leuchars and had a bit of fuel to spare, so we went on a bit of boondoggle around Perthshire and then turned east to coast out near Arbroath and had enough time to have an argument as to whether or not the small vessel we gave a pasting to was a naval ship, a fisheries protection vessel or some sort of coastguard cutter. The great thing about Leuchars was . . . everything about Leuchars. It was close to St Andrews, which was a decent run ashore – not quite world-class but certainly 'up there'. Golfists could use the Old Course. The mess was good, the breakfast was the best in the RAF. The F3 squadrons there were great for trade. But the best thing about Leuchars was that a blind man with no sense of smell could find it. It sat between two estuaries, had a tactical air navigation system, and on the extended centreline out to sea was the Bell Rock lighthouse. We lined up on Bell Rock as the boss led us in for a fourship break.[1] At Leuchars, as you flew your final turn, you could look down and see seals. What a great airfield.

I hadn't been in our new accommodation – in the Britannia Hangar in the north-west section of the airfield – long before the phone rang. It was 'Commander Sea Harrier', just checking we had all arrived safely. I remember the phone call clearly.

I answered 'Hello, 800 det, Lieutenant Tremelling speaking.'

'Oh, hi, Paul, it's Jerry Millward,' came the reply. Jerry was Commander Sea Harrier at Yeovilton and would go on to be the RN Captain at High Wycombe. Wow!

---

1 That manoeuvre you may have seen where fighters arrive in a neat formation and peel off one at a time to land.

A commander knew my name. Weird. We chatted for a little bit, and he signed off by saying, 'Well, the eyes of the world are upon you.' Bloody hell! It had all seemed like a good boys' own caper to me, but he had a very valid point.

You remember we were told not to talk? We went straight to the officers' mess for lunch, and in the entrance hall was a lovely old lady pushing a cart full of crockery. She looked at us and exclaimed, 'Oh, look, it's the Navy boys, come for QRA!' WTF? The fucking dinner lady knows, but I can't tell my mum? Really?

You remember we had to take it seriously, and that the eyes of the world were upon us? We went to the Q shed near the south dispersal and had a nose around. We were met there by Nick 'Candles' De Candole, who I knew from flying training. Now, not withstanding the fact that Candles had always been a loveable character, the conversation I had was 'peculiar'. In a wonderful way.

'Mate, are you a "spread your kit out on the way to the jet" bloke or a "just get your kit on at the jet" bloke?' I asked, because he was only wearing a flying coverall, not any safety equipment, and I had made up my mind that I needed to be fully togged up in my immersion suit all day.

This is a verbatim quote. Candles said: 'Ah, mate, I'm covering for someone and playing Q roulette.[2] I haven't even got my helmet with me!' Q roulette? Fucking hell!

---

2 Q being shorthand for QRA, roulette being a metaphor for taking an enormous gamble.

Why that boy didn't join the Fleet Air Arm I'll never know. Sadly, we lost Candles many years later.

We had deliberately arrived on the Friday, not to partake in Leuchars's fabulous Happy Hour, but to give us a chance to get the two jets prepped for the task on Monday when we would stand up QRA.

However, excitement gave way to frustration and disappointment quite quickly. When the boss and I pitched up at the QRA shed on the Monday, we were met by two FA2s in the prescribed warloads. Not yet snarling but only the application of a bit of AC power away from being absolutely furious! We went about beginning to prep them and our kit when we got told that we couldn't assume QRA just yet as some final approvals had to be gained. This pattern repeated itself every day for a working week before we were eventually told that it was never going to happen. No QRA for us.

Of course, the underpinning argument was ridiculous. In short, we were going to go out of service, and the Establishment had done a good job of proving that ours was a capability that the UK could do without. Quite hard in those circumstances to gain very high-level approval to defend the UK with a capability that had been derided a fair old while. The FA2 could stand QRA. We could CAP higher than the F3, we could intercept higher than the F3. They were faster than us and could go further. Either machine could carry out the role. In retrospect, I think a little bit of the Sea Jet's soul died in those QRA shelters at Leuchars in 2003. Going out of service was going to save a bit of cash, but there was no need to rubbish a perfectly good capability just to make it look like a better decision.

Instead of QRA we spent a glorious couple of weeks working up other units as they prepared to deploy to the Gulf. Glorious in all facets other than that we weren't going.

On one mission I was chasing two Tornado F3s to the north, and they recommitted in a left turn towards me. On my radar screen they showed as two tadpoles. My HUD told me exactly where they were out the front. I was slightly higher than them and just at the edge of my perception could make out the light-grey jets against the cold grey sea as they turned. They would be almost in line abreast. As I looked at it, the right-hand jet would be in front.

Working the radar set, I simulated an AA-10A shot on the leader, with whom I ended up head to head.

'Hellcat 3, Fox 1, F3, lead of a pair BRA 350 at 8.'

Then I brought the nose to my left as I descended and followed up with a Sidewinder shot on the wingman.

'Hellcat 3, Fox 2, F3, trailer, BRA 340 at 5.'

They should have been able to get shots off at me, even from a fairly short-range commit, but hadn't done so. After all, they had four people working on the problem. Just a single incident, but the sort of evolution that made me quite angry that they were going and we weren't.

However, I began to detect in the Fast Air world a general feeling that something wasn't quite right about Gulf War 2. There were reasons for hostilities with a despotic regime, but our leadership was telling us that an aim of hostilities wasn't to force regime change. That meant that the case made to spill blood was largely contrived. An odd place to be. Wishing you were going. Angry that you weren't going. Jealous of those that were, but with a sense of foreboding for the boys and girls at the sharp end.

19. Spanish Night Hop

*We were in Torrejon, just to the north-east of
Madrid, and the run ashore – forecast to
be quite hard work – was ferocious.*

Have you ever had a day (or night) of almost total
confusion that led to everything becoming clear when
you discovered one simple fact? I had one of those
once.

We were working with the Spanish Air Force F/A-18s
and French Mirage 2000D (strikers) and 2000N (nuclear
strikers), who were taking a break from 'city busting' and
were doing some tactical stuff. A couple of things had
been interesting so far. Firstly, it's quite hard to turn a
Sea Harrier launching from Torrejon in time to avoid the
super-controlled airspace of Madrid Zone. Secondly, the
Mirage chaps really didn't like the idea of flying at low
level at our normal 420 knots because it put them in a
poor position for engine relight if they needed it. They
preferred to fly much faster but they were kind enough
to humour us. Thirdly, the Spanish used an AIM-7
variant that on paper we could still out-stick, but in practice it and the AMRAAM seemed to be fairly evenly
matched, and our radars really did a great job of inter-
fering with each other. Fourthly, the Spanish Air Force
working day was simply bewildering. We would brief late
in the day for a morning hop the next day and sometimes not debrief at all because the crews had already

gone home! Lastly, the 800 NAS callsigns of Satan and Hellcat really didn't go down too well with some of the Spanish crews, whose religious views weren't necessarily aligned with us pretending to be the devil himself. Still, I think we found that funny. Perhaps we shouldn't have. They flew as Tennis. Somewhat, er, weak.

The exercise was called DAPEX or similar and had two shortcomings. The first was that there were players involved from Torrejon, Zaragoza and Albacete. In slack handfuls these bases formed a right-angled triangle, with Torrejon in the south-west, Albacete in the east and Zaragoza to the north. The way the flow worked (or didn't) was that we'd fight over Albacete – or up towards Zaragoza – but the jets from those bases would be entering the fights from beneath, which in retrospect could have been used for good training against low CAPs and strip alerts.[1] Instead, it just led to multiple administrative fuck-ups as jets climbed through a fight to join it.

The second shortcoming involved a tanker. There was only one. It was a Spanish KC-130, and when it had been outfitted there was obviously a shortage of proper fuel hoses and hose units. As a result, instead of the thick hose with the big stable basket – with beta lights on the rim – the Spanish one seemed to be equipped with a garden hose and a recently deceased squid on the end. Flying the Sea Jet behind slow tankers such as the KC-130 or the Transall wasn't too comfortable – they couldn't go fast enough for us. Add to that a lightweight

---

1 Tactically placing aircraft on ad hoc surfaces away from major airfields, such as sections of roads.

hose that bounced around and a basket that was small and floppy and you've got a recipe for hard work.

Break, break. What I must mention, however, is that the crew were, as all tanker crews are, magnificent. When we asked for more gas, we got it. When we asked them to drag us off the towline and to some other part of Spain – they did it. They had a female captain whose favourite saying appeared to be 'OK, we can do dat.' Great people – never met them but we still owe them some beers.

Anyway, there's usually a cast-iron way of making something harder in military aviation: try it at night.

The last hop of the exercise was going to be a multiple-aircraft combat search and rescue (CSAR)[2] mission. It was going to be done in 'real time', which meant we had to mount a CAP over the area the survivor had gone down in for a few hours. This meant spreading our assets out and using the tanker. The rescue was going to be done by real soldiers in real helicopters; there was going to be an actual F/A-18 pilot wandering around a Spanish hillside going through his drills. Naturally it had to be done at night to give the baddy militia nothing to shoot at apart from engine noise.

In effect this was for us 'any old air-to-air fight'. The opposition would be the Albacete and Zaragoza bunch using a mix of F/A-18s and Mirage F-1s. The scenario was that the pilot had been downed in a previous strike on Albacete. Our mission was to provide a CAP over the

2 They currently use a different acronym to mean exactly the same thing. Never miss an opportunity to rebrand for no reason.

top of the rescue package. Only two complications. We needed to take over the CAP from someone and hand it off to someone else at the end of our allotted time. This sounds easy but depending on what the enemy is doing can be anything from a complete non-event – 'Hello, mate. Nothing happening. All yours' – all the way up to a stunt 'eight-ship lead' for a few minutes – 'Hello Tennis, Satan targeting north and middle group, Tennis, commit, target southern group, bullseye 090 at 15, head west. Group bullseye 120 at 40 dead, previously targeted' sort of thing. So I'd look forward to handover from and to the Spanish at some point. The rather more critical point was that the 'Rescue CAP' had to be in the right place, for which we needed to know where the survivor actually was as opposed to the broad area of Spain he'd disappeared into/over. That would be provided to us by the on-scene commander at some point.

In a strange break with form, the Spanish Air Force guys actually planned this mission very carefully and professionally with aircrew that seemed content to turn up for the whole day and night. This was bread and butter to us, and as I was working up to go on the air warfare instructors' course, I got to lead. That meant a lot of liaising with the other leaders and in particular the mission commander, who was either doing a fabulous job because there was a general watching, or the general was watching because he was doing a fabulous job. Fuel was an issue. We could cover our period, but only just. No flex whatsoever. That was until we got offered the tanker. Now we had loads of gas available, but it was the wrong side of the 'garden hose/squid' conundrum.

We suggested a compromise: I would lead number 2 to the tanker and get (or attempt to get) gas. Numbers 3 and 4 would launch later and not get gas – but would eke theirs out for the period. Thus we should have four jets of which two would be full, but worst case we'd have two failed 'tankers' who would be there to start with and two 'eker-outers' if things went awry.

There was actually a serious side to this. The KC-130 that the Spanish were operating wasn't actually in our 'Release to Service' (the big book which says what one can and cannot do with Her Majesty's aircraft) as being approved for night tanking, and we had a special dispensation to do it.

When I explained all this to the Spanish leader, he gave me a look that in summary was 'disparaging'. The long variant would be something like 'You can bitch about our briefs and debriefs, you can have a pop at our callsigns, you can drip about our working day . . . but if you aren't prepared to go to the tanker at night, you're a bit of a pansy.' Which put us in a bit of a spot, because we'd already seen that these guys didn't even particularly like fighting in cloud, so the news that the tanker was 'no big deal' wrongfooted us. We stayed firm. They stayed aghast.

In an act of sheer comedy the mission commander turned to a junior guy, who trotted off and returned with a picture of a Spanish KC-130 that had been ripped off a wall. It was still in its frame, and the screws and plugs were still attached. The leader used his pencil to show me where the hoses came out and other points of interest around the aeroplane. Oh my fucking God! I knew how to tank! It was just that doing it behind this crapheap in the dark was 'focusing the mind' somewhat. UK tankers were a doddle at night. Nice hose, nice basket, lit up so you could see them for miles. We were obviously having a conversation at slightly cross purposes, so I left it and went to find my gumshield.

Anyway, the mission got underway. We waited for our allotted time to go, and then the senior pilot and I blasted off from the south-westerly runway and turned east for the tanker towline. Obviously we had no problem finding the thing on radar, but fuck me – this is no exaggeration – the aircraft itself was simply a slightly darker patch of completely dark sky. I inched up to where I thought a safe distance was off the starboard wing.[3] Some of Spain is quite empty, but I found that by using the little cultural light available on the ground to 'backlight' the KC-130 then I could work out where it was. There was a single tiny green navigation light on the starboard wingtip. There was a tiny white light on the tail. Everything else was simply pitch black. This was actually looking like a non-starter. We had one teeny-weeny factor going in our favour and that was that the Sea Harrier probe had a light just under it, which I switched on. I was cleared astern the left basket. With my probe light on I could just about make out enough of the aircraft to move from off the right wing to behind the left wing,

---

3 They changed this later. After years of joining on the right and re-forming on the left it all got reversed. Never miss an opportunity to change stuff – particularly when it involves hundreds of knots and thousands of gallons of fuel.

catching sight of what I thought was the right basket on the way. Always best to stay 'in tight'. I then found that if I sat close enough to the left wing then the probe light illuminated the two propeller discs in front of me. From there I was able to find the hose and follow it back out to the basket. This was somewhere in the part of the Venn diagram where the risky, dumb, simply-not-worth-it bubbles all collide. The dit cauldron was bubbling furiously at number 11.

As I plugged, the senior pilot sat on the right wing. The call he made as I went forward was genuinely a shout: 'WATCH OUT! CLOSURE!', as from his perspective I was going to fly into the tanker. I wasn't, but then when two people can't really see the aircraft they are both flying in formation on, a small difference in perception is understandable!

SP was cleared astern the right, and then came a hilarious call as he asked me, 'Is there actually a right hose out?' To which I replied: 'Well, I definitely passed something on my way over here!' That was how dark this fucking thing was. My number 2 couldn't even tell if there was a hose out.

Low-speed tanking, from an aeroplane we were 'self-illuminating', using that lightweight hose and crap drogue, genuinely unable to see anything apart from the prop discs ahead of us and two lights the size of pen tops, is easily the hardest thing I ever did in my aviation career. Harder than any poor-weather fight, any Red Flag, any weapon drop, any night recovery to CVS or CVN.

Eventually the game of 'keep dimly lit propeller discs in same place' resulted in fuel flow. After some pretty

sweaty minutes, we were full, and this unlit torture could
come to an end. The mission itself was pretty straightforward, despite locating the survivor proving an issue
for the helo teams, and it took us a while to nail down
where he was. Other than that, the Red Air never put
more than four jets up against us at any one time. The
boss and AWI had done a great job of being on time, so
we could cope with the threat and saw out the back end
of the mission. We went home to Torrejon and the usual
rigmarole of logging shot data for the debrief, which was
going to be held in front of the general at about 0300
in the station briefing facility. The general was pleased
as Punch and he managed to start the debrief with an
amazingly stereotypical (but wonderful) address about
how we'd done a great job and something along the lines
of 'being strong like bull'.

We didn't do a full end-to-end shot validation but we
did pick over the bones of the mission to identify learning points from how we planned and flew it. When it
came to be my turn to speak, I said that we had made the
tanker plan work (eye rolls from everyone), successfully
manned the CAP, the handover was sweet, we'd kept
the enemy fighters beyond the desired 'line in the sand'.
I was then asked some questions about the positioning
of our CAP. Slightly confused, I said that I had used the
lat/long given to me by the on-scene commander, but
the line of questioning quickly became one of whether
or not I could see the helos and the survivor himself.

Trying not to sound either stupid or rude, I said,
'No. I didn't see either the helo or the survivor,' which
caused some raised eyebrows. I didn't add 'Because it

was night-time, you fucking dick!' but I was definitely thinking it. The mission commander pressed the point.

'You didn't even see the Firefly strobe?' He was referring to the strobe that the survivor was using to show his position. Not visible to the naked eye, as it had an infra-red filter on it.

'No,' I replied, as I thought the question was somewhere between dumb and ridiculous. 'Confirm that the Firefly is an IR strobe? How would I see that?'

'Through your night vision goggles!' came the reply. Ah . . .

'We don't have any night vision goggles!' I said, smile forming. All of the day's misconceptions were suddenly cleared up. All of the night's pain understandable! They were convinced we had NVGs.

'Oh,' said the mission commander as he melted into laughter, rapidly followed by the Mirage and F-18 crews.

The stupid Brits went to the unlit tanker with no NVGs!

Of course you'd be relaxed about night tanking if you could see in the bloody dark!

Still, showed them who the big dogs were . . .

20. Missile Practice Camp

Stone-cold sober and about to throw a
£200,000 weapon at a target drone.

The best analogy I ever heard for justifying the use of
live weaponry in training was that of a simple plank. If
you put a plank on the ground and ask people to walk
along its length, about 100 per cent of folk would be
prepared to do it. If you laid the same plank over a significant drop or abyss, then fewer would. Same plank,
same motor skills – completely different context, ante,
implications, consequences and heart rate. With live
weapons you can actually kill people, which of course
you can with practice or even no weaponry if you really
wanted to in a fast jet. But there was generally the sense
that you were at risk when operating a fast jet. When
you brought weaponry into the equation, there were
quite a few others you now had to watch out for. Part
of the raised ante was that live weapon events were com-
paratively rare. For air-to-air shots, the vast majority of
people never got a go. There was therefore a perfectly
reasonable pressure to 'get it right'.

My first missile practice camp took place in 2002.
MPCs were run out of RAF Valley in Anglesey. My job
was relatively simple. Take off from RAF Valley with a
live AIM-9M Sidewinder under the starboard wing, fly
down to the weapons range at Aberporth, follow the
instructions of the range controller until I was within

a certain bit of sky relative to a Jindivick target-towing drone and launch my AIM-9M Sidewinder at the flare pack it was towing.

The 9M was a tremendous weapon and streets ahead of the 9L that other folk used. Really good, that is, unless you are trying to shoot a flare pack towed behind a small aeroplane. The 9M was designed specifically to ignore flares and find the tricky target that they hid. This had a fairly obvious consequence when, on the day of the races, you asked it to do the reverse. This was compounded slightly by the fact that the Sea Harrier radar was so good and could be used to cue the Sidewinder well away from the aircraft nose, or 'off boresight', which meant that you could engage a target well outside the HUD. Parts – a simply top-drawer example of human and fighter pilot – had employed his weapon system correctly in the last shoot for an off-boresight shot. The 9M had done its job magnificently: seen the flare, disregarded it and gone for the Jindivick. Result: the Jindivick is somewhere in the Irish Sea keeping all the army drones company on the sea bed. The upshot of this was that we were no longer allowed to shoot off boresight and had to check visually that the Sidewinder was tracking the flares rather than the Jindy. This was easy enough. In the HUD the radar tracked with a vertical cross, the Sidewinder tracked with a diamond.

I drew a head sector intercept. We had practised the profile in the simulator a few times, and it was relatively straightforward. But real live weapons coming off a real live jet are different. The plank lay across the abyss.

Overall it was a great day to be airborne – a tumbling

mirth of sun-split clouds (if you will) made navigation very easy, and I checked in with Aberporth and
was able to enter the range having 'checked switches
safe'. 'Switches safe' for us was 'someone has put a strip
of masking tape over the cover to the pickle button'.[1]
I removed it as soon as I was in the range. To fire the
weapon, I still had to select Sidewinder, open the flap
and push the pickle button. Three things to do was fine
by me. I thought of a fourth as something to get wrong,
so the 'high security' pale-yellow masking tape got stuck
to my kneeboard.

My job was now to do as I was told. Aberporth Range
Control were feeding me instructions, and I was following them. They were also letting me know where the
Jindivick was. If you had a God's eye view of proceedings, you'd see a Jindivick flying in oblong boxes to the
north and me flying in boxes to the south with Aberporth able to shave miles off the legs to make sure that
when we finally set off for the intercept we were perfectly
set up for our '180 by 5' – 180 degrees out, 5 miles apart.
And they did a great job. The only thing that beat them
was the Blue Vixen – as soon as I was turned inbound,
I got my target marker out to 40 miles and made sure I
was looking level.[2]

1 The button that released the store. The Sea Harrier was fairly unique.
Most jets use the trigger to fire missiles; the Sea Harrier used a small
button on the stick top.
2 The target marker was an icon on the radar screen – very intuitive and
was controlled using the 'pizza pan' on the left thumb. The rocker on the
front of the throttle set the antenna elevation. In a 'not brilliant' piece of
'Hands Off Throttle and Stick' (HOffTAS) the only way of changing the

All intercepts were exciting, this even more so because the prize was so cool. The technique was relatively simple. Put the target marker just in front of where you think the target is and wait for it to fly into the electro-magnetic net you've laid in front of it. However, it was time.

'Satan 1, you are clear hot,' called Aberporth just as my radar was telling me that I was indeed 45 degrees off. I immediately got a shrieking tone from the 9M. Damn, these warshots were good. RANGE was printed in the HUD. Everything was perfect. The radar thought so, the weapon thought so. Only there was an issue. My last visual check. It appeared to me that the reason the weapon was so happy was that it had once more found the aircraft, not the flare. It was hard to tell exactly what the weapon was tracking. Was it slightly in front of the flare pack or slightly behind the aircraft? This wouldn't have mattered a jot in combat – that weapon would have been on its way. But in peacetime, against a drone, on an MPC, you get things right, and I just couldn't be sure. Ah – bollocks.

'Satan 1 terminating,' I called, 'switches safe.' Hastily reapplying the masking tape.

To cut another long story short, we weren't entirely sure what to do about this. It turns out I wasn't alone,

---

'scan volume' that the radar was looking at was via touch keys to the side of the radar display. The radar scanned like a TV in bars, and you got a choice of how many bars and how wide. A four-bar search in wide scan gave you a searched area of about 40 degrees vertically – four sweeps of about 10 degrees – and 60 degrees horizontally. This was pretty much the 'utility' scan, which dealt with most situations.

and another pilot, Swampy, had had exactly the same issue. The fact of the matter was that the missile tracking the aircraft was one issue – but telling whether it was or not was completely separate. But how to check? The answer was elegantly simple. We'd check on each other. We'd fly around with live weapons locked to each other's Sea Harriers and see where the diamond actually was compared to the jet! What a heady mix of risk and temptation. Made even more tempting by the fact that Swampy would 'tow' for me – I'd lock him up – first, in the knowledge that he would then lock me up. Quite the game of trust.

That's how it happened. Swampy and I locked each other up. We noted where the Sidewinder diamond was sitting as we gently wove our way through the blue sky down to the range, over the cold grey sea. I then went into the range, and everything worked like a charm.

'Satan 1, you are clear hot.' This time, though, it was time to let the weapon loose.

'Fox 2!' I called as the weapon thundered off the right wing – *sssssiiffff* – and immediately cut to the left to 'head off' the drone. 'Fuck!' I thought, 'it's taking the bloody drone.' Then it appeared to reduce the amount of lead it took and appeared to head for the flare pack. 'Thank fuck for that' had just crossed my mind when, as I stared to the west, it appeared to ever so subtly go back to tracking the drone. I didn't have much time to worry, though: milliseconds later, the target detectors found their target – thankfully the flare pack – and the blast/frag warhead detonated in a perfect annulus of destruction. A bright-yellow circular flash that erupted into a black smoke ring sprang outwards as white-hot debris kept going in the line of the missile's travel.

Fucking awesome!

In the cold Welsh air hung the smoke trail from the Sidewinder engine, clearly showing the three course corrections I'd noticed. The Jindivick pressed on south – seemingly oblivious to what had just happened aft of its tail pipe.

'Splash!' I called. That was brilliant. What a good ship-mate that Sidewinder was.

If the Sidewinder was a good and faithful shipmate, toting the AMRAAM was a bit like having a battleship on each of the weapons pylons. My AMRAAM shot was slightly better in some regards and thoroughly dis-appointing in others. It transpired that, as part of the air warfare instructors' course, I would get to fire an AIM-120B.

I had been in the USA for a couple of weeks vis-iting US Navy and industry and ended up at NAS Point Mugu in California. I must mention that at the time IT was relatively new, and there was a single disc burner at Yeovilton, owned by the Unit Pay Office. I produced a presentation on Sea Harrier ops to brief at the Naval Strike Warfare Centre (pronounced N-Sock) and the Strike Fighter Weapon School (pronounced TOPGUN . . . I doubt that will stick, to be honest, but good luck to them). When I got to Fallon we got an amazing brief on air-to-air comms by a TOPGUN instructor, and then it was my turn to reciprocate with a Sea Harrier brief. I took the stage and then found out that the disc the embryonic IT set-up[3] had burned for me contained six pictures of someone skiing. Gulp.

We were at Point Mugu with two Sea Harriers supplied by 801 NAS from the boat, which was off the Eastern Seaboard. We were also in company with two Tornado F3s from their Operational Evaluation Unit. On the fateful day I was flying the armed aircraft. Jim[4] was leading in the other FA2. We had a Tornado F3 chase aircraft. Jim and I launched and joined the range, flying circles and waiting for the Tornado. Now, the Sea Harrier liked being at height, and the F3 really didn't. So we deliberately went high, ostensibly because the shot profile called for a 30,000 feet shot, but mainly to annoy the F3 crew.

Two things conspired against us. Firstly, and most worryingly, the weather at base started to deteriorate, so it would have been nice to 'get on with things' to preserve fuel for the return to base or a diversion, which was now on the cards. Secondly, the range announced that they had not loaded the correct telemetry crypto – which was needed for a trials shot. This required a range reboot which would take a little while and most certainly wouldn't allow us to 'get on with things'. So we had to wait. The F3 crew asked if we could descend to 20,000 feet, as they were throwing fuel away – they even said that they were having to use afterburner to get around the turns. In the Sea Harrier, so long as you didn't get slower than Mach 0.8 and were relatively gentle, then 30,000 feet and above was a good place to be. So we

3 It was 2003.
4 Not the same Jim.

sat in a race track and 'hung on the blades' at about 70 lbs of fuel burn per minute and waited. And waited. We even had enough time to do some high-altitude ship spotting, as there was a USN Arleigh Burke destroyer milling around outside the range. The weather up here was brilliant. We could see the various San-this and San-that islands, one of which – San Clemente, I think – had launched our target, an unmanned F-4 Phantom. That's right, I was about to kill an F-4. It didn't really get much cooler in peacetime. With the weather being so brilliant, it was hard to believe that it was so bad back at Point Mugu. It was terrible, in fact. The marine layer[5] that no one other than Californians knew was common in California had rolled in. But we didn't really appreciate this. We were boning around in the wide blue yonder with a live AMRAAM on the rails!

My shot was going to be an interesting one. The target was going to be well off to my left. After being fired, the weapon was going to have to find the target for itself very quickly and then whip across my nose to intercept it.

The range was eventually reset. The weather was getting worse at base. The Tornado crew was issuing warnings about how little time they had on task. Then we got the go-ahead to shoot. My shot was supposed to be at 12 miles, wings level, at Mach 0.8 with the target just on my radar screen on the left-hand side. The HOTAS

5 Californians keep the sea surface temperature and the dense fog of the marine layer a secret to perpetuate the myth that they live on a movie set for twelve months of the year.

for AMRAAM wasn't altogether dissimilar to that of Sidewinder. As I closed from the south, the Blue Vixen picked up the F-4 at range – about 30 miles away. Working my HOTAS, I selected AMRAAM, then SINGLE TARGET. Now all I had to do was turn sharply to the right, get the target to the edge of the screen and shoot.

It almost worked perfectly, but with full power I didn't seem to be turning quickly enough – the range was counting down quickly, and I needed to get the target right to the side of my scope, so I pulled a bit more than usual on the stick. Rolling out, I was at 30,000 feet (tick), radar track just on the screen (tick), 12.1 nautical miles (tick), Mach 0.78 (piss). Still, I knew that I had a bit of flex on the range so long as I didn't let the target into the missile-seeker field of view, so I kept the throttle parked and at 11.8 nautical miles flicked up the pickle cover and held it down. I knew what was going to happen. I knew in incredible detail why it was going to happen, but it still surprised me. Nothing happened. Exactly as planned. When you fire an AMRAAM, the aircraft and the missile go through a 'minor domestic dispute' – agreeing on stuff like where the target is, a place that the target isn't that they can both reference, that sort of thing. It takes about a second[6] to come off.

A second, when you're flying a warplane, is an age. An eon. It was long enough for me to check all my switches. My eyes rechecked all my parameters. The delay was so

6 The longest second of my life, which would stand until my time in Afghanistan, when a twenty-second LGB drop seemed to take just over six months.

long that I considered releasing the pickle button, which would have caused a hang fire. Just as thoughts of failure were about to consume me, I turned my head to look at this fucking weapon still strapped to my jet, and as I did, 'BANGGG!' What occurred was akin to an explosion under my starboard wing followed by an enormous amount of physical mayhem as the weapon leaped snarling off the rail. That thing 'went'; the jet shuddered, and I ducked involuntarily at the violence. The whole of my aircraft was consumed in exhaust plume as it went across my nose – the F-4 being well out to the left – so quick I genuinely didn't see it. I tracked the plume and stared down the bearing to where the F-4 had to be and I saw it! There it was, just as the weapon stopped burning. This was going to be epic – a missile detonating just at the edge of my visual range on a fighter-sized drone! And then, for the second time in a day, nothing happened. And this time it was really, really bad. There was no explosion. I thought I saw the faintest white scratch in the air, almost as if the weapon had passed so close to the target that I saw it, or maybe it genuinely impacted and caused a small fuel leak – or maybe I was just making things up, and it was time to go home!

We knew that the Tornado crew had been burning a lot of gas at 30,000 feet and that fuel burn was about to turn their recovery into Point Mugu into a minor emergency as the Californian marine layer rolled in. I knew that there were two seasoned aviators and good lads in the jet so never doubted that they'd crack the recovery through the unexpected gloop; but I also knew they were working hard and would be willing their fuel gauges not to drop. Fun as this was, it was a very small compensation for having watched my AMRAAM miss the F-4 after the euphoria of the launch. I think we can still call it a minor triumph for the single-seaters, who got back just fine.

The weapon firing was actually a highlight of the air warfare instructors' course, a pretty intense period during which I learned inordinately more about the Sea Harrier and its weapon systems than I had picked up on my passage through 899 as a student and on my first tour. It's an emotive subject, but a huge number of people don't ever complete more than one frontline tour. I would argue, from experience, that it's only in your second or third frontline tour that you really approach the zenith of your capabilities. At the end of the AWI course I stayed on 899 as a flight commander,[7] before heading back to the frontline as AWI 801 Naval Air Squadron: the Chequered Death.[8]

---

7 Promoted to acting lieutenant commander.
8 Demoted back to lieutenant, before being repromoted to acting lieutenant commander to do a desk job. It's the thought that counts.

21. Seeing Off Tornado F3s (Accidentally)

We were in the Moray Firth,
and the beers could wait until later.

It was night-time, and we were embarked for an exercise called Neptune Warrior. It was big, involving a multi-national fleet and aeroplanes mainly from the UK, but the French and Germans used to pitch up as well. We had managed some really good training with the RAF Tornado F3s from 25 Squadron, RAF Leeming. They were coming again this evening. We had a tanker which we were going to use before the mission, and our job was to defend it against the F3s, who were now also carrying AMRAAM missiles, the big stick. We had code words to tell the tanker captain how well or how badly we were doing, and when it looked like we were going to be overwhelmed we were planning to transmit a code word which simply meant 'scram', get out of here. Tanking and fighting are training evolutions that rely utterly on trust and honesty. You launch on time because you trust the tanker crew to be there on time with the right fuel load. They do exactly the same. They trust you to be professional around their aeroplane. If you mess up, you're expected to hold your hand up and admit it, otherwise the trust cannot continue and won't be there next time – with a possible result that there won't be a next time.

The deck cycle hadn't worked two days before, when we caught the news that the tanker had cancelled as we were sat waiting to start. No tanking for us meant less fuel, so best to wait. I talked to the ship and asked to slip our launch time. They agreed and kept us out of the arguments that followed, but essentially the ship's navigator was fuming that he'd got the ship up to launch speed only to be told that he'd wasted his fuel and we'd be going in half an hour. Once I'd agreed new launch and recovery times for us all with the ship, we sat in the cockpits to while away the time until we had to launch.

'Vixen 1, Chariot 1.' My second radio sprang to life. Chariot 1 was the opposition lead, and he had somehow got onto our squadron chat frequency.

'Good evening, Chariot, go for Vixen,' I replied.

'Hi, Vixen, we launched on time but have just heard that the tanker has cancelled. Is there any chance we can bring the fight forward?'

Ah . . . this was going to be fun. We'd moved our launch back to cater for the lack of tanker. Now we had opposition who needed trade sharpish and had no way of refuelling to make the original start time either!

'Chariot, Vixen – we'll make it work. Call you back,' I transmitted, before using the main radio to talk to the boat, where my name would now officially be mud.

'Flyco, Vixen 1, we've just heard from Chariot. They need us to launch ASAP. Could we start the engines now and launch at 2100 please?'

I imagined the look on the navigator's face. He'd got the ship up to speed for plan A, then accepted our plan

B, which was to wait. Now we were on plan C, which was get off ASAP. The four mighty Olympus engines deep down in the ship began to rumble once more. The ship's team were going to deliver.

There's something special about flying to the boat. The almost romantic notion of finding Mum, that little floating piece of the UK at the end of the sortie; the fact that when the fighting's over the land-based guys switch off, just as you have to switch on. And if mastering the game by day was something to be proud of, then night flying was something completely different altogether. Undertaken with a glee that meets every professional challenge, mainly to cover up the nerves, but also because if you can land a VSTOL fighter on the deck at night you have done something that very, very few people can say they've done. With exclusivity comes prestige, and rightly so. We commenced night deck ops only after completing seventy deck landings by day. I achieved my Initial Night Qualification (able to land on the deck at night) in my first tour. My Full Night Qualification (able to do it after high-intensity tactical sorties) after becoming an air warfare instructor would follow tonight's mission. And if we got to completely rot the night up for some Tornado F3s along the way, so much the better.

Everything takes longer at night, everything is more difficult. As I walked to the aeroplane, I knew that it would be trickier than in the day. I used my torch to identify the aircraft lashings, which keep the planes stuck on the deck and in a pretty much fixed location. Now lurking in the darkness ready to trip me up. I played my torch along the fuselage, making sure I had the right jet. Using my torch to highlight all the things I needed to check, I made my way around the aeroplane, each check requiring concentration, because my peripheral vision was no use in the dark. I paid close attention to the pins that needed to be removed from the wing tanks. I left a pylon safety pin in on one night walk round. If I had launched and needed to punch off the tanks in an emergency, it would have prevented me from doing so. One tank would have gone, but not the other. The asymmetry would have been a major, possibly uncontainable issue, making whatever emergency I was trying to cure a whole load worse. I was saved on this occasion by a very professional then PO, Mickey Oates, checking everything one last time before I lined up.

The walk round had to be split in two, as the jet's tail was protruding over the sea. This was normal for day operations too on the CVS but was another reminder to concentrate more than I would by day. The deck's more dangerous for everyone at night. As I looked up the dimly lit runway towards the ramp, I knew that the normal number of people were there, but I couldn't see them. That meant I wasn't able to supervise and monitor like I could by day. They would be there when the rain started to fall, the deck pitched and I ran my engine up to check it pre-flight. I knew that a maintainer blown overboard by a jet blast during the day stood a fighting chance; at night there would be no chance at all.

As I mounted the steps to the cockpit, I switched the nav lights to STEADY and DIM. Steady dim, someone's in. When ashore, you could make your seat live[1] whenever you fancied, really. On the boat, if you were strapped to a jet, then you needed a live seat. I moved the pins for the seat and canopy. As I couldn't use hand signals to tell the plane crew what I needed, I flashed the nav lights to tell them that I had reached 'the next step'. The first flash meant that I was going to start the auxiliary power unit to get some AC power on the jet. The plane captain made an A-frame shape with his wands to acknowledge. At launch minus ten minutes I flashed the lights again to say, 'I am starting the engine,' and received a circular movement of the wands in return. As we got to launch minus six minutes, I signalled for the high-power engine runs by waving my finger torch back and forth. The plane captain mimicked my signal, meaning that I was clear to run up. As the jet reached 55 per cent, I snatched the nozzles back to the stop. Invisible people outside checked that they were at the correct angle for ramp launch. I got two wands held up, which meant that the ground crew agreed that my nozzle rigging and trim were good. I nozzled back to 10 degrees and went to idle. Good to taxi. I moved my light switch from STEADY to FLASH. Looking around, I could see the other jets' lights start to flash. Four of us all ready to go. Not a word spoken.

Following the marshaller's signals, I switched on the auxiliary landing light, which made a puddle of red light

---

1 A live seat is ready in all respects for ejection and is therefore at the same time a lifesaving device and incredibly dangerous, as misuse or accidental ejection could well be fatal.

for me to taxi into. I made my way to the centreline, carefully applying brake as the ship heeled in the swell. Once lined up, I felt down beside my left buttock for the switches. Nav lights STEADY; ready to go.

I watched as the traffic light beside Flyco went green, the FDO raised his wand, and I pushed the throttle to the stop. Dimly lit superstructure and parked Sea Kings whisked past on the right as the familiar thrust of the Pegasus propelled me to the ramp. At ramp exit, I snatched in the nozzle as I blasted into the abyss. Just my HUD to see out the front. No ambient light, no dimly lit ship, no idea where sea finished and sky began. I now had to make two more light switches. Nav lights to STEADY BRIGHT and red anti-collision light ON. Staring at my HUD and the inky blackness beyond, I moved my left hand down to the switch tray once more. Second row back, second and third switches in from the right.[2] I pushed both forwards. Time to get ready to fight – which first meant getting to the tanker for a quick suck of gas.

---

2 If you move your head to look for the switches, you risk giving the inner ear all sorts of accelerations it isn't used to. Disorientation follows. There were two separate fatal crashes in Sea Jets at night that I am convinced resulted from this. It's a well-documented phenomenon called the somatogravic effect. If you turn your head by 90 degrees while accelerating forward, it experiences a lateral acceleration, not the longitudinal one it is expecting. This feels exactly the same as tumbling. If you think that you're tumbling and take corrective measures you will crash the aeroplane. Similarly, the only time your head is programmed to experience G going straight back is when you are lying down, face up. For that reason, when you accelerate in a jet, it can feel like you are rotating backwards. These effects are killers, and the only way to beat them is cast-iron discipline and adherence to the instruments.

Off into the blackness on this particular night, no need to join in pretty formations, best to get straight to the tanker and just meet up there.

'Freddie, good evening, Vixen 1, with you looking for Tartan 34, please,' I called our own squadron fighter controller.

'Vixen 1, good evening, Freddie, Tartan 34 is in the tac towline to you east at 15 miles, flight level 200.'

It took seconds to motor the radar scanner onto the tanker and to sort out the intercept geometry.

'Vixen 1, radar same, Judy.' I told Freddie that I could see Tartan and was happy to run the intercept myself.

We had a radar mode perfect for joining the tanker, which actually gave you steering to a position astern of the target. It was designed for our original primary role of intercepting and identifying Soviet snoopers.

Tartan was lit up like the proverbial Christmas tree. That wonderful big Vickers VC10 with all the gas you could want, and some bloke in the capacity seat making sure all his charges got what they needed at the right time. I have never met an unhelpful tanker crew, quite the opposite, and some of the things they did for us in Afghanistan many years later were awesome. With our small fuel load you would never find a Sea Jet driver with a bad word to say about tankers. I am no exception.

'Good evening, Tartan. Vixen 1 with you joining, visual,' I called the tanker. There followed the staccato radio transmissions required to get that precious fuel into the jets. Tanker running the show, me acknowledging their instructions.

'Vixen 1, clear astern the left.'

'Vixen 1.'

'Vixen 1, clear contact left.'

'Vixen 1.'

Having topped up to full, I sat by the tanker, waiting for all four of us to get through the hoses. Red anti-collision lights washed each other and the tanker in soft red waves. This was the night team, so no Mummy's boys here. The boss, the senior pilot, the American exchange instructor and me, the AWI. This was a chance to get myself set up exactly as I wanted to be. All lighting turned down in the cockpit to an absolute minimum, allowing me to use all my cockpit displays and instruments. I moved all switches back to live from their safe position, which is mandatory around the tanker. I brought my radar back to life with a single push of a button on the throttle. As 3 and 4 called complete, I pushed the throttle forwards to climb the mandatory 1000 feet clear of Tartan.

'Tartan, Vixen 1, many thanks for the gas. Vixens and Tartan, let's all push tactical,' I directed. 'Vixen, Tartan combine, Freddie channel 12 push.'[3] This ensured that everyone was on the tactical frequency, rather than the one we'd just used to tank.

'Freddie, Vixen and Tartan 34 all up with you on channel 12,' I called.

'Freddie copied,' came the voice from the ship, somewhere in the complete darkness below.

---

3 Very geeky but if you 'push' to another frequency you do not expect to check in once you get there. Some communities loved checking in. We preferred to do things without comm if possible.

The four Sea Jets, occasionally washed by their red anti-collision lights, set off for CAP. We would defend the tanker, which was moving to a position north of Aberdeen. We would CAP north of Lossiemouth, and the F3s would come at us from the west, from somewhere between Wick and Cape Wrath. At night we stuck rigidly in our sanctuaries. These were pre-determined 1,000-foot-high blocks that you owned; no one else was allowed in them. You had a sanctuary in every 10,000-feet block, so if you owned 12,000 feet, for example, you also owned 22,000 and 32,000 feet. If you needed to change to one of your higher or lower sanctuaries then you had to do it quickly, and make sure that everyone was at least 10 miles away before you did. On this night, we would fight as two pairs, the wingman in each pair behind and above the leader, able to see him on his radar scope. Leaders would call their headings to help keep the formation together. In the day, your eyes would have done all this, but at night they were no use.

People fire weapons at you when they think that they can kill you. If they fire at absolute maximum range, and you keep going in a straight line, then their computer will have got it right, and you and the missile will meet just as the weapon runs out of speed. If you manoeuvre during the weapon's flight, it will miss you, unable to generate any more energy to complete the intercept. So you hold on to the weapon until you think you have a good chance of a kill, maybe half of maximum range. That way the baddy will have to take extreme avoiding action to defeat your shot.

We had a feeling that we knew when the F3 would

be shooting. And we wanted them to shoot. We needed to get them to fire and then defeat their weapons. If you did it enough times, they would run out. We also wanted to get in close and start using our weapons against theirs. But they had AMRAAM, and we, as their Red Air opponents, were simulating a warload of Russian AA-10A missiles. Big stick plays small twig. Our tactic was therefore simple: run in and then deploy into a different formation, defeat their shots and make them make decisions. Maybe that way we could get a leaker through.

'Freddie, Vixens ready in the east,' I called.

'Vixens, Freddie, Chariot ready in the west, fight's on, fight's on,' called Freddie. That tingle again.

'Vixens, Freddie, single group, bullseye 270 at 80, hot, hostile.' Freddie let us know where they were, and that they were heading our way and up to no good.

'Vixen commit.' I put our plan into play.

Freddie kept up the familiar patter.

'Vixens, single group, bullseye 265, 60, hot, hostile.'

The F3 formation was coming at us as an unruly mob. They had chosen to mass firepower up front and were going to make the first presentation count. Our plan was to bracket the unruly mob and make their life hard. The Blue Vixen had no problem breaking them out. Now, as I watched them on my radar screen, I just had to wait until they got to a certain range.

'Vixen 1 section, execute!' I called as calmly as possible. I was working on the assumption that there were weapons in the air targeted on me and it was time to defeat them. Rolling to 150 degrees and applying 4 G, I pulled into an aggressive abort. I needed to let 2 know he was safe to follow.

'Vixen 1, out south, passing 26,000 for 20,000.' He could now leave his sanctuary at 31,000 feet in his abort, knowing I was below him.

Hauling the jets around to the east in a hard turn, we had charged toward the F3s, lured them into firing and were now running away. Their simulated shots would fall in the sea behind us, and with any luck they'd still think we were up at 30,000 feet.

'Vixen recommit,' I directed. We'd now turn to the west – I was in the south, so would go right; 3 was in the north so would go left. That would put us in a wide presentation and put Chariot in a pincer.

With radar moved hard over to the right and level for an early pick-up on the F3, I racked the jet round. If I could get my radar looking directly at one of theirs, my 'wiggly amps'[4] might interfere with theirs. However, no sooner had I found them again on my radar screen than my RWR sprang into life. Time to defend. Quickly working out the maths, if the guy I could see was the one targeting me, he bore 294 from me . . . therefore I had to crash down to 10,000 feet and fly on 204 to get into the doppler notch (a clever way of saying 'flying at 90 degrees to the radar'). With no closure, their radar set would struggle to pick me up, as I would blend in with other stuff not moving towards or away from them – Planet Earth, for example. I was also trying to get below

---

4 Electromagnetic energy. Part physics, part witchcraft, which leaves the radar, bounces off something and comes back with all the info you need.

the F3s. No radar likes looking down,[5] and even the F3 guys would admit that in their Foxhunter set they didn't have the world's greatest bit of kit. Flying as aggressively as possible, I pulled level at 10,000 feet. All this was done without daylight's intuition. With the sky as black as the sea, indistinguishable in turn from the mountains. Sweating in an immersion suit in the familiar warmth and electric hum of the cockpit, when actually I was hurtling around in the cold night air, at 420 knots plus, max performing the aeroplane through the sky to get into my sanctuary in the next block down.

But it was always going to end in one inevitable way. A kill was called on a Red Fighter – one of us was dead; from the position it sounded like they'd killed Critter, our American exchange officer. I was getting very close to one of the Tornados in the south, which probably meant he'd lost me, and I tried in vain to unleash the simulated AA-10A 'terror weapon'. Freddie was working really hard to keep the picture, and the scene he painted was of us about to be overwhelmed. This was it, we'd lost, so I issued the mission's last code word.

'Tartan 34, scram, scram.'

Credit to this tanker crew – they had really welcomed the chance to be involved in the defensive plan. My call was immediately acknowledged by the tanker crew;

---

5 A radar will struggle with returns from the earth/sea due to the main beam hitting the surface. This is called main beam clutter, and by notching (flying at 90 degrees to the radar) and by being lower, you were both acting like MBC and maximizing it.

I could even hear their engines spooling up over the radio as the captain turned his aircraft towards Norway and lit the coals. Freddie was now telling me that the game was up, I was being targeted by at least one aeroplane, and the fight in the north seemed to be nearing its logical conclusion as well. My Sky Guardian radar warning receiver burst into life, giving the squeaks and crackles that told me a Foxhunter had me illuminated. I put out all of my counter-measures, all my chaff to try to drop the radar lock. All my flares to deny a heat-seeker shot. This was a twin-edged sword at night. Flare bloomed amazingly under the aeroplane, a huge magnesium brightness, reflected on the aircraft belly and in my mirrors. It destroyed my night vision and gave every fighter in Christendom my position. But it was better to be seen than be dead, and it bought us time – time for Tartan 34 to head east.

Kills were eventually called on the remaining three Sea Jets. We had been overcome at last. But we'd done our job, both real and simulated. In an actual fight, our job had been to stop the HVAA being shot down, which we'd done. In peacetime, our sole job was to give the F3s a realistic simulation; the Blue Air training aims were the absolute priority. I felt we'd given them a decent work-out. We set up to go back to Mum. Mum was due north of Lossiemouth at about 20 miles; all we had to do was close the throttle and mosey back to the cakestand.[6] The F3s came up on our frequency.

6 Holding jets, flying in circles, all stacked up, looked a bit like a cakestand.

'Hi, Freddie, Chariot 1 with you looking for Tartan 34.'

'Chariot, Freddie, Tartan 34 is to your east at 84 miles, heading east.'

'Confirm 84 miles?' came the reply in a slightly pan-icked tone – hmm, that didn't sound good. 'We don't have fuel for 84 miles!'

Suddenly, it dawned on me. Mum was under the tanker towline for the exercise. The F3s needed to join it to get enough gas to go home, they were below their fuel state for Leeming. The F3s had assumed it would stay in its original position, a perfectly reasonable assumption on their part, so had worked out that they only needed a small amount of fuel to reach it. How could they possibly factor in a 'run east' plan they knew nothing about? We had drawn up a realistic plan to protect the tanker without considering how much the opposition were going to need it after the 'terminate' call. Their fuel plan would have been based on getting to the tanker and in the unlikely situation that they couldn't find it, or plug in, they'd have just enough gas for a quick nip to Lossiemouth. We had moved the tanker and also got him to run away. The tanker was, quite literally, fucking miles away, still scramming east, the captain getting his teeth into his first tactical scenario since officer training. Loving every second.

As I settled myself down for one more night recovery, I had a last look to the east. Blue Vixen had an 80-mile range scale. I could see the tanker at about 60 miles. A lone jet was chasing it at about 30 miles, one was going to high level, stating under-confidently that he was going to try for Leeming, but would probably go to Leuchars. Two jets were biting the bullet and were already inbound to Lossie. Excellent, we'd be in the bar by the time they had even found a fuel bowser. By playing the game and being such a good lad, the tanker captain had run away from the very guys he was meant to be refuelling, and they'd all, for the purposes of keeping score, run out of petrol as a result. I'd call that a draw. But the laughing could wait for the debrief; it was time to switch on.

As I descended for 2,000 feet, it was time to get the aircraft and head set for a night recovery. An important bit of this was flying using the head-down instruments. The head-down artificial horizon was the critical instrument and was partially obscured behind the stick.[7] I kept up this habit pattern as, if you had a HUD failure close to the boat, your night was about to become incredibly hard. I didn't fancy refreshing myself on head-down flying at that point, so always had a go on the way back to the boat for practice.

As I approached the ship, I could see her on radar and could see the two red line-up beacons on the left of the flight deck. That was it. Paying absolute attention to the radio altimeter, I crept up the left side of the flight deck.

'That's a nice height.' The LSO's soothing voice confirmed my instruments were good. I could never relax in the hover at night. I put it out of my mind that I didn't have enough fuel for another go or to get to the diversion; this was it. Gently pushing the stick to the right and with a smidge of power, I inched across the deck – able to make out the dimly lit superstructure, the runway lights and the wand being held by the brave soul marking

7 Because flying the Sea Harrier wasn't hard enough already!

199

my spot. The performance octagon told me that I had plenty of thrust in reserve as I set up the descent. Smack. Bit of a teeth chatterer. Throttle idle. Brakes on. Now to obey the wands and really start to concentrate as I was marshalled towards the graveyard. This is a game for the big boys, and we all wanted to be big boys.

Another night, another exercise. It was common for fights to end and teams to go home with some sort of jibe. Why couldn't they stay longer? Why not one more fight? Stay and fight, or are you scared? I remember being off Leuchars on an inky-black night, the Scottish coast looking bright off to the west, where orange sodium lights marked out roads and habitation. To the east, just blackness, no horizon, nothing. But somewhere in the nothing was Mum. Leuchars was my favourite RAF airfield, scene of many happy detachments. We were fighting the F3s again, but the fun and games were drawing to a close. We were out of time.

'Venom, this is Horseman. Have you got time for one more run?' asked their leader, who was a rather splendid chap called Macca.

'Really sorry, Horseman, no. We need to set up for recovery now.' I think I probably smiled under the oxygen mask when we told them that we weren't going to play, that we had to go. And not a sound from them, no banter, no quips. They all knew that they were going to a well-lit, static airfield; we were going to a dimly lit mobile bath tub with a tarmac roof. I really appreciated that last call from Macca and the boys that night: 'Thanks for the trade. Take care.' Perfect in its understatement.

22. Downtime: The Case of the Dead Air Commodore

We were in Lossiemouth, most of us were sober, Wilky had had a couple.

In 1997, the RAF embarked some of its Harrier GR7 aircraft in HMS *Invincible* to go and help out in the upcoming hostilities in Iraq (which I don't think actually upcame in the end). An RAF pilot crashed into the sea attempting to land on the carrier at night. The (contested) RN view of the story was that our light-blue brethren had tried to bite off a little more than they could chew, that the progression to night flying was a little quick and that the pilot had got himself into a little bit of a pickle that could have been avoided had he simply overshot and had another go. He was also trying to land off an approach type advised against by the RN. The important bit of the story is, however, the generally accepted pseudo-fact that he had ejected under water (how is beyond me – but not to worry) and so had an MRI scan to check which bits were still in alignment and which weren't. The scan found a brain haemorrhage, from which, the story went, the good officer sadly died. The other really important thing to mention is that I wasn't there and so can only go on what I have read about the accident . . . and the HUD video we were shown at some point.

Wilky wasn't there either.

Now, what is generally forgotten about the Sea Harriers coming under RAF command and control as part of 3 Group is that, whilst we probably were told that it had happened, we never actually paid any attention to it, didn't listen at the briefs and therefore ended up with knowledge about the RAF, their group and the personalities in it that could accurately be called 'scant'.

It was 2003. We were in Lossiemouth to take part in tactical leadership training. The vehicle chosen for TLT is the COMAO[1], Balbo[2] or gorilla[3]. Call it what you will, it is still a whole load of aeroplanes all going to fulfil the commander's intent by blowing up their allotted target.[4] I am prepared to bet my starboard spherical man-bit that the UK never launches its own organic, coordinated strike from a single base for a single mission led by one bloke. I can see us doing it using a Combined Air Ops Centre, I can see us doing surgical strikes with a little bit of coordination required, but a COMAO? On our own? No.

Still, it was bloody good fun, very demanding, and it gave the Air Warfare Centre staff a chance to pick holes in your plan, and it was done in a very British way:

---

1 Composite air operations: different aircraft operating as a team.
2 Named after the Italian who first thought of aeroplanes ganging up. Code for aircraft operating as a team.
3 Big ape. Code for aircraft operating as a team. Usually (in fairness) coming towards you as an unruly mob.
4 Technically we were supposed to have the correct effect on an allotted target. This much-drummed-in point is a little superfluous, as, given that warplanes carry bombs, the effects they can have are pretty much limited to blowing stuff up. Still, it's the thought that counts.

quote 'unrealistic, but great training'. Seriously? A person of sound mind actually said that. When I say of sound mind, his nickname is actually Mad Mick. QED.

The COMAO is interesting because so long as it's just fast aeroplanes it's a doddle. The twin-seat community stop wandering around as a herd and do all the trivial jobs, like deciding where to go, how high to be, who's going when and all the other George. The staff make you plan and replan to make sure that it's so damn safe the seventy or so aeroplanes will never even see each other. Then you go and fly it. People drop out, people go late, people react to SAMs and to the Red Air baddies, people get lost, some have two goes at the target, and before you know it there are aeroplanes all over the shop in what rapidly becomes an all-comers bun fight. Great fun, and every now and again, in the debrief, you find out that what happened closely resembled what you thought happened. For the lion's share of the time, your sense of reality and what occurred are so amazingly different you could be forgiven for thinking you'd gone to the wrong debrief. So what makes it tricky? Helicopters and heavies. Trying to integrate the fuckers into a seamless plan is nigh on impossible. What invariably happens is people keep shouting about integrating them, when actually what's happening is there are three plans; Fast Air, helo and heavy, happening simultaneously, in parallel with a feigned level of connection. But it keeps everyone happy, and every now and again there'll be a helo guy who can work the photocopier or maybe a heavy guy who can make a good coffee, so they're more than welcome.

So there we were. In Scotland, planning for a mission (which in Sea Harrier days involved checking what bullseye[5] we were using, what frequency the chat/shouting would happen on,[6] when we thought it best to start firing some AMRAAMs at Red Air and when we were going to fit into the taxi pattern of endless Tornados – each containing twice the number of people that are strictly required to fly an aeroplane). This mission must have involved helos at some point.

Mid (three minutes in) plan, in walked this polite high-ranking RAF officer of some description. The RAF wear small barcodes in place of insignia of rank, so it's quite tricky to work out what they are, particularly if you're from a force that considers lack of knowledge about the air force to be a laudable quality. Being equally polite officers, we stopped what we were doing (i.e. looked up from the map).

'Hello, sir, how are you?' I said.

'Hello, chaps. I'm Air Commodore JFH,' he replied. Which was, of course, wonderful. Joint Force *Helicopters* (I think) is what they've all been bundled into these days.

'Oh really, sir?' I replied. 'The helos are at the far end of the building, in the hangar.' This was a bit of a stretch. The helos were in a tent in the hangar, which doubled as a briefing facility. The building was actually a few Portakabins. Why in God's name would the RAF have a

---

5 Tactical reference point. One would usually get told where the baddies were as bearings and ranges from this point.
6 Really the only big question in COMAO planning. All on one net, or muds on one, air defenders on another?

building in which you could plan, brief and debrief a decent mission, for Christ's sake?

Now the senior officer looked at me quizzically. 'I'm Air Commodore JFH,' he said for a second time. This basic repetition was, I thought, a relatively sound tactic, so tried it myself.

'In the hangar, sir. Sea Kings, Chinook, Lynx, all sorts.'

'J – F – H,' he spelled out. Jesus, we're really not getting anywhere!

'In – the – hangar,' I replied, conscious that I might be beginning to sound a little contrary.

'Joint Force Harrier,' he asserted. Ah, the sound of one big dropping penny. It would be fair to say that I felt a little bit stupid at this point, a touch embarrassed and red of face – and, true to form, the ground didn't swallow me up. Still, can't be a bad thing annoying the RAF, and the rest of the formation obviously thought it quite funny.

So we showed him the plan, which was a map of Scotland with Lossiemouth ringed on it, the push point (where it was all going to kick off) and bullseye on in pen. It took about twenty seconds to explain the basis of our plan. We go to the push point, ahead of the muds, go first, kill everyone, come home. Which would have been the plan, and might have even happened, had it not been for that perennial turd in the punch bowl, the weather. Fog was coming but was forecast to get to the coast, not the airfield. The coast and the airfield are about 4 yards apart. Cue lots of anxious formation leaders coming up with great diversion plans and us trying to work out whether doing a completely illegal, self-vectored approach and just believing our nav kit was in any way sane. We decided it wasn't, but as we couldn't really come up with a plan B it had to do. The engineers weighed in with a minor unserviceability issue, and before long it became clear that Milhouse and I would be on our own. Various aircraft types started inventing reasons not to go, but I seem to remember the Tornado GR4 community were prepared to give it a crack, holding a ridiculous amount of petrol to get to Waddington, when the whole, 'land when the nav kit says so' plan came clattering down around us.

We briefed, we changed, we got to 'the line'. This is where you sign over the aeroplane from the engineers using a book thicker than a telephone directory which only really has two useful things in it: how much petrol they have shoved in and what broke on the last hop. The fog was there, you could see it at the perimeter fence. In the time it took to sign out the aeroplanes, it stormed through the airfield boundary. It was so thick, finding our way back to the car was hard. Finding the jets would have been impossible. This was, of course, the best possible outcome. We had for all the world looked like we were game to go on a night when others weren't, and then it all got cancelled anyway. Win.

So, no real need for a debrief and just enough time to get to the hotel and go out with the chaps. When we got to the hotel, there was news that a team was already ashore but we would all press on to the Chinese at some point. The air commodore was there and was only mildly offended when Swampy took one look at his spectacular pullover and remarked, 'Oh brilliant, Christmas jumpers,

I'll get mine!' So out we went. When we got to the Chinese, the others were there. It became clear quite rapidly that Wilky had already had a few. He also, for reasons that aren't clear to this day, had a bee in his bonnet about RAF night work-ups on the boat. We (on the other hand) were fucking boat ninjas, we practically lived there, and they all loved us . . . or something. Cue Wilky, who wasn't night-qualified himself, but anyway . . .

'Sir, the crab[7] night rules are rubbish. You go night flying too soon, and it's all going to end in tears.' The usual deathly silence followed. At this point the junior officer usually remembered stuff like he was in the military and shut up, but not Wilky. 'Seriously, I don't want to speak ill of the dead, but the guy who crashed by *Invincible* was over-confident, the work-up was rushed, and he shouldn't have been doing what he was!'

The air commodore had been goaded into action. 'What exactly do you mean, lieutenant?'

'Well,' Wilky continued, 'he was doing a night visual recovery to the boat, he had rushed his work-up, so he must have been over-confident, and, well, that's it – I don't want to speak ill of the dead.'

'Ill of the dead?' the very nice RAF officer enquired. 'Ill of what dead?'

'Oh, you know,' went on Wilky, 'he had a brain

---

7 Our impolite but well-meant nickname for the RAF. Actually taken as a compliment in JFH, where I once heard a wonderful squadron leader remark 'I don't want to be a shipmate – I'm quite happy as a stinking crab.' Still possibly not the way to address the RAF when talking to a one-star officer.

haemorrhage that they found after the ejection and the poor bugger died.'

Silence. My penny dropping earlier a mere tinkle compared to the massive gong that was going off in all our heads.

'Lieutenant,' said the air commodore with a wonderfully firm voice, keeping a magnificently measured decorum. 'I don't consider myself over-confident, I didn't feel rushed, I thought the manoeuvre entirely appropriate . . . (drum roll) . . . *and I'm not dead!*'[8]

The senior pilot entered the fray with an astutely placed order: 'Get out, Wilky!'

Proof, if any were needed, that you really ought not to spin apocryphal dits. BZ,[9] Wilky, top stuff.

---

8 Read *Harrier Boys* 2, which contains the pilot's account, and which wasn't written from beyond the grave, Wilky.
9 Bravo Zulu, which, for some reason, means 'well done'.

23. What On Earth Is FTC?

We were in the North Sea. Somewhere near Newcastle. We were probably having a couple of drinks most nights.

None of the following is a whinge about RN career management or how I felt treated. It is a simple scene-setter for what happened next.

For the initial part of our careers, there was simply too much going on to worry about our careers. We lived day to day. To think too much about our future could even be seen as arrogant, as we had so much to prove in the here and now at that stage. However, this leads to senior folk on squadrons being exasperated by junior people who don't know what they want to do next, don't have any idea how to fill out preferences on a form and don't know the basics about career progression and the prerequisites for follow-on jobs. Long may it continue. Young pups should be worried about only one thing – learning their weapon system and being the best warfighter they can.[1]

---

1 My joy was unbounded in the ready room at NAS *Meridian*, where I had the privilege of pinning USN wings to an RN lieutenant's chest and afterwards listened to CNAF (Commander Naval Air Forces) tell the winged aviators that he wanted one thing from them and one thing only: 'Learn your weapon system and be the best naval aviators you can possibly be. Nothing else.' That was their job until they had enough experience to 'come up for breath'.

We all got a bit muddled by careers choices, which boiled down to whether or not to volunteer for a longer commission. The carrot was a possible F-18 exchange, which would mean flying with the United States Navy and living out the TOPGUN[2] fantasy we all harboured somewhere. The stick was the longer commission. After much thought, this actually became simple. If jam tomorrow was an F-18 tour, then I was a volunteer. Despite it being quite important, I volunteered and then forgot about it. Bearing in mind the fluid nature of appointing plots at the time, the chances of me going on F-18 exchange appeared to depend on jam tomorrow made in a factory that might, in due course, be built on reclaimed land in a location yet to be determined, or drained, from as yet ungrown fruit to a currently undefined recipe. I went about my business as a Sea Harrier pilot. You might think that's a little cavalier or 'gash'.[3] Well, if you are one of the low-capacity types in the surface fleet who has to think at walking pace, and for the first couple of tours is not let anywhere near a weapon system, then you probably have enough time on your hands to worry about trivia. If you fly Fast Air, you are expected to lead four-ships and missions in the wide blue yonder from the get go, are presented with numerous opportunities to kill yourself on most days, and are expected to be master of the Blue Vixen, AMRAAM, Sidewinder, 1,000lb

2 For the record. There is only one TOPGUN. It's the US Navy's Naval Fighter Weapons School. There is no such thing as a human TOPGUN. Even if there was, it would be strictly limited to graduates of the Fighter Weapons School, not any turkey who happened to fly a warplane.
3 A handy term to describe someone not necessarily up to speed.

bombs, 540lb bombs in high explosive and inert guises with retard tails, freefall tails, a variety of fusing options, practice weapons, cannons, counter-measures and ESM systems, as well as having all the duties any other officer would have. Things like promotions and pensions tend to slide down your list of priorities.

I went to the RAF electronic warfare range at RAF Spadeadam with Monkey on my wing. We only (thank God) had 3kg practice weapons on board and were training with JTACs[4] doing close air support in one of the open spaces on the range. CAS involves getting all the necessary information to make an attack on a target and then setting off (in this case) from an initial point and the JTAC 'talking you on'. My target was a pair of trashed old aircraft in long vegetation.

I let the JTACs know who we were and what we were carrying: 'Good morning, Mayhem, Satans are with you, two by Sea Harriers with practice weaponry, yours for three zero mikes,'[5] before slipping into 'soldier speak' to let them know our playtime was thirty minutes.

'Satans, Mayhem, good morning, stand by rear brief,' came the reply from the JTAC, who filled us in on the scenario that they were working to.

'Satans, ready nine-line,' I said, telling the JTAC that

---

4 Joint terminal attack controllers. We used to call the same people forward air controllers or FACs (pronounced 'fax'), but the Americans changed the name to JTAC (pronounced 'jay-tack'), and we followed suit for no real reason other than it sounded cooler.
5 Communications brevity code for thirty minutes. Numbers have to be spelled out to avoid confusion.

I was ready to receive the nine bits of information we needed to talk through before my attack.

'Mayhem,' came the reply. The JTAC read out the nine-line CAS brief. I read back to the JTAC the bits that he needed to know that I had transcribed exactly. After having a look at my map, I knew which area we would be in. Sure enough, I was able to confirm that the target was 'in Spadeadam', so made the correct switches to give me a 3kg weapon sight up, all the while positioning so as to be wings level, on heading, leaving the initial point in good order.

I always found it hard to keep my head 'out of the cockpit' when there's so much to crack in the cockpit – and the stuff that can kill you is all outside. Thankfully, in the Sea Harrier, the weapons selections were simple, and by moving the single switch above my left knee I made my pylon live, and the single button push gave me the sight for a weapon delivery. The bomb sight was given to me as an inverted T in the HUD, and quite simply I now had to put the intersection of the two lines on the target and press the pickle button. The bomb would hit it . . . assuming that the target and the ground below you were at the same altitude. Despite various rumours to the contrary, the FA2 had a cast-iron bombing solution, and if you 'put the thing on the thing and pressed the thing', then the bomb hit the thing. It took some special inputs to fuck it up. Please read on.

'Satan 1, IP inbound.'

'Mayhem, copy. Your target two parked aircraft in the open.'

There's essentially cock all to say to each other for

the first bit, because the JTAC's given you the brief, and at low level you can't see anything worth asking about, and he can't see you. However, as you go down the run, the pair of you can start a 'bat and ball' dialogue about what you can see, and when he gets eyes on your aircraft he can shout out where the target is. The thing that I forgot, though, was that we were talking to the JTAC but operating within Spadeadam, which meant that the JTAC talked you onto the target, but the range controller gave you clearance to drop. Usually when you called 'Tally target!'

'Mayhem, visual, 12 o'clock, 2 miles,' called the JTAC – he could see me, and I had about fifteen seconds to find these bloody aircraft and make an attack.

In I came, speed pegged at 450 knots, maintaining 250 feet and staring through my HUD, looking for aircraft in the open. I saw the aircraft at the very last second, actually just after the very last second, and to my eternal shame still tried to press the attack. They weren't dead ahead and would have passed just down the right side of the aircraft had I not seen them. This could have gone one of two ways. The least likely of the two was 'well'. By rolling right, unloading and 'stabbing' my velocity vector at the moorland above the aircraft, I did get the bomb sight to travel through the target, but it was swinging wildly with the aircraft movement. If the weapon-aiming computer could have verbalized what it was thinking, it would probably have shrieked, in a high-pitched voice, 'I can only do so much, you clown!'

'Satan 1, tally target!' I shouted in a lame effort at multi-tasking.

Pickle cover up, pickle, and I dropped my practice bomb. Two issues: 1) Even the most advanced weapon-aiming computer likes stability as opposed to being flung around; 2) No clearance to drop. I was so maxed by finding the target, and so euphoric to have found it, that I simply 'got on with the attack'. I realized my mistake immediately and apologized profusely to the range control officer as I made my switches safe and flowed south for the next attack – theoretically there might not be a next attack, as range controllers kick you out for stuff like this. In fairness, they were supposed to monitor the exercise and shout 'Clear hot' when you acquired the target. There had been no time for that, and I shouldn't have made the attack. They were actually pretty sanguine about it.

'Range, this is Satan. Apologies, I just dropped without clearance.'

'Roger, Satan, yes, no clearance was given. Satan 1, you are responsible for getting a clearance to drop on each pass.' I said sorry again. I said sorry to the JTAC. When we were done, I said sorry to the JTAC again. I said sorry to the RCO as I left the range to go back to Mum.

Once we'd landed, I hurried downstairs to the briefing room to find the CO, who had authed the trip, and apologized to him. The CO was his usual great self and said something like 'Oh, I did that once!' Almost immediately, though, I was told that I would fill in for someone else in the next mission, so I needed to brief. As I was still in full flying kit, I went to sit down, and no sooner had my arse hit the briefing room seat than there was a bellow from the back of the room.

'Where's Tremelling?' I saw the surprise on other faces and turned around. The captain had just entered. The ship's captain. The grand fromage. 'Where's Tremelling?' he repeated. Fucking hell! I'd only dropped the fucking thing thirty minutes prior and I'd said sorry to everyone involved, and now the bloody captain was asking for me! I stood up and timidly raised my right hand.

'Here, sir!'

The captain rounded the front row of chairs and stood a metre or so away.

'You're on the FTC!' he said.

'Oh,' I replied. That sounded serious. What a day I was having. I wondered how FTC played out – summary punishment in my smart uniform or something? It sounded bad, though.

He then looked at me quizzically and said, 'You look guilty as hell!' Which was true but probably not the best starting point for a defence. 'Anyway – be in 4T at 1930 – see you then.' 4T[6] was the skipper's quarters at the aft end. Feck – an evening bollocking for one bloody 3kg weapon, not much bigger than a bottle of lemonade!

As he left, people became very relaxed and jovial – notwithstanding that we needed to brief, everyone seemed quite excited. I closed my eyes. How had today gone quite so badly? It was the senior pilot who spelled it out to me.

---

6 Ships decks are numbered from the flight or weather deck downwards. 1 deck has the runway on it, 4 deck is three below that. The ship's compartments are labelled alphanumerically bow to stern – so T was at the very back. Nice view!

'What's FTC?' I asked – dreading the answer.

'FTC? FTC? You're on a full-term commission, you twat!'

I should really have known that. It certainly makes sense now that the skipper hadn't seemed too cross. Great news – I'll take that over a court martial, I thought!

Now I was going to stay in the Royal Navy until the cows came home – with any luck bearing an F-18 exchange with them. Until then, though, with the premature retirement of the Sea Harrier upon us, I would be converting from the Sea Harrier FA2 to the Harrier GR7/9. I was going to become a mud-mover.

24. Sea Harrier FA2 to Harrier GR7 and GR9 Conversion

Peculiarly, I had to fight to get onto an FA2 to GR7/9[1] conversion course. I was suffering the necessary ignominy of a staff tour after being an air warfare instructor on 801. I was serving at Strike Command[2] at RAF High Wycombe, where the job was essentially one of elegantly deleting the Sea Harrier and bringing the Joint Force Harrier in its new 'mud-moving only' guise to maturity. I enjoyed the job and thought it absolutely necessary, but it did show me a couple of things. Mainly that the frontline complained a lot about a lot but never said thank you. On the plus side, as ever, there was a team of great people on the No. 1 Group Royal Air Force staff. In particular, the 1 Group RAF 'chief of staff' area under a wing commander with a simply phenomenal work rate.

My duties were first being the FA2 desk officer[3] and, only a matter of days later, when the SHAR was no more, Jack of all the jobs that no one else wanted.

Under the direction of the chief of staff, No. 1 Group

1 The GR9 brought with it many improvements in avionics, for example better radios and better navigation equipment.
2 It became Air Command while I was there.
3 Desk officers have simple duties: sort everything out for your 'chosen' platform – funding, upgrades, investigations, reports, training, exercises . . . the list is probably endless.

started planning for a future that included the F-35. This system was going to be truly revolutionary for the RAF. The jet was being developed by the US Navy, US Air Force and US Marines, and there was a variant planned for each of them. We were going to buy the short take-off vertical landing (STOVL) variant along with the US Marines. It would operate in a similar joint force of RAF and Royal Navy personnel and would be able to operate from the new carriers being developed in parallel to be specifically tailored to the F-35.

We had an exceptional place in the programme due to some expertise we contributed along with a significant investment. The ability of the F-35 to sense its surroundings, fuse all available information and present it to the pilot is world-beating. As a low observable platform, it can enter airspace in which older aeroplanes would simply be shot down. No. 1 Group was therefore concerned not only where this formidable capability would be based, but how it would change the way we fought, trained and even thought about air combat.

I was given the job of being the first ever 1 Group F-35 man – which was an amazing opportunity to get into that programme. The (phenomenal) COS arranged it, and my duties included development work in simulators and basing studies for the aeroplane. Years later, I would be the F-35 desk officer. Let me summarize. The F-35 is simply incredible, and whilst everyone is allowed their opinions,[4] having a striker that can trespass enemy air

4 Mainly on costs. When I say everyone is entitled to his or her opinion, most who opine will have simply 'no idea what they are talking

defences, whilst others cannot, delivers relevance to an air force that would be irrelevant without it. Whilst teaming with other assets, for example, Typhoon, is important, the irreducible minimum is the F-35, not its stablemate. Air forces now fall into only two buckets: those with F-35, those without.

Fortunately, I also had the spare capacity to go about tunnelling my way to Wittering for my conversion to mud-moving – as we had moved a modicum of mud in the FA2, I wouldn't be a complete newcomer to the game. Tunnelling was made easier by being in the HQ and therefore knowing who the training officer was – and where his desk was and what the plot looked like. I even managed to get him to put my name in a course slot. It was made harder by a perplexing line from the RN captain there at the time, who thought I was irreplaceable – despite my protests that I really wasn't. This argument quickly degenerated into one about 'RN Fixed Wing drivers always wanting their own way and having tantrums' – and my counter-argument that I wasn't after a pay rise or better shoes, I was asking to be sent to a place called Afghanistan, not famed for adding to your quality of life. Harriers had been deployed to Afghanistan since 2004 and were giving a phenomenal account of themselves, in the main flying close air support for the heroes on the ground. Eventually my

---

about'. Sadly 'they' are numerous and don't ever shut up. Why is it that most subjects (finance, professional sport, the weather) insist upon professional pundits being relevantly experienced experts? Why is it that warfare stands alone as the one subject anyone can gob off about or write about even if they've never seen it or done it?

appointment came through, and I ceased being one of those sorry souls who walked to work looking at the wide blue yonder, yearning to strap a jet to their arse.

This time it would be different. This time I wouldn't be flying a jet that was being retired impolitely early and which people were therefore actively attempting to keep out of operations. I would be flying the aircraft deployed into the thick of it. There was a massive poster on the wall in 1 Group. It said something like '1 Group assets are deployed in bitter combat operations. Do not leave work until you have done everything in your power to assist them.' Carve me off a slice of that! That poster was put there by the air officer commanding No. 1 Group, an RAF two-star who had a reputation for being brusque, completely un-Joint and occasionally asking for things that might be thought of as lunacy. An example was the time he asked assembled RAF aircrew whether or not they would fly into an SUV to kill a Talib commander. For the record, he was the finest two-star I served under or with. He was an amazing orator and had an encyclo-paedic knowledge of military history. He was as Joint as they come – but there were two new issues to be faced with retirement of the FA2 that brought with them another disappointing episode of inter-service nonsense – with 1 Group seeming to be the fulcrum.

Firstly, there was now a paucity of jets to keep decks warm and carrier flying skills high. Secondly, there was a wrangle about who actually controlled the jets in peace-time and war. The FA2 had been a bit of an orphan within the RAF chain of command, and the dark-blue force had, in a way, masked to the RN the fact that they owned people but no longer owned any aeroplanes. The retirement of FA2 brought this into stark relief. If you don't own any aeroplanes, don't expect someone else to lend you theirs when they are actually deployed on actual warfighting operations. AOC 1 Group understood what a deployed Harrier force could and couldn't do at a time when the RN just wanted jets on a deck. It wasn't his fault that the RN had handed over its jets and then watched them be retired. The RN better understood that pilot skills were but a building block of a carrier strike capability but didn't have any levers to pull as regards getting the jets embarked and keeping them there. To perpetuate a capability required the Air Group, ship and wider Task Group to be worked up – not just the Harrier force personnel. However, to have done so would have detracted from the skill sharpening of a force already only just able to meet its own internal training requirements while it was in a three-unit 'war–recock–work-up–war' cycle.

The command and control of 1 Group Harriers was actually elegantly simple. They were RAF aircraft and, no matter who flew or maintained them, they operated under 1 Group Air Staff Orders and would be apportioned to the Air Component. The RN flat tops being reduced to the status of 'basing option' was, in my opinion, a circumstance that the RN had constructed for itself. The notion that you could create a set of circumstances whereby jets absolutely needed to be commanded and controlled from someone actually on a ship was fanciful. The RN had relegated itself to being a stakeholder in the first couple of per cent of an aircraft's combat radius. From now on Harriers would exist in the RAF world and really only enter the RN bailiwick when they turned finals to land on the boat. Drivers and maintainers at the coalface, however, simply had to acknowledge that, whilst our spiritual home was 'the boat', our life's purpose was war – which rightly took priority. As ever, at the tactical level things just worked. JFH delivered. People of all services delivered, uninhibited by the petty squabbling that seemed to exist in a sphere inhabited by very senior officers (who should have known better), very junior officers (who didn't know better but no one should listen to) and armchair experts, whose right to an opinion I question!

That all led to 20(R) Squadron and the conversion course. Going to a new aeroplane can be seen as a bit of a tightrope walk. You have to be confident in your ability and the relevance of your experience but humble about the need to ingest and learn. It's about picking your moments to be front-footed if you need to – to show a few folk you aren't going to be pushed around. It's about being seen to learn and contribute at the same time. I contributed by instructing the current weapons instructor course about how radars and air defence tactics actually worked. The 20(R) hierarchy encouraged me to do so. I worked hard on learning – being unprepared for a brief or sortie is too easy a kill to give away. When I needed to fight my corner, I did.

Following a 1 v 1 air combat hop I got about halfway through the debrief – which was being run well – before I felt I had to bring up the key point. We had had five fights. I had won all of them. The other aircraft had appeared to gain a shot opportunity on me once, so I had simulated deploying counter-measures. Five-nil with only one counter-measures event was a bit of a clobbering, and I felt that the debrief needed a little 'reset'. In fairness, the instructor took the hit. Good lad. The reason I bring all this up is that some people had had horror stories going through 20(R). I wasn't there, but I suspect it was because some of them just weren't good enough. The net at 899, the Sea Harrier headquarters squadron, didn't catch everyone, and there were a couple of 'borderline cases' let through in the latter years. Some folk may have been complacent and ill-prepared. Some people may have overcooked their status as previously qualified VSTOL pilots. Obviously, there's also a chance that 'local celebrities' who didn't necessarily welcome the formation of a Joint Force made life difficult for them, and some of these might have been poor instructors. Some combination of all of the above easily mounts up to a poisonous atmosphere in which good, healthy, inter-service rivalry becomes a very negative force. Not for me. I worked hard and was treated very well.

The jet was great. Easy to fly, dead easy to hover. Actually a little bit cumbersome in the hover. I missed the radar, feeling naked without the ability to 'look out' using my 9(ish) GHz eyes and ears. I missed nozzle nudge in the VSTOL regime, as the ability to quickly flick your nozzles forward or aft by an extra 10 degrees was very useful. I missed one or two other bits and pieces. There weren't many challenges to actually flying the jet. The bigger wing really helped, and evolutions like the conventional landing went from being a bit of a pulse-raiser to a non-event. This did lead to a small disagreement with one of the trimmers, who viewed my decision to land downwind using the conventional technique 'dimly'. When I remarked that it was a doddle and even with a couple of knots up the chuff I was nowhere near the tyre limit or in danger of running out of runway, he viewed that equally dimly! He had a point, but it felt to me to be from the 'just because' school of reasoning, whereas my 'at first look a little bit gash' approach was actually based on aircraft performance knowledge.

And never let it be forgotten that the winner of the Joint Force Harrier Red Nose Day bombing competition in 2004 was 800 Naval Air Squadron flying the Sea Harrier FA2. From this you might be tempted to conclude that, of the myriad bombing modes possessed by the GR, every one of them was less accurate than the way the FA2 went about it.[5] Just thought you ought to know. The science of dropping a bomb depends on knowing where you are relative to something and how high you are above it. So long as you knew what your jet was doing for both, things were straightforward. The GR7 and GR9 both had an array of modes for dropping weapons that you could tailor to all eventualities. And you could still use the old-school technique of putting the thing on the thing and pressing the thing . . . which was nice, and it worked. (*Cough*, just not as well as the Sea Harrier . . .)[6]

_____

5 Clearly I am talking about unguided bombs!
6 The Sea Harrier had a very tight height feed into the weapon-aiming computer and could (sometimes but not always) use the radar to be

While in many ways the jet was significantly better than the Sea Harrier, whoever decided not to give it a radar set needs a kicking. Not least because it would have got rid of the TV on the nose that was responsible for the more complex weapons modes and, in my mind, not responsible for any increase in accuracy. Indeed, we could have used air-to-surface ranging with a radar which was tighter than a tight thing instead! The bigger wing was better, it had more weapons stations, the jet could carry more fuel, the refuelling probe actually folded away.[7] When not being used just to make you work hard, the automatic bombing modes gave you a night and poor-weather capability. Another significant improvement over the Sea Harrier was the forward-looking infra-red, which allowed you to see in the dark – incredibly handy at night, in dust or when there was a low sun. The system was very clever and would come in handy at the boat and in Afghanistan.

Things that were not taught on 20(R) but left until the frontline and which were absolutely critical were targeting pods, of which there were two, and the bigger engine. Nothing conceptually difficult about using a targeting pod – in fact, it was so simple that I spent a lot of time wondering what it was I was missing! I think that there were about twenty trips in the TIALD[8] targeting pod

---

precise about the range to the target; and the weapons were very well modelled in the machine.

7 The FA2 probe was simply bolted on, and it really did affect the handling.

8 The imaginatively titled Thermal Imaging and Laser Designation pod. Good for bridges and stuff, for which it was designed.

work-up. I did two – including the second, which was a heavy weapon drop on a barge. I was justifiably proud to find out that I had hit the barge-mounted camera that was supposed to film the event. There were about ten trips in the Sniper pod[9] work-up. I did two. The systems were intuitive, and turning more fuel to noise wasn't necessary to get to the standard to deploy. The same is true of the big engine – just more engine limits to memorize . . . on top of the GR limits that were themselves different from the FA2. In retrospect, the art of mud-moving isn't actually that conceptually challenging. It all comes down to getting into weapons parameters at the right time – having fought through or evaded whoever is trying to stop you. In fact, so long as you could choose between speeding up or cutting a corner to make up time,[10] mud-moving was for you!

I was sent to a newly rebadged unit. The Royal Navy had failed to provide enough suitably qualified people to man two squadrons. We therefore formed the Naval Strike Wing in place of 800 and 801 Naval Air Squadrons. NSW was the same size as a traditional RAF squadron, which was a little bigger than the Sea Harrier units had been at Yeovilton. I think the idea was to re-emerge as 800 and 801 at some point when we achieved the right level of personnel, but history got in the way a long time before that could happen.

9 The next generation of 'bad ass' pods. Looked evil, performed brilliantly. Perfectly named.

10 For some reason being late was a problem about 95 per cent of the time and being early a welcome novelty on the few times it happened.

25. The Great North Sea Wind Hunt

*North Sea. A couple the night before
but still razor-sharp for night flying.*

Despite other pressures on Joint Force Harrier, we did manage to take the jet to sea, just with a reduced frequency. Having previously been a night-qualified pilot FA2, I was very much towards the top of the pile when it came to carrier experience.[1]

The vast majority of deck operations were the same in the GR9 as they had been in the Sea Harrier. Small differences included the inconvenience of not having a radar or MADGE[2] to help getting back to the ship. Other differences were positive. The bigger wing of the GR9 made the ramp launch far better and, as ever, the jet was more stable alongside. With fewer embarkations, corporate knowledge and ability did wane occasionally, and the perennial challenges of landing on ships were still there. In the wrong hands, a ship could still make your life very hard indeed.

The ship did a great job of making the approach harder the night of the 'Great North Sea Wind Hunt'. This saw me pitted against a critical mass known locally as the

1 Really not much to shout about compared to others, but I flew my 198th deck landing in a Harrier. People were considered experienced in JFH if they had flown somewhere around the thirty to forty mark.
2 Microwave aircraft digital guidance equipment, a ship-to-aircraft system that allowed the pilot to get back to the ship on his own.

'chubby subby', subby being short for sub-lieutenant, and chubby being a cruel (yet accurate) reflection of his BMI. I can categorically state that no one in the air group coined that phrase, but it seemed to be worth adopting at the time. So, what happened was . . .

We were in the North Sea and we were flying at night, which always seemed like a good idea and you really wanted to be part of it, but night VSTOL at sea is (in my humblest of opinions) about as high-end as you can get, so the whole team needs to be on their game. I was in a GR9A, which meant that with the big engine I had a stack of performance and wasn't going to struggle to hover at the end of the mission. There were a couple of other foibles that we lived with on the great jet that came home to roost here. The first was the 'deedle-eedles', the sound that the secondary warnings gave. There were loads of them, and though you tried to maintain professional discipline, it was sometimes the case that you got numb to them. As I entered the ramp and blasted off into the inky blackness, I got the not abnormal deedle-eedle. Something had gone wrong – but not enough to worry about right away. At night off the boat you get yourself sorted, away from the sea, then worry about trivia. I tidied the jet up and had a scan around for what was causing the deedle-eedle, which was repeating itself, almost as if the jet were testing whether or not I was going to keep flying the aircraft, which of course I did. Eventually my eyes settled on the cause of the mystery. Above my right knee, my fuel gauges were showing zero. Fuel indication issues were not wholly uncommon in the GR9. There is a very clear indicator that you still actually have fuel – which is that your engine is still running. The simple fix is to use normal engine settings and fly for less time than you usually would. Easy. Only that – in this case – at the far end I needed to land on a ship (at night) and that required me to be below a certain fuel weight and above another. What to do . . .

Here aircraft knowledge and the bloody good bloke that is Bollard came into play. Just like the Sea Harrier could dump down to 2,200lbs, the GR had internal fuel groups that were slightly larger so you could dump down to 2,800lbs. Between us we came up with a plan. As I sorted myself out at 2,000 feet, which was the lowest height from which you made a recovery (1,000 feet was always reserved for anyone who lost their radio), we made our way out towards the bit of sky Mum would marshal us in to make our approach. My plan was simple.

'Mate, if I stick the dumps on, we should both be able to see the fuel go,' I said to Bollard, using the second radio, which made gash R/T discipline permissible. 'When they stop, I have to be at 2,800lbs, don't I?'

'Yes, mate,' came the reply.

Sweet. We'd ask for a landing in about ten minutes' time. It took six minutes to fly the procedure from 15 miles, including the hover and landing at the end. It also took about 600lbs of gas. If I started dumping fuel now – or as soon as the ship agreed to the plan – I would have enough time to get organized and at six minutes to run the indication that I had jettisoned all my fuel, other than the last 2,800lb, would be the dumps switching off automatically. At that point I'd know what fuel I had, and I'd know that I would be alongside with 2,200lbs, which would mean I could hover . . . Gentlemen, the war's as good as won. The plan was agreed to by the ship and worked like a treat. Only that, somewhere out ahead of me, a brooding presence was forming: the officer of the watch had decided that night-time fuel emergencies were getting a little too simple for his liking and he was going to spice this one up somewhat.

This is actually a classic case of giving someone enough knowledge to be dangerous. The OOW had got it into his head that the FW guys liked wind over the deck. That was true. What he hadn't read (or been told – probably our fault) was the small print that said, 'Not to the exclusion of all else, you flaming idiot!' That night in the North Sea we had launched into a light breeze coming from the north-east. We had therefore benefitted mainly from Mum making the most of the wind herself using forward speed. No issue, she could do the same for recovery. If she stayed on DFC to the north-east, all would be well. But she didn't, she turned hard to starboard.

I was just about to start the final descent, listening to the professional, measured tones of the talk-down controller, keeping me on centreline. I had descended to 1,200 feet, as one did upon leaving the cakestand, and very shortly the controller would start to read me my advisory heights as I closed the boat. Out at the cakestand, the directions could be of any magnitude – tens if not hundreds of degrees – but at these ranges it was usually a heading change of 2 degrees or so. Maybe 5 if things weren't going well.

'Come left 10 degrees for centreline,' came the call.

Eh? I thought I was on the centreline . . . hmmm . . .

'Come left 10 degrees for centreline, you're at 6 miles. Start your descent now.'

I made the power correction that would settle me on the glide slope. Out the front, only inky blackness.

'Satan 1 at 3.5 miles, 1,000 feet, come left 20 degrees for centreline.'

Eh? Why was I correcting so much to the left? I should have been in the invisible tube leading straight to Mum, but that tube seemed to be moving off into the darkness to my left. Rapidly. How was I going to make a controlled approach to Mum if she was playing some form of hide and seek out in the darkness?

'Satan 1, come left 20 degrees for centreline!'

Wtf is going on?

Andy then said the first thing that had made sense for a while.

'Satan 1, you are passing through the centreline at 90 degrees at 2 miles, we're going to have to break this one off.' Damn right. Always easy to be cross with the ops team, but Andy was actually doing a phenomenal job of trying to keep me in the right bit of sky – the ship was moving that bit of sky around on a long moment arm.

The OOW had turned the ship through about 60 degrees, chasing the light ambient wind. I had therefore always been to the south of the approach path as it moved away to the north – like a long, straight tail extending back from the ship. Instead of being south-west of a ship heading north-east – both of us aligned – I'd ended up due west of a ship that was now fucking off to the east – and I was heading north!

I immediately applied full power and settled at 2,000 feet. Nozzles aft, gear and flap up. Throttling back. Then came the pearler.

'Satan 1, have you got fuel for another attempt?'

I'd never encountered a boat trying to 'throw me off' before, so I was actually giggling when I said 'Homer, Satan 1. I haven't known how much fuel I've had for the last fifteen minutes!'

Actually, I was overstating the case a little. I knew I'd left the cakestand with 2,800lbs, so by rights I should have had about 2,200lbs. Just enough for another go, which would mean no diversion to Newcastle, with all the associated palaver if the pattern went smoothly, and they turned me in early. My maths told me that, 'give or take', I would probably still be back alongside with 1,600lbs, which 'broadly speaking' would mean I had maintained my diversion fuel to Newcastle until the appropriate point. Can't possibly be bollocked for being below diversion fuel if your fuel gauge isn't working, can you?[3]

I made it home on the second attempt. Short patterns aren't ideal for night flying when it's all about calm and collected aviation, but so far this hadn't been calm or collected. There was simply no expression of regret by any of the bridge team. For some reason the air traffic heroes seemed to think that they were at fault when we mustered in the bar later. Of course, they weren't – they'd done an amazing job. You were never after

3 Fleet Air Arm answer: no, of course not. RAF answer: absolutely, you can.

The business end. Live AIM-120 on the rail as we prepare to take over Northern QRA (Chapter 18). No matter what anyone ever tells you, try not to leave home without an AIM-120 . . . the wingman of choice.

Low Slot Port off *Ark*. I am leading Donald. The idea with the Low Slot was to be as fast as possible, at or lower than Flyco as you passed the ship and broke to land. Only to be attempted once you had a few normal approaches under your belt.

Low Slot off *Invincible* with a USN *Arleigh Burke* in the background. It wasn't uncommon for ships to snuggle up on the port side to get a good view of the recovery/buffoonery.

This is supposed to look square! A night deck landing where the ship's team didn't quite get the wind right and my attempts at being neat obviously failed! Night VSTOL to the boat is about as high-end as it gets. (Chapter 21)

My wingman en route to the weapons range in Oman. Air-to-surface in the desert – not necessarily the Sea Jet's spiritual home and probably not a capability most thought we had. If you ever get a chance – go low flying in Oman . . . you'll see why.

The deck landing. I have my gum shield in for a suitably firm arrival. Firm = likely to stick, which is a good thing.

My last go in my beloved Sea Harrier, leading a fourship against RAF fighters in Wales. There really was no need to be decorated in baked beans upon my return but I appreciated the effort the boys and girls went to.

The new steed. The GR9 armed with Enhanced Paveway 2 Plus weapons at Kandahar – the leader's weapon load until we got Paveway 4 (Chapter 29). When we got there the temperature was above 40°C, but soon we were into cold weather gear as snow arrived on the hills.

The JFH board at Kandahar. Evidence that the force restructured and the RN contingent relabelled from 800 NAS to Naval Strike Wing – but the Joint Force continued to deliver for those heroes on the ground.

Every unit will always have a creative genius somewhere and their prime role is to ensure you leave your mark.

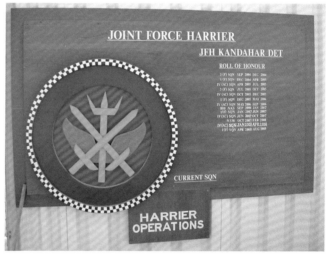

My wingman and I make for the tanker after attacking Talib positions. The frangible cones on the rocket pods are gone, shattered by the first rounds to leave the aircraft. The mixed load of rockets and 540lb bombs complemented my GPS and laser-guided weapons. (Chapter 28)

A picture of me in the lead aircraft as we set off to complete a reconnaissance task. Teeth-extractingly boring, but the product was excellent.

The RN failed to achieve the personnel levels required to break out into 2 Harrier squadrons. JFH kept the sensible and proven 3 unit model and we rebadged as Naval Strike Wing. I ended up as Senior Pilot.

Me taking a quick suck of gas in a break from supporting troops in contact in Arghandab.

The new Paveway 4. NSW were the first to carry and employ it on operations. We were dreading 4 Squadron RAF replacing us and dropping it first, with the RAF news headline '4 drops the 4' writing itself. Luckily David hoofed one off.

Always good to spend as much time as possible with the aeroplanes – which wasn't easy given that the ops room was over a mile away. Here whiling away some time, spinning some great dits to a couple of rocket pods.

Wingy in close on the way back to KAF from Tarin Kowt. This particular chap ended up in the Red Arrows. I put precisely none of it down to my expert tutelage.

Upside down over Uruzgan. I accept that there were probably better things to be doing than taking happy snaps – I was going to the tanker and it was a very quiet day on the ground.

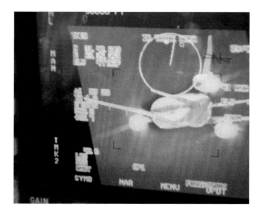

Little-known fact. You can use targeting pods in the air-to-air role. Here helping me to ID a USAF tanker. Had I done this one fateful day, I wouldn't have ended up chasing a BA jet on its way to Hong Kong.

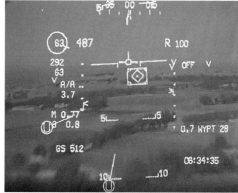

My HUD during a show of force. Very useful for scaring the enemy rather than employing weaponry. Top left is speed, and the bombs could take 495 knots, so I have 8 knots in hand. Top right is height; at 100 feet I am as low as we were permitted to fly.

HMS *Ocean*. My home for most of the Libyan job once she was fitted with the correct computers. An odd experience, contributing to Maritime Strike from the wrong boat with the AAC heroes doing the striking.

The world's finest self-escort strike platform. Everything about it was simply superb. Termed the Rhino in aviator speak, as getting 'Super Hornet' into a ball call when working hard behind the boat was unlikely to result in success.

VFA-25 Rhino on the catapult. From the moment the yellow coat beat his hands on his chest to the moment you were off the front – probably the most exciting thing an aviator will ever do.

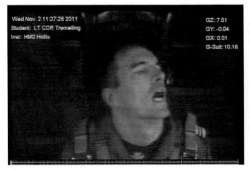

A view of an aviator not necessarily enjoying 7.6 G. Pre-Super Hornet with no jacket or mask in the USN centrifuge. Still, just the 'looking over the shoulder' run to go.

Lights out. Looking over your shoulder – as you would in air combat – closes certain blood vessels and makes the job of fending off G harder. My first attempt was unambiguously sub-optimal.

Approaching the deck at night. I thought this simplified things as you could only see the three things that mattered! Go to the aircraft's DATA page, select BLOOD TYPE, box ICE.

Enjoying some sightseeing on the way home from the Fallon ranges. Around the boat you used your jet's number – 405 here – to identify yourself. All Fist aircraft started with a 4. A minor issue once in USS Carl Vinson when another unit did the same.

Sometimes things just get a little too tough. I was in the back of the tanker for VFA-25's flight to Hawaii and we managed to get a squadron photo exercise done on the way. Beautiful jets, premier-league operators.

Returning from Hawaii. Brain wandering from tanking, to the sheer size of the Pacific, to survival chances if we ejected, to the game of battleships we played to while away the hours.

In the cockpit for my last flight in a military jet. An air-to-air mission to Fallon, followed by an attack with an inert 500lb weapon, followed by my friend Blut kicking me around the sky in BFM.

And we'll call that a day. Flying with the USN and VFA-25 in particular was a rare treat. As the saying goes – if there's no squadron cock, it's probably you. I give you: the squadron cock.

someone birch twigging themselves to death. But the aircrew world was built on brutal honesty, and if you've fucked up you had better own up before someone calls you out. The OOW in the case of the 'Great North Sea Witch Hunt' didn't even register that he'd done something wrong!

Good stuff. Another successful game of naval aviation.

But whilst embarked operations still held their challenges and were something we were justifiably proud to be able to perform, at the time we had a higher calling. War.

But first, a little light relief from one of the junior fellows . . .

26. Downtime: The Dangers of Minimum Regulation Compliance

We were in the North Sea, and I had drunk three, gusting four, glasses of wine. Someone else had drunk enough to kill a carthorse!

In military aviation we are bound by rules and regulations. There are absolutely hundreds of the things. The documents cascade from one to another, so that as one descends into book after book the rules are tightened and tightened until you find yourself in a vice-like grip. In the UK, the highest-level rules are in JSP (Joint Services Publication) 550. It used to be JSP 318, but someone changed it, for some reason, and probably got a huge promotion for doing it. The next level of regulation for us Fixed Wing types is Group Air Staff Orders (GASOs). An RAF officer has to tell you what you may, or may not, do with his precious aeroplanes. He does it through GASOs.

In among some, in my opinion, overly restrictive ASOs are some that actually make a fair bit of sense. One of these concerns alcohol and flying, or rather how to separate them. It's simple. You can't drink within twelve hours of flying and you are advised to minimize alcohol in the twenty-four hours before flying. The guide is five units. It was written carefully as a guide, but some took it as a hard limit. I was once witness to someone who set out to see, scientifically, how these rules actually protected you, and to what degree. The results were unambiguous . . .

I had had the good fortune of having dinner with the captain on board *Illustrious*. I cannot think that it was due to anything I had done; it was in all probability due to the fact that my boss had been asked to nominate someone, and he couldn't be arsed to go himself. The dinner itself was a huge privilege, and my fellow guests were from a Guild or Company of Something or Other from London. One gentleman had brought with him photographs of his microlite on board an RN ship, one of the carriers in the 1980s, I think. He couldn't fly the festering thing but had a pilot to do it for him. His idea had been to use it as a communications relay. The idea wasn't bad – in so much as a comms relay is a good idea. However, he had made the mistake of trifling with deck ops. Carrier aircraft need to be far more durable than their shore-based counterparts. A microlite on deck in a gale or at sea state 6 would last seconds and probably lead to the injury or death of anyone involved. The skipper did a great job of seeming to at least be listening and then, with a perfect blend of etiquette and authority, he politely yet firmly told us it was time to go. I went to the bar.

For the following day, plan A was medium-level work. Plan B was a low-level strike. We'd make the call in the morning, because basing anything on the weather relied upon trusting the met men, or women, who have an awful job, because when they get it wrong we beat on them and when they get it right we don't say thanks. And, let's be fair, they're always wrong.

Kelp[1] was on the strike. Well, that was to say that he would be if the weather was shit. The strike would launch at 1320 the next day. He was a little drunk but for the next two hours and twenty minutes he had a tenuous defence: he would still be outside twelve hours from his flight.

'Mate, you do know you're in the middle wave tomorrow, don't you?' I enquired.

'Well, I'm not, I'm in the reserve, and even so, I can drink until 0120 and still be GASO compliant!' he retorted with a Gallic shrug and not an inconsiderable amount of trouble.

'Okaaaay.' I fizzled out and went off to bed. Kelp didn't notice the time creeping into his protective twelve hours.

So what of our hero? Was he lucky? Er, no. The weather in the medium level was rubbish, the strike was called for. Kelp was called for. Kelp didn't fly but got a damned good hiding instead. Good lad, young Kelp, the sort of chap you want in your trench.

I think that the phrase is something to do with rules being there for your safety, and that of your team . . .

---

1 A very unkind nickname. 'Lower than a bottom feeder'. Actually a top bloke, superb aviator and best wingman ever.

27. Afghanistan – I Went Too

*The Naval Strike Wing were in Afghanistan, and all
we had to drink for four months was 'Near Beer'.*[1]

This is where it all came to a head. Where it all mattered.
Where the lessons from everyone I'd met were brought
to bear. The need to know one's stuff inside out, to not
give up, to know the difference between the vital and the
trivial. To brief and debrief with brutal honesty. To keep
focused on the task. This was Afghanistan.

Afghanistan, for a lot of people, is hell. It was hell for
the Soviets, it was hell for our infantry, it was even worse
for the poor bastards who simply just got born into a
country where hardline militants beheaded the innocent,
and foreign fighters on both sides of the fight flooded
the country. We were there to support a government
everyone knew was corrupt and to attempt to enforce
Western-style freedoms on a tribal society that was
fine without them. We were there because if we didn't
fight the Taliban and three (or four, can't really remember) other recognized insurgent groups, plus Al-Qaeda,
in that country, we'd soon be fighting them at home.
Afghanistan is a hell of blazing heat in summer and shiv-
ering cold in winter. I believed, and do to this day, that we

---

1 This non-alcoholic nonsense didn't stop us going through the time-
honoured traditions of 'having a beer' after a day's work or a tough
mission. It even had its own placebo effect, which is a bit weird.

were absolutely right to be there, but this shouldn't have been a military campaign. This should have been a multi-faceted campaign of which the military was a small part. There is the spectre in Afghanistan of a flapping stable door and the sound of distant hooves. If we'd done the job properly in 2001, we might have been back home a long time ago. No one ever actually told me why we were going, but I worked it out for myself.[2]

For me Afghanistan was heaven. A chance to do what I had always wanted in the simplest of frameworks. Get up in the dark, go to work, plan and fly a mission, get back, gym, eat, bed. Repeat for four months, go home. For those not lucky enough to have read Paddy Hennessey's excellent book *The Junior Officers' Reading Club*, here is my four-sentence review. We need wars, because that's what we joined for. We need the excitement and don't like to take glory in killing, but it has to happen, and we want to be there. Without wars we wouldn't have a story, and in wartime you want for two things: you want it to end and at the same time you want to be part of it for ever. The person trying to kill you and those that you kill are absolutely essential.

My vision of the war in Afghanistan is that of a close air support pilot. I never saw friends and enemies alike mangled beyond recognition, I never smelled the rotting flesh in the intense summer sun. So were we brave or gallant? Probably not in the classic meaning of the words,

---

2 For anyone thinking that this might be an attempt to align my thoughts with more recent news – I can prove electronically that I first wrote that paragraph in 2010.

probably not by any standards. You cannot be brave in a fairly benign environment. What an infantryman was faced with requires amazing physical bravery. The CAS pilot requires skill, quick thinking, depth of knowledge on all the procedures, rules and instructions we operated under and the cool head to deliver heavy weapons close to friendlies. Hand-to-hand fighting is incredibly tough, and to do it at all requires bravery of the highest order; to keep doing it is incredible. For these experiences, we traded anxiety; in place of the infantry's amazing physical courage, we needed a cold moral courage. For we ran a very real risk of notching up friendly casualties as well as the enemy body count . . . of which I am still not a major fan.

The worst that can happen when you drop a 1,000-lb bomb with its heady mix of high explosive and forged casing is inconceivable. The soldiers 150 metres away, the children unseen 200 metres away, the mother and child in the building next door. All, some or none could be scarred, wounded or killed in even the most professionally conducted attack. And the potential exists for an incorrect strike on a misidentified target or an honest mistake. These could be absolutely disastrous. A Talib killed could bring victory a few hours closer, a child killed could perpetuate the conflict for eternity. That level of responsibility was with us in all we did.

We left home in July, the temperature at home rising to 25 degrees as we packed up. In Kandahar it was 40 plus. The other-worldly experience of at last being on operations was added to by arriving at night in a blacked-out Tristar, body armour and helmet on. A couple of hundred souls alone with their thoughts as the truck drivers took us to war.

Kandahar was a very well-established base. Everything you could want, plus more dust than you'd ever need, and it stank. We were replacing 1(F) Squadron RAF, who had come to the end of their tour. They looked after us brilliantly, from squaring our beds away to making sure we had all the reading we needed on day one to go flying on day two.

The first trip was a 1(F) Squadron lead with me following. It was a very boring reconnaissance flight for me, and the only pulse-raiser was a bit of tanking in the middle of the sortie. However, I couldn't shake one nagging feeling. We were over some pretty unappealing terrain, and some very unappealing opponents, should the worst come to the worst and we ended up abandoning the aircraft.[3] The mission passed without incident, though, and despite a savage crosswind back at Kandahar there wasn't much to talk about in the debrief.

Shortly afterwards, I was over Sangin in support of the 16 Air Assault Brigade heroes. Places I'd heard of for all the wrong reasons, now the towns and green zones we circled over. I had a full nine-line from the controller in Forward Operating Base Inkerman and the weapon, a 1,000lb E-Paveway 2+ laser and GPS guided munition, and was ready in all respects. I turned inbound towards the target, an enemy rocket team. In training we tried to be punchy, to turn tighter than other aircraft types, to be

3 Ejecting, banging out, taking the furniture, being 'in the silk', conducting a Martin-Baker letdown . . . you get the idea.

seen and heard to move quickly. Here it was imperative —
shaving a half mile off the run-in could be the difference
between those bastards getting another rocket off or not.

'Recoil 51,[4] in hot.'[5]

'Clear hot,' came back from the JTAC on the ground.
The HUD symbology told me that I was within the right
parameters. I made the Late Arm live and held down
the pickle button. *Clunk*. Half a ton of pain left the
aeroplane.

Dropped from around 16,000 feet, a weapon takes
about twenty-five seconds to fall through the air, electronic 'eyes' watching out for correctly coded laser[6]
before it begins its final journey to impact the desired
target. Twenty-five of the longest seconds in the world.

'Please just fucking hit.'

With rockets or freefall weapons aimed through a
sight in the HUD, there is no leap of faith. You put the
symbology on the target, at the correct speed and dive
angle, let the weapons go, and they fall ballistically onto
it. With precision weapons, I was relying on the magic
pod under the aircraft divining the correct coordinates
for the target. These are passed to the mission computer,
through witchcraft, and they somehow find their way
to the bomb. I had checked on the stores page that the
bomb was going to go to the right place.

My eyes focused on my right screen. Using my left

---

4 Not bad as callsigns go, but not a patch on Satan.
5 I am 'in' for an attack, and it is 'hot', i.e. a real weapon's coming. In
training we would call 'in dry' if we were just simulating weapon release.
6 Unless, of course, you're just going to let GPS handle the guidance;
the times and emotion are the same in any case.

thumb, I made the pod track my target and then held the smallest button on the throttle down to fire my laser. Somewhere below me the bomb 'saw' reflected laser and dived towards it. The seeker, fins, fuse and warhead all functioned correctly, and the target – a Taliban team still firing at our troops – took the full force of the weapon. Dead baddies, live goodies.

Anyone can keep a crosshair on a target on a screen, but to be in that position in the first place I needed the wherewithal to fly a combat aircraft in a warzone. All the rest just had to work; hence, I would sit watching the screen, able to check all my switches were in the right place multiple times, as the weapon plummeted earthwards.

'Please just fucking hit.' I am sure I said it out loud on a couple of occasions.

'Good hit, smoke obscuring, stand by BDA,' came from the JTAC, amazing people who you simply have to hold in the highest regard. BDA, the battle damage assessment, how many baddies were now no longer with us? The unimaginable would be to kill an innocent. The next most unimaginable would be to have gone through all that training, all those years, that last fraught five minutes, and not contributed.

Some of the boys had been here many times before, many more than me. These guys presented the complete spectrum. Some had had enough of being there, some were sick of the killing, some were ambivalent, some loved it. Some of us had been unlucky and had been ready to deploy for years, just never had the chance. Some were fresh out of the box, but out of the box and into a war, the close air support facet of which Harriers excelled at. Rather unashamedly I really enjoyed the job, loved the tension and delighted in getting pain down onto the most evil of enemies.

No one can go to war on their own. If they tried it, they would find it very painful and quite short. You go everywhere as teams. Teams look down on some teams, up to others. They dismiss some as being rear echelon, or fat, or unprofessional. War creates some severe myopia. Those who wear the Herrick[7] medal and actually fixed bayonets are very few, but to them, and in particular the JTACs, infantry, EOD[8] and Special Forces, I raise my hat. They can have my medal if they want it, because they really have deserved it. And I had enjoyed something far better in the coffee queue at Timmy Horton's, the place that grizzled, isolationist land-types say is all that's bad and phoney about war in Afghanistan. An infantryman enquired whether or not I knew who had been flying as Vapour 41 the Thursday before.

'Yes, that was me and Simon.'

'You saved our lives, boss.' The reply meant more to me than any promotion, bonus or award, although at the time I couldn't remember doing anything special to earn such praise. When the paras, those fabled hard men from Colchester, left theatre, they had a photograph taken with their weapons, in front of our jets. That's how

7 UK ops in Afghanistan are called Operation Herrick, from the Celtic word 'Heric', meaning four months plus in a dusty hole with Near Beer and the occasional mortar bomb to liven things up.
8 Explosive Ordnance Disposal. The bravest of the brave, end of story.

close we had come to one of the UK's finest fighting units. My friend Simon and I were invited to be in the photograph. We had worked a lot with 'Nowhere 53', their JTAC, who would be rewarded with a QCVS, and had bombed, rocketed and bombed again on 15 August 2008 until the baddies 'left the heroes alone'.[9] What a privilege to sit among those warriors, even if we had got the wrong end of the stick by turning up in sweaty flying coveralls, with tatty, different T-shirts and no hats. No disrespect intended, we thought we were just showing them the jets.

Simon and I actually managed to get stuck in a bit of a rut. A rut of destruction. For some reason the Gods of War smiled on us in August 2008 and let us have the lion's share of the trade, if only for a little while. We had started well. I had been on Simon's wing a week before our efforts with Nowhere 53. We got sent to a troops-in-contact (TIC) in Now Zad, the first time I had experienced the excitement of being told that we were going to a fight. The command and control guys had called us, giving us a place to go, and someone to talk to. As best we could in the Harrier, we piled on the coals and got there in best time. The JTAC was a US Marine, Noose Callsign, who was with a large USMC patrol. They had come under fire from a particular compound in the centre of Now Zad as they approached from the north-west. They talked us onto the compound, and we made quite hard work of it initially, Simon using the laser search on his pod with little effect as they marked it for

9 Died.

us.[10] I found the laser spot using the aircraft's own laser spot tracker, which had a wider field of regard than the pod.

'Mate, I've got the target – good spot and matches the description,' I told Simon on the second radio. 'The compound is sticking out into the Green Zone in that big cut-out on the western side of town.'

'Yep, agree,' said Simon before calling the JTAC.

'Noose, Vapour 41, we are tally target, a compound orientated north–south, main building is in the north-east corner. We are visual multiple personnel outside the south-west corner of the compound,' called Simon.

'Noose copies, target point is enemy at south-west corner,' came the reply.

I liked operating with Simon. He was healthily 'forward leaning' when it came to giving the troops what they wanted, and the Taliban what they deserved. Simon ended up with more operational sorties over Afghanistan than anyone else in the Harrier Force. He was my immediate subordinate, although he sometimes seemed to think that the roles were reversed . . . Still, somewhere above Now Zad . . .

They came up with quite a good plan for the attack, Simon would hit the baddies with a 1000lb GPS- and laser-guided weapon, I would follow up with a 540lb airburst weapon. I'd then set up with rockets for anyone that was still up and about. At the time, the new

---

10 The pod had a very small field of view, not great for searching for laser spots. Marking using laser usually speeds things up.

lightweight bomb hadn't arrived yet,[11] so we had com-
plementary types of armament distributed between the
aircraft. These procedures were all to be conducted from
medium level.

I ran through my air-to-surface checklist, using a
single button push to bring the jet into air-to-ground
master mode. I selected the correct bomb on my stores
page. Now I had the symbology I needed to make an
attack, I needed to make sure I was at the correct entry
height and speed for the pattern.

Simon's LGB attack would be a level run at about
15,000 feet. He'd select the jet into air-to-ground mode
and push a button to select the 1,000-pounder. He'd
be staring at the target using his pod, the picture displayed on one of his TV[12] screens. On the run-in he
would fire the laser at the target using a small button on
the throttle, depressed by his left thumb. He would tell
the pod to track the target by pushing down on a bigger
controller, again with his left thumb. Once satisfied that
he had the correct target and the displays had settled
down, he would push a castle-shaped switch on the stick
forwards with his right thumb. This put the target position into the bomb. With his left hand he would move
the weapon master switch on the left 'dashboard' up to
make everything live. Now all he had to do was check
that he had enough airspeed (the fuse required it), and

11 Paveway 4, our new bomb, had failed its acceptance trial due to the
unreliability of a new technology.
12 Technically a multi-purpose crystal display (MPCD), but you get
the drift.

when the bomb said it could make it, he'd depress the big red button on the stick with his right thumb (having got clearance to do so from the JTAC, who, as we termed it, 'bought the bomb'). Once the weapon left the jet with a satisfying metallic clunk, he'd track the target again and ensure that the laser was still firing. He'd get to a point over the target at about the same time as the bomb, which would detonate and bring hell and derision to bear on the enemy. For a couple of reasons we didn't fly directly over the target but offset slightly to one side. So that was his attack.

The first one went badly. Not at all because of anything he did. The bomb just simply refused to work. It hit the right place, it just didn't go bang. Horrid moments these, mainly because you always suspect that it's something you've fucked up. In this instance there was no case to answer, so he reset for another go. This had two implications for me. The biggy being that I was now going in first. The second was all about the target.

As I pulled in for my 30-degree dive attack, I was expecting to see a big cloud of dust — left by Simon's bomb — just to confirm that I absolutely, definitely, had the right target. Obviously there was none, and this was my first attack. Simon had managed to confirm the target with the JTAC while I listened in. I was sure I had the correct target, but that last veneer of confirmation would have been nice to have, for the first-timer.

The 30-degree attack is dynamic. With all switches ready to go, I set up running in at a slight angle to the track I actually wanted to end up on, the feeling in my stomach not dissimilar to being 'pre-deck landing nervous'. At the correct distance to go, with neck craning to stay visual with the target, I rolled the jet almost to inverted and pulled back. My anti-G trousers inflated. My combat survival waistcoat and life-saving jacket on top of it were pushing down on me, but I scarcely noticed. Every ounce of concentration was going into the attack and all the things that needed to be right.

I transcribed a massive J with the nose. Down the long bit, under the target and back up to it. This meant that I got the nose well below the target and brought the weapon sight onto the target under positive G. The jet, freed of the effects of the turn, accelerated towards my delivery speed.

Once I'd set the correct angle between where the aeroplane was actually going and the target, the task became one of monitoring all the parameters of height, dive angle and speed that needed to be right in order for the attack to work. As the speed increased, everything looked good. The aiming sight would arrive at the target pretty much exactly on the planned parameters.

'Vapour 42 in hot,' I called to the JTAC, trying to sound professional. But there is nothing matter-of-fact about your first live weapon drop.

'Clear hot, clear hot!' came the excited reply.

My jet was 30 degrees nose low and accelerating towards the patchwork of an Afghan town, mainly grey, with splashes of colour where agriculture was being attempted. Small compounds and buildings were the main constituent of the conurbation, with paths and roads, large and small, between them. Our target was an isolated building, in a prominent 'indent' where desert met town.

I watched as my bombing sight arrived at the building we'd been talked onto. The building that the USMC confirmed was the target by using a laser pointer, which the aircraft was clever enough to find. The building around which the enemy had firing positions. The enemy were still firing their weapons at Coalition troops. Anticipating the arrival of the symbology to guard against the bomb going long of the target, I pressed the pickle button with my right thumb, as hard as I could, and left it there until well after the thump of the weapon leaving shook the aircraft. My locked right arm kept the aircraft exactly steady at the *moment critique*, now 30 degrees nose low, wings level and speed going up through 450 knots. With the button still depressed, I pulled back on the stick to get the aircraft away from my own weapon. (That thing was going to go bang, and it would be somewhat miserable if I shot myself down.) I let the button go as I made the weapon master switch safe, and then found that I couldn't resist the urge to see what was about to happen. I should have pulled to 20 degrees nose high at 4 G to reduce the chance of fragging myself, but this was my first drop. This is what it's all been about, and I couldn't suppress the urge to roll inverted and crane my neck to see the target. The target is men. Real men. Real live men. Men that had twelve seconds from the time I released the weapon to the time it went off above their heads, showering them with thousands of metal splinters, enveloping them in whirling dust, debris and pain. Blast and fragmentation. The weapon detonated exactly where I had aimed it, which was exactly where the JTAC wanted it. And then came those wonderful words 'Vapour 42, direct hit. Vapour 41, you're cleared in hot,' as the JTAC declared the attack a success and at the same time allowed Simon in for the second go. Simon's second attack was a complete success, and the 1,000lb weapon finished off this particular pocket of insurgency.

It was at about this moment that I realized I needed to get the aircraft back in order, and the place to start was a fuel check. Even speeding up the maths, I had about ninety seconds to play with, and my immediate concern was that this wasn't enough for another attack if one was needed. Simon was the leader and somehow had enough fuel to get to the tanker, but I really didn't. Not by a long way.

'Mate, I can make the tanker, but I have to go now,' he said.

'Not a hope for me, I'm afraid – I'm going home,' I replied. We liked to operate in pairs, but two big boys could look after themselves without any drama. Not much more we could do, really. And so I set off for Kandahar, to give it its real name, climbing high into the thin air, where the sums worked in my favour, and it began to look like I'd make it home without having to declare any sort of fuel shortage. We had to tell the command and control teams about weapon drops on the way home, so that all the HQs and legal guys could start combing over it. I told them that I had dropped a bomb and while I was on the C2 frequency heard that the next pair, the boss and young Kelp, were haring towards the TIC to replace us.

And on the way back to KAF I was simply overjoyed.

I had finally done the job for real, finally got some pain down onto the enemy.

I then took my mask off and shouted to no one other than myself, 'I dropped a fucking bomb!' What goes on in one's own cockpit and all that . . .

28. A Dusty Valley and Every Close Air Support Pilot's Dream

We were in Afghanistan and had drunk absolutely nothing more exciting than espresso for about three weeks.[1]

We were off on a fairly boring mission. Flying the Harrier should always be a thrill, and flying over some pretty fearsome terrain with a number of murderous inhabitants should perk things up no end, but there is a natural predator of the pilot's *joie de vivre*: the reconnaissance pod.

The festering thing is strapped to the bottom of the aeroplane, completely out of place alongside menacing targeting pod and bristling weapons, all desperate to leap off the rails and into the fray. It's chubby and rounded and its photographic soul peers out through a window the size of a piece of A4.

Planning to use it is tedious, actually using it is worse. The former was like a rubbish game of join the dots,

1 Not that we ever drank anything intoxicating or even interesting in Afghanistan. We'd only been there for two weeks. Green Beans'[1a] vanilla frappuccino is fairly indulgent and was probably the high point of liquid intake for the entire tour. There was the odd exception.
[1a] A US-based coffee firm that appears to pride itself on ethically sourced products sold solely to warriors in morally dubious (or at least debatable) areas of operations.

while the mission itself was an incredibly boring piece of flying in straight lines for a long time, checking stuff. And to cap it off, the pod was heavy and had low tolerance to G. So no hard manoeuvring. The best way to describe flying reconnaissance in the Harrier is 'It was shit.' As far removed from being a fighter pilot as it felt like you could get.

But here was the rub: the photographs were excellent. The ground forces loved them, and in some cases considered them absolutely mandatory for planning. The counter-IED[2] world loved them, as we could photograph a whole stretch of road, tens of miles long, in one go and get it home and processed in no time. We even had a list of a few hundred targets that we called the 'ad-hoc list': targets that people didn't have footage of but would love to get hold of some – if we had time and megabytes left.

Today, we were to fly into the depths of the country for mission 'Godforsaken Task'. We'd take a whole pod's worth of images, before joining up with one of the tanker aircraft to grab fuel then pop off to Sangin to talk to the heroes of 16 Air Assault Brigade and our old friend Nowhere 53. Only, something else cropped up . . .

I was wingman to Simon, who was leading the formation. The recce was over 100 miles north of Kandahar, flying high in the cold sky above pink granite mountains

---

2 Improvised explosive device. For example, a roadside bomb. In fact, there's very little improvised about most of the purpose-built, Iranian-supplied devices – but the moniker has stuck. P-BI-SED doesn't have quite the same ring.

that glowed in the dawn, yet now, at about midday, were stern brown lumps which simply looked very big and had a distinct 'painful to parachute into' look about them. We always took pictures in the middle of the day, to minimize the shadows, and called ourselves Photo 43 and Photo 44. We carried a full warload of bombs and rockets, but recce was our primary task. The Photo callsign was designed to remind the command and control (C2) team that we had a priority task, and that retasking us would prevent us from doing it.[3]

The villages and towns up in the highlands are dispersed but are all in the valleys, near any available water. The recce lines therefore tended to follow the valleys. This meant that you were flying in a line either along or near the ridge on one side of the valley. These ridges are incredibly high. It is no secret that if you take a missile to the top of a hill it works very well indeed, vastly extending the range of the weapon. We felt very vulnerable, as we flew predictably in that environment. The day was a peculiar one, as up here we were in clear air, but down south the join-up had been painful.

We always took off as singletons. To take off in formation, you need the wingman to be able to call upon more thrust than the leader, so that he can adjust his position. This isn't possible if the leader is at full power, and in the thin air of Kandahar that was usually the case. We also always wanted to leave the airfield in different directions, just in case one of the bad guys had finally decided to act

3 How we longed for a retask! And never missed an opportunity to remind C2 that we were fully armed . . .

out his fantasy of downing an ISAF aircraft as it took off.[4] Joining us after take-off was usually fairly easy, but today had been different. Today was dusty, dusty enough to hide a fighter. Above the dust was cloud, up to about 16,000 feet, having started at about 12,000 feet. Dust and cloud were both perennial issues, but both together is very rare. Eventually, though, and with far more radio chat than we were happy with,[5] we joined above the cloud.[6] Putting all this to the back of our minds, we set off to the north, cruising through cold, clear air.

Flying long straight runs over as many targets as possible, we took photographs, before looping lazily around at about 20,000 feet to start a new run. Tedious as it was, we couldn't accept bad results, so any run affected by banking the aeroplane, or being slightly off course, had to be repeated. If you didn't, you could bet that they'd tell you to go and get the very same photos the next day. At this height in Afghanistan, the sky was nearly always a piercing blue, with no cloud at all above us. The cockpit conditioning worked wonders, and you could pretty much choose any temperature you wanted. As in the UK, I always flew at max cold – it kept me awake and reduced the sweat when things began to get exciting. It

---

4 This would require operating the Russian-made, Iranian-supplied missile he didn't know how to use, but felt like the king for possessing.
5 Part of the 'I am a fighter pilot, I can do everything' psyche is the notion that extraneous radio chatter is a cardinal sin for which one will burn in hell.
6 Cursing yet again the RAF, which had bought a jet with no radar then denied it a data link – toys which would have made the join either easy or unnecessary.

also cooled my water bottle quickly, small things gaining great importance in a single-seat, single-engine fighter, far from home.

At last, the task was complete, and we set off to the tanker. In this case, an American KC-10 Extender. Tankers are absolutely critical. Tensions always rose in periods of high intensity, when the call went out that there was no more gas in the AO.[7] Great work between the C2 boys and the tanker crews regularly saved the day for CAS pilots, in desperate need of the nearest available petrol. With high heart rate and nervous stomach, looking at a dwindling fuel gauge, you would disengage from your CAS task at the last possible second.

'Iron Rod, this is Photo 43, out of TIC Alpha Delta and very short of gas.'

'Photo 43, Iron Rod, I have gas for you in Towline Fagger, roll out 050, your height 190, tanker is Fluter 32 at level 200. Fluter is 40 miles on your nose. He's leaving the towline to pick you up, call visual.'

Awesome and humbling.[8]

As we closed on the tanker, we got the glory shot we'd been hoping for all day: troops in contact. Over a secure frequency we took down the 'TIC words' from C2, all the information we needed to get to the fight. Who? Where? What frequency? We were off to help some American Special Forces,[9] and from the grid it appeared

---

7 Area of operations.

8 Someone must remind me to buy both the C2 guys and the Tex heroes the many beers I owe them one day.

9 The Americans, bless them, call their SF 'SOF' or Special Operations Forces. Same difference.

they were down around Sangin. Excellent. One quick plug into the tanker and then we can get into the war!

It turned out that this was exactly what Simon had in mind. With his characteristic and absolutely spot-on attitude to delivering 'the rain', as we called our HE goodies, he had decided that it would be more expeditious if I refuelled from the KC-10's single hose while he went straight to the fight, 'pushed the fuel a bit'[10] and came back for petrol later. By the time I arrived he would be on minimum, but the guys would have had the cover they needed.

'Your hose, mate, see you at the TIC,' he said as he swept away to the south-west. I double-clicked the transmit button, an unofficial 'Roger that'.

With a satisfying clunk my refuelling probe connected with the trailing hose. Filling was probably only going to take about five minutes, but it was an age when all you want to do is get to Sangin and get involved.

I watched the fuel gauge record the rush of fuel into the tanks, listening to Simon on the second radio.

But something was wrong. He was coming back.

He couldn't raise the JTAC and had run out of fuel while trying. He was inbound to the tanker, and I was full. It was time for me to set off and see if I could sort out where or what the problem was. The tanker was now heading south-west, directly towards Sangin. I disengaged and climbed to establish a mandatory 1,000 feet

---

10 No one in the world would ever go below minimum fuel, but knowing what actual, no-shit minimum is, and staying on task until the last possible micro-second, is what sets apart the average from the warriors.

separation above the tanker, then opened the throttle. I saw Simon joining from the south as I said thank you and goodbye to the Tex before pushing tactical to the south-west.

I went back to Iron Rod to confirm the frequencies and position of the TIC, and it quickly became clear what the problem was: a duff coordinate. Simon had been given an incorrect location for the fight, so far away that radio comms, once he'd got there, were impossible. I had taken the grid myself, and it wasn't anywhere near Sangin, but north of Qalat, a town well to the east of Kandahar, a 'mere' 120 miles from Sangin.

'Confirm that grid is in Killbox[11] 87CL?' I demanded from Iron Rod.

'Affirm. Clear to contact Eastern C2.' And that meant the Aussies. Essentially the Brits controlled anything west of Kandahar, the Aussies had everything to the east.

I pulled the nose around to the left to head east, passing close over the Tex and Simon. Simon was left in total confusion. Why the fuck was his number 2 turning away from the fight and buggering off in the wrong direction? As a big 'thinks bubble' filled his cockpit, I transmitted on the second radio – the one we never changed from our own private 'chat' frequency.

'Mate – the TIC's in 87CL, I'll give you the grid once you're done, from here it's about 090 degrees at 60 miles.'

---

11 We divide the world into boxes of air, about 30 miles by 30. They are called killboxes and are numbered south to north and lettered west to east. Basically squares on a map, handy for quickly getting to the vague area of a target, or booking airspace around one.

And with that I set off, chopping to the Aussies and telling them that I was en route. As I headed for the killbox, I could see a line of bad weather ahead of me. 87CL was going to be masked by cloud and hidden in dust. My weapons all had to be aimed by eye in dive profiles, I had a crap targeting pod. And for some reason, comms with Eastern C2 were perennially poor.

This was going to get interesting.

87CL was the other side of the line where the implausible dust/cloud combo was making life hard. This meant that I would have to get down through the cloud and fly around in the dust. There was a massive problem with this. Massive hills. In any form of aviation you only fly around in cloud down to a sensible minimum. For small hills this is 1,000 feet more than the ground, which gives you a buffer. For really big hills this is increased to a 5,000 feet margin, which allows for all the pressure differences mountains can bring. Each killbox has a handy height in the centre of it, the minimum you can fly in cloud safely. I knew that the cloud went down to about 12,000 feet. The minimum for 87CL was 13,900 feet. Oh crap. I would be doing something that every pilot has beaten out of them from day one. I would be doing it on purpose and if I smeared into a hillside trying to break cloud, my mum would be told simply that 'Your son died because he was stupid'! I would be below the safe height, relying on my map and GPS. I would have to trust that my kit was working and aim for one of the valleys between the hills, flying through the cloud to pop out in a dusty valley where the tops of the hills on either side would still be in these same clouds. Achievable, but illegal and fraught with potentially fatal pitfalls. Obeying all the rules here would mean not getting the job done.

Just to add spice, the French were on the frequency in hurried, anxious tones explaining that they were Winchester (out of all munitions) and needed RIPing[12] as soon as possible. The situation on the ground was dire, and air support was required ASAP. So, as long as I could ensure separation from Anger, the French boys, while getting a handover from them, get under the weather, into the dust, talk to the JTAC and get into the fight soonest, then successfully employ weapons, all should be OK. Hardly a 'war's as good as won' moment.

One thing at a time, then. Except that every one of them needed to be done at lightning speed in quick succession. But was I fazed or disappointed? Hell no. This was it! What we'd always wanted, a high-demand scenario, and that was just to *get* to the fight. And all the while, the boys on the ground were taking a kicking. Our *raison d'être*, to dig the heroes out of the shit. I had no doubt that they were giving as good as they got, but they needed more air-delivered weapons. They needed Photo 43 and 44 right now, and sooner if at all possible. This is the stuff any fighter pilot dreams about. And dear old Simon was still attached to a tanker somewhere.

Time to prioritize. First, let's get rid of the French. I asked Eastern C2 if I could use their frequency. Getting only static and a broken transmission in reply, I cracked on.

12 Relief in place – taking over someone else's job when they could no longer do it.

'Anger 21 from Photo 44, I'll enter 87CL from the north-west at 10,000 feet or below, you're clear to elevate to 11,000 feet and above and exit to the west, I am now level at 10,000,' I called as the desert below disappeared, and my jet was engulfed in a grey cocoon of cloud. That should get them away from where I needed to get to. In thickly accented but perfectly clear English they confirmed the plan.[13]

'Go with the handover,' I called back.

'Ze friend-uh-lees are een a steep valley. Zay are surrounded and are takeeng a big amount off fire.' It sounded like I needed to get a move on.

'Ze friend-uh-lees are split up, all our bombs were danger close!'

So, multiple friendly positions and the baddies close by. It sounded like this was now going to go one of two ways. Either the boys on the ground, with help from me, and Simon when he got here, were going to be able to sort this out quickly, or this was going to turn into something newsworthy for all the wrong reasons, a Coalition patrol surrounded, separated and chopped up by the Taliban.

Anger 21 gave me an updated coordinate for the fight, which I punched into the mission computer as I continued my descent through the cloud, catching occasional glimpses of the ground below. Flying in cloud can be incredibly disorientating. You have to trust your instruments, as the human ear can play all sorts of tricks

13 In direct opposition to the international press-fuelled stereotype, I have nothing but good things to say about the French.

on you, convincing you that 'up' is 'down', etc. You guard against this by continually concentrating on your instruments and breaking up all other tasks into small chunks. You do one chunk, then back to the instruments, another chunk, back to the instruments. This is fine if you are doing something boring or routine. When what you are doing needs to be done quickly and is, quite literally, a matter of life and death, well, you get through chunks pretty fucking quickly.

Dust is weird. For all its impenetrable qualities when trying to look through it sideways or on a diagonal, straight down can be easy. I tried to tell Eastern C2 that I needed to push to the tactical frequency but with such bad comms I couldn't get through. I decided to go anyway. So here I was, flying around, able to see down but not across, now under the clouds, very close to the hard stuff, which I couldn't really see, unable to talk to air traffic. This is (and rightly . . .) uncharted territory for most pilots. And for those of you in the aviation fraternity who are currently sucking your teeth thinking, 'What in God's name is this bell doing in instrument conditions, well below safety altitude, without a service from anyone, performing a self let-down into a valley based solely on GPS?' I have an answer: I was doing my fucking job by attempting to relieve the withering fire being poured onto guys fighting for their lives whose boots I am not even worthy to lace.

'Cougar 12, Cougar 12, this is Photo 44,' I called.

The reply was startling.

I had expected a calm conversation between two professionals on a quiet radio frequency. Cougar was professional but he wasn't calm, he was gasping for breath. The radio frequency wasn't quiet. Automatic fire filled my headset, outgoing guns roared, while inbound weapon impacts from something heavy could clearly be heard. In the background were shouted infantry orders, and interwoven among all this I could hear the shouting of wounded men. Cougar struggled to get his update out, but we did get a coordinate sorted, and I was very close, in the right valley.

'We are taking large amounts of direct and indirect fire!' he shouted, gulping down air between words. 'My command element is isolated forward of my position, a section of my patrol is also isolated and out of communications. We have Whiskey India Alpha. Are you visual friendlies?'

I looked down through the murk. I could see the valley, clearly in places and masked by the dust in others. The friendly grid was right below me, so I uncaged the pod, and sure enough the old TIALD could identify cock all. Not its fault, it was designed for something else, I told myself, but unhelpful all the same.

Rolling the aircraft almost onto its back I looked over down through the canopy to see that I was in a steep valley. I had a few seconds to take in the scene. The valley led north. At the bottom was a river. The valley went north for about a kilometre from the position I had been given. At this point it went due east for about 500 metres and then went north again. This gave three easily identifiable sections. The two bits that were exactly north–south, and the bit that separated them, going east–west. Cougar 12 was in the first of them. Here, a small village stretched along the eastern side of the river;

with it was a small green zone, probably only 30 metres wide. At the edge of the green zone was a dirt track, as all roads other than the main ones were in Afghanistan. There were Coalition vehicles on this small road running north up the valley.

'I am visual the friendly location,' I told Cougar. 'Confirm which Humvee you are actually in.'

'Third one back, third one back!' he shouted. Excellent. I could see where he was. Now we were in the game, but, rolling the wings back level, I knew we had our work cut out here. In most scenarios you were able to sit in a nice relaxing orbit well above a fight. With the autopliot flying the aeroplane in circles that barely got above 1 G you were free to scribble down notes and targets, work the pod and look out of the window. Here it would be different. The weather was keeping me clamped inside the valley. The valley sides were steep, and with the ground so close it was absolutely no place to be using the autopilot. This would have to be a tight, manually flown orbit at about 2 G, all the while talking to Cougar and playing my part in the team effort that would save the day.

Things were going to get a little fraught and somewhat sweaty.

'I need an immediate gun run on the west of the valley!' he shouted. 'Enemy on the west of the valley!' This was a start, but the west of the valley was a big place, and I had no gun. Should I ask for a coordinate? Should I ask his view on using rockets instead of a gun? Should I just crack on? The firefight I could hear on the comms wasn't getting any quieter.

At this point Simon turned up. Which is when just

as I'd been thinking things couldn't get much harder, they did.

Simon checked in, and I cleared him to enter the area at a height above mine, warning him that the weather was pretty awful, but descent was possible. He called for an AO update. Absolutely right, he needed all the SA that I had gathered. After all, I thought that I had a fair handle on the ground situation. How best to put this? I paused for a beat to put together a brief for him. Then, as I touched the transmit, someone else started shouting.

'Photo 43, Photo 43, this is Endless 41, we are cut off from our rear element in a steep-sided valley!' came the frantic call. 'We are taking heavy incoming and are cut off from our command element! We need immediate close air support, call ready for nine-line!'

Now who, in the name of all that does not suck, was this guy? He sounded in exactly the same state as Cougar 12, but the voice was different. That being said, he appeared to be describing the same battle.

'Mate, are you getting this?' asked Simon, the note in his voice telling me that this was the first that he had heard about the severity of the situation.

'Affirm, stand by!' I replied, probably quite abruptly. 'Endless 41, Endless 41, this is Photo 44, I have the Tac Lead, I have been passed this update by Cougar 12. Are you co-located with Cougar 12?' I asked, my voice rising as the tension took its toll, my tone becoming ever more aggressive. This needed sorting quickly. If there were two separate fights, then we could go to one each. If there were two fights in the same location, we would have to be careful. If there were two JTACs in the same patrol, well, they needed to get a grip.

'Negative, negative, sir, we are detached from Cougar, Cougar is in the rear element, I am in the forward element, we are separated and have no comms!'

All right, now that probably wasn't too bad a thing, it just meant that things were a little complicated. Up until now, I didn't think it possible to have too many JTACs.

'Have you got the SA, mate?' I asked of Simon. He replied that he had.

'In that case you have the lead back. I can't give you a hard height due to the weather, I'll just avoid you, all right?' Usually we would both have 'hard heights' separated by 1,000 feet. This was impossible today. The answer was simple and flexible, but again added immeasurably to the workload. Simon was going to fly in tight circles below the cloud. I was going to do the same, but I had responsibility for ensuring that we didn't clap hands, while he became the focal point for comms with the JTACs.

'Cougar, we'll take your target first, ready to copy nine-line,' called Simon.

'I need a gun run, a gun run down the west of the valley!' shouted Cougar. Fuck me if the firing hadn't got a little worse. We were in a very delicate situation. We needed at least a position to attack, by the rules we needed a whole nine-line, the nine bits of mandatory information that a JTAC had to give you prior to an attack.[14] We were happy to bend that one slightly (well, gaff it completely, if need be – so long as the constituents were there), but 'just attack the west side of a valley' – nope, that wouldn't stand up in any court of law. Simon therefore had to extract the information from a soldier under fire, working his nuts off, without sounding like he wasn't being helpful, or patronizing.

'We need the enemy position,' said Simon, his measured tones betraying the urgency of the situation. Inside the two Harriers we maintained our tight circle inside the dusty valley, uncomfortably 'belly up' to the hills at all times.[15] We craned our necks to keep the friendlies in our view. We needed just a shred of information and then we could pounce, but that shred of information was hard to come by.

'They're in a hoody-tun,' came the reply. Now what, in the world of sport, was that?

'Sorry, a hoody tent?' said Simon.

'Yes! Yes! A hoody-tun,' came the reply, now in a half shout, half scream. And still the automatic fire around Cougar could be heard every time he transmitted. Simon tried to calm the guy down, even asking him to get into cover and get us a grid of the target. It was impossible. The guy was pinned down, absolutely unable to move.

'Mate, the only thing I can see of any relevance on the west of the valley is a track that leads up the hill about

14 A point to come from, a range and bearing from it, target height, description, location, anything marking it, where the friendlies were, actions on egress.

15 So without direct line of sight of the ground that we were most at risk of flying into.

50 metres,' I said. 'If they're taking fire from the west side, that just has to be it. Looks like a rocket job.' Rockets were going to be perfect. The position was about 50 metres from the river, which was about 30 metres from the road. Maximum diagonal range to the friendlies was below 100 metres. Rockets were our lowest-yield weapon, they were also mine. Simon had only the 1,000lb bombs.

Simon was quick off the mark. 'Cougar, this is Photo 43. We can only see one potential firing position on the west side of the valley, we're going to attack it with rockets.'

'Clear to strike, clear to strike!' came the reply. Usually to get a clearance you had to take and read back a nine-line, confirm the target out the window and then call 'In hot' for clearance. Fuck me, they were desperate down there.

'Let's get the commander's initials,' I said to Simon with a small amount of unease setting in. You absolutely had to get his say-so for an attack this close. Simon immediately requested them from the JTAC.

'Unable, unable, command element is isolated. You are clear to strike!'

Oh, holy shit. To attack within Danger Close is a high-anxiety moment. Statistically speaking, the outer ring of Danger Close is the mathematical line where 1 in 1,000 troops will get hurt by your attack; 80–100 metres was somewhere around the 1 in 100 mark for rockets. Here we were, then, about to attack with rockets, at a range where hurting friendlies was mathematically highly probable, given that I had thirty-eight of them. And we couldn't even get permission to do it. Mull it over in your mind: strike? Risk killing and wounding friendlies? Don't strike? They'll be overrun. You can hear the firing, you can hear the shouting. What do you do? Will you sleep at night again if you kill a friendly? Will you ever sleep again if you sat overhead as a Coalition patrol was overrun? Think about it from the comfort of wherever you are, take as long as you like. You will come to your own decision. I quickly came to mine as I orbited in that valley, arms weighing two or three times their design weight, neck aching, lungs pulling air-mix through the mask as quickly as it would come. I decided when I heard their voices and the fire they were under. These boys were going to get every shred of help that I could give them. No lawyer or armchair quarterback was ever going to dissuade me, and never will. There was only one person to whom I would even have thought about listening and he was Simon, in another Harrier, doing, hearing and feeling the same thing. In two cockpits in a dust-filled valley north of Qalat, we both came to exactly the same conclusion.

We were going to fight.

We were knowingly breaking the rules. We had come up with the target ourselves, we didn't know where all the friendlies were, and we had no commander's permission. We were about to flagrantly smash through the golden rules of CAS. Full stop. Without these bits of information, you simply had to sit on your hands and wait for them. But there is a small issue with this. Whoever wrote those rules probably didn't do it while listening to men fighting for their lives.

'Right, let's go!' called Simon. 'You push out to the north for the attack, I'll get you a coordinate on the firing position.' We knew that the friendlies were in three places, and we assumed that they were all east of the river. Throttle wide, I set off for the cloud base to the north-east, over the zigzag of where the river went east then north. I needed to be about 15,000 feet above the target at about 4 miles for a 30-degree dive. I wasn't going to be clear of cloud at that height. I was not going to get the height, so I needed to be closer. Simple geometry. I was going to have to get things in order quickly.

'OK, mate, I'm in air-to-ground, I've got rockets selected, Q1M1,[16] I've set the sight to 77,[17] forward throw[18] to plus 40, I haven't set the RADALT, my tape is running, and my flares are ready, Late Arm ON.' I went through all the checks as quickly as I could.

'Sweet,' called Simon and read out the target grid. This was easy to enter as it was very close to the friendly grid. As I punched in the figures to the computer, the cloud started to descend around the canopy. I looked at my tactical display – I was about 3 miles from the target, pointing north. From me the target bore about 200 degrees, somewhere over my left shoulder.

It was time to bring the rain – the moment when all

---

16 This meant I'd get eleven rockets in a salvo – our normal opening gambit. Quantity (how many) 1, Multiple (Off how many wings) 1. We had four 'goes' with the rockets in the GR7. This was one go, Q4 M2 would have been all four, from both wings all at once.
17 Depression in mils.
18 A mathematical fudge to refine the sight setting for the exact type of rocket and dive angle. (Long story.)

the years of training and hard work are put to the test, and you find out whether or not God put enough 'Right Stuff' inside you.

Full power and 90 degrees of bank to the left, jet trying to slow down under the aerodynamic forces and weight of warload and 4 g[19] as Mk107 Pegasus pushed it through the air. The attack was going to be almost exactly north–south by the time I had gone around the corner. I had to keep the nose up, had to get the dive angle steep, even if that meant a really late acquisition. Pause, two, three and down. Sight onto the target area, murky in all this fucking dust.

'Photo 44 in hot!' I shouted. Not quite a 30-degree dive, but from inside 3 miles you can't expect wonders.

'Clear to strike, clear to strike!' came the immediate reply. Not quite 'Clear hot', but heavily laced with the tempo of the combat.

I could see the zigzag in the river clearly, so knew I was on target, even if I couldn't make out the exact point yet. My nav kit placed a waypoint, a green diamond in the HUD, exactly where I knew the target was; Simon's grid was sweet. Down through the desert-coloured dust, unable to see where it ended and the dust-coloured desert began. Speed building nicely through 400 knots, now to track the target. Sight saying range was now inside 4,000 feet, inside our usual range, but this was not a usual day. Come on, target, show yourself! And there it was, through the murk. I held the button down as eleven CRV-7 rockets left the pod at Mach 4 with their

19 Fucking reconnaissance pod.

characteristic *phoo-phoo-phoo*, as one shot earthwards every sixty milliseconds. Almost immediately their usual bright-orange burning signature, turning to a dark-grey and black.

Fuck me, they were hitting the desert!

I was far too close, I had pushed the attack well inside minimums. Hauling back on the stick, I craned my neck around to make sure I wasn't pulling up straight into Simon. Four G out of the fragmentation zone for the weapon, I made the Late Arm safe, all weapons were now firmly on the rails again. I had a feeling that the rest of the weaponry circuits might as well be left exactly where they were – we were going to need more weaponry before this one was put to bed! I overbanked to stay level and got myself back into the circle above the friendlies.

Anxiety, sheer anxiety. What had we just done, what had we attacked? The rockets were absolutely on the money. The deafening silence probably only lasted a quarter of a millisecond.

'Good hits, good hits. Photo, this is Cougar. We're still under heavy fire, stand by!' He wasn't lying either. How much ammunition had these bastard insurgents brought with them? But even as the huge relief of a successful strike, carried out against all the odds, washed over us, we were anxious for more trade. We were building some momentum. And at this precise moment we got a call from Endless 41. 'Photo, Photo, northern element now taking heavy-calibre fire from firing positions immediately south-west of a compound to the north-west, request you get your eyes on!' Endless was talking very quickly, very quickly indeed. But he seemed to have a better handle on the fight than Cougar.

'Ready for talk on,' called Simon.

'The compound is to the north-east of the bit of river that flows north-west, marking with 50 cal!' called Endless.

This was odd for two reasons: first, because there was no section of river that flowed that way; second, because although the dust seemed to be clearing slightly, we couldn't see any weapon impacts from our level. We explained this to Endless: we could see two compounds to the north of the river, where it went east–west. Could it be one of those two?

'I can see the two compounds to the north of the river, where it bends,' I told Simon.

'Yeah, me too,' came the reply. 'But the river isn't going north-west.' He was just as confused as I was. Two calls to Endless 41 later, and we were none the wiser. This is where Simon really began to take the fight by the throat.

'OK, Endless, we're going to descend to very low level, I want you to tell us when I am over the target!' he called, offering himself up as a human target marker.

From the southerly point in the orbit he rolled out, heading north up the left-hand side of the valley. I followed on the right, about a mile away and slightly behind. We flew up the valley, hugging the rising ground to the east and west. We were very low. The valley sides towered over me to my right as I aimed to fly over the eastern point of the zigzag. So close to the mountain, my radio altimeter alarm went off repeatedly. As I was just about to get to the eastern edge of the zigzag, Simon flew over the western end and over the westerly compound.

'Photo, Photo, Endless 41, you are overhead now!' called the JTAC. To my left I could see the friendly position: three Humvees on the southern bank of the river. And I was also absolutely certain that I knew which compound they were talking about, even if I couldn't see their marking fire.

'Photo 43, tally target,' called Simon, as sure as I was.

'44, tally target,' I replied.

'Request immediate rocket attack,' called Endless. 'Clear to strike, clear to strike.'

Simon was very quick off the mark. He had already used his kit to get a coordinate.

'OK, Endless, we're going to give you a rocket attack on open ground to the south-west of a compound,' he called and confirmed the grid. Even as he was doing so, I pushed the throttle fully open and pulled back on the stick. Once again, I set off for the cloud base. I was passing the target compound, going north, only a mile away or so to the west of me. The quickest way to get ordnance down was going to be a tear drop around to the right, 270 degrees of turn.

'Late Arm live, all other switches the same,' I told Simon.

The weather seemed to be marginally better, with the cloud breaking a little, which allowed me to get more height coming from this direction. I pulled the aircraft around to the right. I could see the target in my right 2 o'clock. My parameters were good, and the weapon system all set up. Advancing the throttle to full power with my left hand, I brought the nose around to the right, this time letting it drop immediately onto the target area. The attack was going to be much the same as the first, but managing to eke out a little more height meant I could begin attack run from further out. The visibility was going to be about the same, but getting the aircraft into a steady dive would be easier.

'Photo 44, in hot.'

'Clear to strike, clear to strike,' came the same non-standard reply. With the sight coming up towards the target and range counting down, I plummeted earthwards as the aircraft accelerated through 400 knots. Maybe in later years it will dawn on me that doing this in an aeroplane in poor visibility probably deserved more conscious thought. Almost at the firing range, almost exactly on speed, and with a split second to go, my peripheral vision picked up something in my low right field of view, from north of the compound. Something bright yellow and twinkling.

Firing! My right thumb held down the pickle button to unleash the rockets. *Phoo-phoo-phoo.* The eleven rockets left the tubes, again smashing straight into the desert. Again, I immediately applied 4 G to get out of the frag. But my head and eyes were drawn to my right, to the yellow twinkling, which I could now see, quite clearly, was an enemy weapon, and quite a big one, engaging me.

To be shot at is a little bit strange. We always train for it, as anyone in the military trains for the enemy to actually fire back. It would be ridiculous to think that people were going to roll over and die without a fight, but the first time it happens is still a bit of a shock. There is really

no way of adequately explaining the epiphany of realizing that, just as you are trying to bring your weapons
to bear on the enemy, he is doing the same to you, that
there is a human being doing everything in his power to
kill you. I have no complaints about it, of course not,
but thinking that someone with gritted teeth and shaking hand was letting fly with large-calibre ammunition,
and his target was me, was a peculiar feeling.

As I pulled the aircraft nose out of the 30-degree dive,
I could see he wasn't alone. The line of the attack was
taking me parallel to a row of compounds about 300
metres to my north: the heavy weapon with the distinctive yellow muzzle flash at one end, then, at two or three
other points along the southern face of the compounds,
now in my 3 o'clock and very close, I could see more
muzzle flashes. These ones were noticeably smaller and
paler in colour. And a lot faster than the ponderous rate
of fire from what I assumed was a Dushka.[20] I guessed
that they were small arms, AK-47 or similar. Either way,
there were three or four Taliban who had definitely had
enough of us.

We'd been briefed that if you could see the muzzle
flash, the chances were that the enemy was tracking the
aeroplane. That meant, though, that he wasn't allowing for forward travel of the jet during the bullets' time
of flight and probably hadn't allowed for gravity drop
either. This should mean he would miss behind and low.
So, what to do? The truth was, very little. By pulling up
at 4 G I had already further complicated their aim. I was

20 A Soviet-era anti-aircraft cannon.

probably pretty safe; however, a little muscle memory, or maybe even a piece of grey matter that just wanted to survive the day, moved my left hand to the 'pinky switch' and deployed flares. I knew even as I did it that it was a nonsensical defence against weapons that were almost certainly being aimed by hand. And while it wasn't the worst idea in the entire world to pre-empt the possibility of something nastier, I'd actively selected only the most inappropriate kind of flare. Doing nothing seemed inadequate, and so I instinctively did something. Something scarcely more useful than nothing. The shame still burns. But I was already forming a plan to do something far more meaningful.

Fighting back was something I was still eminently tooled up to do. I had sixteen rockets left. I had an impact fused 540lb bomb and an airburst one as well. And I was actually under attack myself and was therefore in the realms of sheer and unadulterated self-defence. Someone was trying to kill me, and it was only fair that I attempt to return the favour. As I hauled the jet around to the right, I prepared to attack the gun crew with the heavy weapon first. An impact 540 is what would sort those fuckers out, I thought. And that was when Cougar 12 spoilt all my plans by jumping onto the comms net with some top-drawer JTACing.

I'd fired rockets in support of Endless, but it was Cougar 12, the original JTAC, who was now talking to me.

'Photo, Photo, good hits, good hits. Main enemy firing points 100 metres west of last rockets. Come west 100 metres!' This was more like it. My personal vendetta would have to wait for a second. We now knew after two successful attacks that we were able to put some fire down onto the main body of the enemy.

Perhaps this marked the turning point in the battle. My blood was up. We'd done the dangerous bit, taken some gambles, and they had paid off. We'd put some pain down onto the enemy positions, but now we could really go to town on an enemy that was firing back. Now in possession of the targeting information we'd needed all along, I wasn't too bothered about a perfect attack. This was about getting it in quickly, 100 metres west of the last one. I only had to move two switches. I would use everything I had left in the rocket pods, all at once. I craned my neck to look down into the zigzag of the valley, trying to judge the earliest possible moment to cobble together a successful, if neither pretty nor text-book, attack.

Simon chipped in: 'Hey Tremors, fuck the parameters, get another attack in!'

As the jet's nose sliced around to the right, all my switches were made, and I allowed myself a smile. Great minds and all that.

'On my way, Photo 44 is in hot heading 270!' I called.

'Clear hot, clear hot.'

Now, in retrospect, this wasn't too bright. I was coming down exactly the same track as before, but the troops were still under fire, and we were here to support them, and they were going to get this attack no matter what. After bleeding off speed in the climb, I was still slow as I dived back down into the dust. Third time around, and the novelty wasn't wearing off. But it really shouldn't have surprised me that if I did exactly the same again, then so would the enemy. As I approached my firing parameters, something yellow whisked past the window from low 2 o'clock to high 10. Tracer round, from the same place. My dear friend the Dushka gunner was back in the fray, firing from exactly the same place. My fault really, because so was I. I pressed on. Steady on the target and pickle. Sixteen weapons raced off the wings speared towards the desert. I racked on the G and pumped out flares.[21]

The effect was immediate.

'Good hits! Good hits! Right on the money!' exclaimed Cougar, his voice noticeably calmer from the relief of no longer being shot at. Three attacks in God-awful weather had bloodied the enemy's nose, but, judging by the tracer at least, they'd come close to getting rounds on us. The battle was far from over. We still had trade, because the enemy in the northern positions, the guys firing at me and Simon, began to reposition. The ones in the south were no longer an issue. The rocket strikes had seen to that.

'Photo, Photo, this is Endless 41.' The boy's voice now calm, if still out of breath. The weight of fire in the background now down to what sounded like outgoing deliberate and controlled rifle fire.

'Go for Photo,' Simon replied immediately. I saw his aeroplane ease out of low level, and we both climbed to the relative safety of the cloud base, which was now breaking nicely, the dust below giving way to the sun

---

21 The right ones, this time . . .

as it streamed through the emerging gaps. Simon had stayed low throughout the fight. I wondered how much fire he'd taken and immediately berated myself. In all the attacks I hadn't got a single call out to him that I was taking fire. *Idiot.*

'Photo, repositioning enemy command unit leaving the fight to the north, squirter on a motorcycle is PID[22] enemy and has a PKM on his back!'

'Confirm clear to hit the squirter?' Simon replied immediately. Since his arrival he'd run the battle brilliantly. The teamwork required between him, the JTACs and me had been the reason this fight was now going our way.

My last target was hustling up a road about 200 metres west of the position that I'd seen the tracer streaming in from. On a motorcycle, the enemy commander, still armed and probably looking for somewhere new from where he could continue to direct the battle.

'Confirm the squirter has just turned north on the north–south track, directly north of the last target by 200 metres?' I shouted, probably sounding a little bit too loud and excitable. I knew I had been engaged by something belt-fed, and this fitted the bill: the PKM was the Soviet version of the general purpose machine gun, and while I still think that the real culprit was something larger, this guy needed some attention.

'Affirm, affirm, clear hot, clear hot,' called Endless.

'He's on the –' came from Simon.

'On the what, mate?' I called. Nothing came in reply.

22 Positive identification.

'Photo 43, from 44 radio check.' Still nothing. Fuck, radio failure! Not now!

'Endless 41 from Photo 44 radio check.' I was heading west across the valley just south of the zigzag, climbing for the cloud base. A 90-degree turn should put me into an attack straight up the road, where, right on the edge of visual perception down through the dust, I could still see the squirter, gun on his back.

'Photo 44, loud and clear!' called Endless. Excellent, that meant Simon's radio had failed, not mine. Being comm-out in this weather wasn't going to be nice, and I had to find Simon and get him back in some semblance of order. But first there was a job to do.

Full power, roll right, bringing the nose down, all switches live and ready for a 540lb airburst attack. Speed of a motorcycle? About 20 knots on that shitty track, 10 metres per second. Time of flight about twelve seconds, aim about 120 metres ahead and let the air burst fuse do the rest. But as I settled into the dive, I saw the motorcycle stop. It had stopped right at a distinctive kink in the track, so I knew my eyes weren't tricking me. Thank the Lord, this was now a static target. I had a second or two to sort out the attack and I reduced the angle of the dive to compensate for the rising ground. Too little time in the air, and it wouldn't arm. Up came the cross of the bomb sight on the HUD. As it came onto the target, I pickled. With a clunk from beneath the wing, a quarter tonne of pain flew earthwards.

Seconds later, the patch of desert around the motorbike erupted. Splinters of metal and a shock wave smashed into the desert floor with the target just to the north of the epicentre. The weapon had gone off exactly as advertised, and, dare I say it, with the 30-degree attack it looked like a direct hit. No one could possibly have survived. The command element and his PKM, still warm from firing at Simon and me, were no more. And all was now quiet in the area: we'd won, and they'd lost. They'd tried to kill us and failed, we'd tried to kill them and done quite an efficient job of it.

'Great shot!' came from Simon. Total confusion now, I thought he had a radio failure!

'Endless, Cougar, we've taken out the squirter,' I said, my head craning around to try to find Simon. 'Just give me a second to get together with Photo 43, I think he has a radio failure,' I told them.

'No problem, Photo, we are no longer under fire. When you are ready, request you keep eyes on the valley to the north. We will regroup and move north,' called Cougar. Adding, 'Thanks for those attacks, Photo, good job.'

'Photo, this is Endless, great job,' added our other new best friend. Mutual back-slapping can be a little cheesy, but it definitely has its time and place. And this was both. All the same, I threw in a very British 'Our pleasure, guys, glad to help.'

As the radio went quiet for a second, I circled just at the cloud base and searched for Simon. It didn't take long. I saw his Harrier off to the west by a couple of miles in a right-hand turn. Soon he'd be coming towards me and he simply had to be able to see me. I put out flares and began waggling my wings. One would get his attention; the other was the universal signal for a comms failure. Bursts of static confirmed that he was trying to contact me.

'Tremors, from Simon, have you got a radio failure?' Ah, the penny drops. Simon had an intermittent fault in his transmitter, so I could only hear him occasionally, but his receiver was completely broken so he couldn't hear anyone.

I levelled the wings and soon Simon was alongside me.

'Tremors from Simon, I think you have a radio failure.' I shook my head vigorously. It is more than possible to exchange signals between aeroplanes, but you have to make them nice and big. I pointed at his jet, then at my ear piece and gave a thumbs down.

'You can't hear?' he enquired in a quizzical voice. The penny certainly hadn't dropped in his cockpit – how could I tell what he's saying without hearing? I vigorously shook my head again and repeated the signals. Pointed at him. You. Tapped my earpiece. Hearing. Thumb down. Malfunction.

'Er, you can hear me?' he said, even more perplexed. I stared at him for two solid seconds and repeated the drills, this time with a real vehemence. Pointing repeatedly at his aeroplane. Slapping the side of my helmet with my gloved hand and then looking back at him to give many exaggerated thumbs down. Silence. And then . . .

'I can't hear? I can't hear! It's me, I can't hear!' I had to laugh – a real belly laugh. I took my mask off and nodded. Beaming at him through the perspex. He did the same with a broad grin. I was still chuckling as I reattached my mask. The tension was gone, the killing was done, flying around in the dust was finished for now, and we were back together.

But the boys were still in that valley and still needed our support as they cleared the compounds to the north, and so I contacted Cougar once more, and we talked about what I could see up the valley, and despite us finding one lone man that simply had to have been involved in the fire fight, given he was on the north shore of the zigzag and had either been in or under almost all the fire, he went unassailed. I told Cougar that I was just chopping to Eastern C2 to try to get a RIP. They'd be far better off with two fighters with working radios and preferably two decent targeting pods; we only had the one, and Simon was using it. I was passing him points of interest as grids, holding my fingers up to the window, and he would acknowledge over the radio. We had given the guys about twenty minutes of overwatch when we got the call from Switch 33.

'Photo 43, this is Switch 33, we are RIPing you at TIC IC,' came the American voice. Switch was a Hornet callsign. These guys were from a flat top somewhere off the Pakistan coast and had come up 'the boulevard' to support Operation Enduring Freedom, as they called it.

'Switch, from Photo 44, good afternoon, we are out of TIC IC. Friendly position is now at TB 870 150 on the southern side of the river. We have attacked multiple enemy forces and believe the AO is now cold. If you're happy, we will egress west before climbing. You have the AO.'

'Switch has the update, many thanks. Switch has the AO.' And so our work was done.

Simon closed on me on the starboard side. We had to punch through a bit of cloud as I talked to Eastern C2 to book our transit altitude home. I asked them to let KAF know one of us would be comm-out.

Coming into Kandahar, I contacted the tower frequency for clearance for both aircraft to descend, Photo 43 down first, comm-out. I looked at Simon. I pointed at him and then pointed down and made a landing motion with my hand.

'Confirm I'm going down and I am clear to land?' he asked. I had just started nodding when his jet rolled inverted and pulled towards the desert. Ten seconds later I did the same.

Back on the ground at Kandahar, I made a point of thanking the ground crew. Thirty-nine weapons had gone earthwards, and every single one had worked. Then I walked slowly around the aeroplane. Surely there had to be a hole *somewhere*. But there was nothing. Next, we were debriefed by the squadron executive officer, my great friend Kris. At first it seemed almost reproving – we had, after all, broken a few cardinal rules – but he quickly realized why we'd been low, and why we simply had to do everything we did. So what looked as if it was going to be a fairly firm ticking-off turned out to be quite the opposite. Although we were about to break another rule.

You don't tend to sleep very well after days like that.

Luckily Simon's dad knew the score. He was an airline pilot, a world far removed from ours, but he was obviously on the right wavelength. He'd sent Simon a litre of port in a Ribena bottle. Still coursing with adrenaline, we stayed up and chatted the night away. It took us quite a few hours to reach a point where our beds beckoned, both of us still both wondering how all those bullets had missed us.[23]

23 Simon received a Commander Joint Operations Commendation for his exemplary leadership on that day in August 2008. I received a Mention in Despatches for my part in the battle. Both are very minor awards in the scheme of things, but I am very proud of both. However, neither of them really mattered compared to that first transmission from Cougar after the firing had stopped. That was special.

29. The Big One

Afghanistan, and although I hadn't now had a drink in two months, I still managed to wake up feeling hung over – possibly dehydration, potentially just a rut I'd got into.

I woke with a torch in my face and a hand firmly rocking my shoulder to and fro.

'Tremors, mate, you need to get up.' Brian spoke in a whisper, but there was no mistaking his voice or its urgency.

There are only three reasons for someone with a torch shaking your shoulder. Most likely you'd managed to oversleep, and there was now a 4 x 4 full of pissed-off people waiting outside because of some numb nuts who wasn't cleared to operate an alarm clock solo. Not a good look.

The second possibility was that the night team had been scrambled for a GCAS (ground close air support) and needed someone to man the ops desk until dawn. But if I'd been the nominated reserve for this duty, I'd have known before I went to bed. And it wasn't my turn.

The third reason for getting a flight commander – that's me – up in the middle of the night was that something had gone sub-optimally, badly or disastrously wrong. In Afghanistan there was little middle ground; bad news was likely to be very dreary indeed.

'Mate, you've got to get up. We've got a priority target,' said Brian, adding, 'Can you get Kelp up, please? I've got a small snag with the cops. You need to be ready in five!' And with that the torchlight receded, and Brian left the dark room. *Fuck.* I rubbed my eyes as I sat up on my bunk. A priority target, a big fat juicy one. Now you're talking. Leaving aside the fact that one of my flight had an issue with the local feds, this sounded quite exciting. No tired trudging up and down the corridors today with the blurred eyes and fuzzy thoughts that came towards the end of a tour in Kandahar. My mind did the right thing unbidden, all systems fired up and ready to go.

Brian would have jumped at the chance to go himself. Asked once back home whether he ever felt guilty about all the Talibs he'd killed, he barely understood the question. 'Er, no, they are the enemy,' he replied. The only guilt he felt was when empty fuel tanks meant he had to leave the guys on the ground. He flew hundreds of trips in theatre. Guys like him who had been there and done it, and given the choice would have done it for ever, were the ones I admired. Others had done the same number of trips, dropped the same number of bombs but had grown weary of the whole caper. I had little time for their complaints. Luckily, we were blessed with plenty of good lads to make up for the odd one or two who had let their motivation drop. With a team that included the likes of Mental, Bollard, Paul, Bernard and Simon, we had enough yin to outweigh the odd purveyor of yang. And we had some high-quality young pups as well; in fact, to a man the young guys were keen as mustard. One such gentleman warrior was Kelp.

I went to find him.

Kelp. Half fighter pilot, half jolly-faced clown. A perfect addition to any trench. When called upon to fight, he was there, at your shoulder, sharp as a razor. When not called upon to fight, he was a clumsy, booze-fuelled idiot with an uncanny ability to make a complete tit of himself, with all the edge of a beach ball. He was also a great lad.

And waking him was going to be a treat. Kelp slept with his eyes half open in a pair of horribly tight floral-print briefs. Killing was a fraught experience, the mortar attacks were nerve-racking, but nothing got into your soul quite as much as wondering what your torch might come to rest on when you had to get Kelp out of bed.

So, a priority target. In a symmetric[1] war this would be a bridge, or a missile silo, or a communications node. In Afghanistan, a priority target is a person. There is absolutely no chance whatsoever that this person is unaware that his activities have been noticed. To become a priority target you need to have done some pretty shady (understatement in the extreme) things and to have done them a lot. At a tactical level, Taliban commanders could become priority targets for local units, but to get on the score sheet as one of the ones the whole theatre was after took some effort. It was impressive for all the

---

1 Normal or gentlemanly. Asymmetry (the opposite) was a word dreamed up to explain why conventional forces kept getting bested by guys with an ounce of guile or cheek. It is commonly accepted in dogmatic lunacy that we are only ever the victims of asymmetry and to use it ourselves would be unfair. Much like taking people by surprise, a little unjust and frowned upon.

wrong reasons to be a strategically important target. It might be due to your competence as a commander of an area of provincial size or greater that got you onto the approved targeting list. A degree of notoriety in supplying, making or using weapons, IEDs or partaking in atrocity would seal your place on a sheet of paper which made your untimely (or timely, from the Coalition point of view) demise probable if not certain.

We were being stood-to in order to bring to an end the life of one of these characters, thereby denying the enemy command and control, denying them expertise and giving them a capability gap. We were going to cut the head off the snake. What could be better for morale on our side and worse for morale on theirs than appearing out of the wide blue yonder and surgically removing 'the boss'? This looked set to be a great mission, so best we didn't fuck it up.

After wrestling young Kelp from his pit, I grabbed a quick shower,[2] and we were ready to roll, well inside the five minutes that Brian allowed us. Then the small issue of the local constabulary reared its annoying, small-minded, pointless head.

With a fleeting chance to nail an enemy commander, Brian had come to get us quite quickly. He had gone past a police patrol going over the 20 km/h limit. He'd then compounded this 'recklessness' by not stopping for them, after making a call that snake decapitation was a strategic issue and that the feds could wait for an

---

2 To this day, Brian thinks ill of me for this aquatic adventure. He denies all knowledge of giving me five minutes to be ready.

explanation. Apparently, they couldn't, and apparently the KAF speed limit was actually far more important than polishing off a Taliban commander for such trivial crimes as murder in a public place and multiple IED strikes on friendlies. Luckily the police were backing down by the time I approached, and we were then free to continue to the 904 Expeditionary Air Wing operations building. Sodium lighting illuminated the thick concrete blast walls beneath a black sky.

Entering Harrier ops brought its usual release from the dust, sweat and darkness turning to air con and fluorescent light. Psycho Mike, our intelligence officer, was there to greet us. You have simply never met anyone with a stronger work ethic than young Michael. He quickly brought us up to speed using a map annotated with a hand-drawn cross and a disconcertingly scruffy bit of scrap paper with the details of the mission scrawled across it. This might sound unprofessional, but the reverse is true; you have to be good to be gash, as the saying goes. It takes an absolute professional to make things work with non-existent planning time and short brief. And Psycho Mike knew exactly what we needed. No chaff or bollocks. Codes, radio frequencies, attack profiles and the like were already done. This made things incredibly simple. We had a position for the centre of the area it looked likely we'd head for, a frequency to contact our controllers on, a back-up, a second back-up and codes for our transponders. After months in theatre that was enough.

Everything about operating in Afghanistan had become second nature to us. Very, very little needed to be said in the brief except to clarify the rules of engagement we'd use to nail this bastard. Everything else was standard: actions in aircraft emergencies; actions in the event of system failure; weapon malfunction drills; weapon settings. We had a quick look at the position we were expecting to be scrambled to and noted the height of the ground and the rough distance and bearing from Kandahar. We then talked with Simon, our qualified weapon instructor, about how we were going to take this guy down.

Our intelligence was fairly simple: our priority target was in a vehicle in the desert to the west of Kandahar. As soon as one of the assets out looking for him had a contact, we'd be put onto cockpit alert and we'd launch as soon as someone had corroborated the position from another source. So, while our problem was quite simple, the solution probably wasn't. We could hope for a static target but might have to cope with a mover.

Ideally, we'd want to use Maverick, an American missile, for this sort of thing. The trouble was that loading Mavs took a long time. Failing that, we'd have liked bog-standard Paveway laser-guided bombs. The new model was a little too clever in that it went to a very exact coordinate, and for a moving target this was actually counter-productive. We just want the thing to fall off the aircraft at an appropriate moment, anywhere in the 'laser basket', and pick up laser energy being shined onto the target. The fact of the matter was, however, that we were primarily in theatre to support troops on the ground and, because Mavs and LGBs were less useful in that capacity, we didn't carry them every day.

We needed a bit of notice to prepare the jets with weapons designed to hit moving targets and we had received no notice whatsoever.

So, what we needed to concentrate on was how to stop and kill a man inside a moving vehicle using the Harrier's standard load. Luckily, the Jedi Knights of the Air Warfare Centre at RAF Waddington, all experts in bringing baddies to account through the medium of blast and fragmentation, had come up with a plan. Even better, it had been drawn up by a staunch Harrier man who went by the name of 'Killer'. In all my many dealings with him, he'd only ever spoken sense, and this document was no exception.

The combined attack he'd come up with meant I would acquire and track the target with the Sniper pod and fire the laser at the car. Kelp would then fly towards the target from behind using the laser spot tracker in the Harrier's nose to look for my laser spot, fly over the target in a shallow dive, following the cues displayed in his HUD to make the attack. By detonating an airburst 540lb bomb above the car, we hoped to stop him in his tracks before I delivered the *coup de grâce*: a 1,000lb Enhanced Paveway 2 Plus. It would make mincemeat of a stationary vehicle.

So Kelp and I would use a bit of teamwork to stop the car and then destroy it using the weapons available. If anyone escaped into the desert, we had rockets to make sure they didn't get far. For anyone travelling with our target, the goose was cooked. The ROE and legal teams would only allow us to attack if they were sure that all occupants of the car were fair game. If there is one good thing to come out of Afghanistan, it is that the British public has been shaken out of its Gulf War-fostered opinion that war is about TV screens, quick, painless deaths or collateral free strikes. War is a rough old game.

The sun was rising slowly, turning monochrome to colour as we walked out of the ops building onto the airfield where the wagon was parked. To our left were Brit Apaches; immediately next to us were the wonderful little OH-58 Kiowas flown by the Air Cavalry. According to our friends on the ground, they flew in a manner which paid due heed to their cavalry background. These guys were aggressive and got the job done, taking casualties doing it if need be. Next to the OH-58s were lines and lines of twin-rotored Chinooks: Brit, US, Australian. There were French assault helicopters – a Puma derivative of some sort – and US special mission Blackhawks. Then more Apaches, American this time. We threaded our way through as many as eighty helos. There were rows of big multi-engined transports too. Immaculate Coalition military airlifters and civilian charters that were anything but immaculate. They were all weather-beaten Soviet types and were universally in a poor state, often missing panels or growing mould on the inside of windows. On approach to Kandahar they'd belch out thick soot from what appeared to be diesel-burning engines. If I could see them for miles, then so could the enemy. And the fact that they never bothered to fire at these easy targets reinforced my conviction that there was no SAM threat at Kandahar airfield. The air was still cool as we arrived at Panther dispersal. The jets were waiting for us beneath sun-shelters, or hides.

After pulling on the last of our flying kit, we signed for the aircraft from the engineers. As we did so, we were bombarded with questions: 'Who is it?' 'Where is he?' 'How'd they find him?' Almost none of which we knew, but we were in a position to give them the only news that really mattered. 'Boys, if you give us aeroplanes that work and bombs that fuse, leave the rest to us and we'll blow this fucker to kingdom come!' Nothing like a bit of 'Team America' foreign policy to get Jack[3] in the mood.

With that we walked out into the dawn covered in flying kit and carrying our bags of mission essentials, such as all our mapping and information booklets. The jets stood impassively in their shelters, facing south, brought to life by the maintainers plugging in the external power supplies, diesel generators – the only sound at this quiet end of the airfield. There were eight hides in total. And in each lurked a Harrier, its wonderful anhedral wing signalling the presence of one of the world's best CAS platforms.

As I completed the walkaround checks, the jet hummed. Machines may not have souls, but you couldn't help feeling attached to the one that would take you into battle. Some developed a deep and irrational devotion to their chosen machine. I'm all for having a soft spot for your steed, but when that becomes

---

3 The collective nickname given to sailors in the Navy. We'd show them videos of the mission if we could. Things like this make a massive difference when you're part of a team working so far from home. For us, the boys bringing us cold water after long missions was a prime example.

an obvious over-confidence in, or even dishonesty about, its abilities – it's probably a bit counter-productive. And yet here the Harrier was absolutely in its element, and anyone that argues against it knows nothing about CAS.[4]

I checked the ejection seat – something you simply couldn't be complacent about – and then jumped into the cockpit and strapped myself in. Time to check the radios. I pressed the transmit button to send a short beep out over the air waves. This allowed Kelp to get his radio hopping in time with mine. This meant that it would start hopping through pre-set frequencies at the correct time. It takes a relatively swept-up enemy to listen in to your speech when you are frequency hopping. The Taliban had no such capability.

'Mickey sweet,' he called. He had got the beep, or Mickey as we called it.[5] The equivalent of synchronizing watches.

'Active go!' I ordered, meaning come off this frequency and onto a frequency-hopping net. I did the same.

'Canine 51 flight, check active.' On active, the sound of our voices was ever so slightly disjointed, almost as if you're hearing the frequency changes – a sure sign that the kit is working.

'52's up,' replied Kelp. Sweet work. If you could get

---

4 Close air support was up there with air defence as the sport of kings, the crucial difference being that you get to do CAS for real. AD guys go for decades without trade.
5 It was actually called a TOD, or 'time of day' – but only a geek would actually call it that.

through a Havequick (the code for active) check-in, then you could crack most things in the Harrier.

We were all set. And with that, I shut down the jet and climbed down to the waiting crew. We were ready to go. All we could do now was wait.

'Everything all right, boss?' the plane captain asked.[6]

'Perfect, thanks, guys. Hopefully see you again shortly.' I hung my helmet and LSJ on a wing pylon. The jet was set up exactly how I wanted it, I had signed for it, she was mine. I and only I could touch her.

'Thanks, boys,' I called as I jumped in the wagon to pick up Kelp. How these guys kept their motivation up amazed me; all they ever saw of Afghanistan was departing jets and the inside of the walls. It was absolutely crucial that we kept appearing at the aircraft line to see to it that they were well, and for continued squadron morale we owed a huge debt of gratitude to some very strong senior rates.

We did our bit by playing the theme tune to *The A-Team* full blast and wheel-spinning our way out of Panther in a cloud of burnt rubber to grab some breakfast.

Behind us, the sun was edging over the south-eastern horizon, and the mountain to the north had made its way out of the grey dawn. Large signs blocked the ladders to the cockpits that warned in unambiguous red lettering: GCAS JET, DO NOT TOUCH.

---

6 In the Fleet Air Arm 'boss' is a perfectly acceptable term for a lad to address an officer by. We have a far better 'all of one company' ethos than the fast jet operators in our sister service who, in my experience, seem to run an 'us and them' relationship between pilots and engineers.

The call came soon enough.

Obviously they couldn't call us before or after break-fast; the mobile came to life just as we were sitting down. A few garbled words through the static, and we were off, running to the fire escape through throngs of Coalition personnel wondering why two guys in kit were running away from their steaming piles of food. Expecting to burst into the dawn light, we were brought to an unexpected and painful halt. The fucking fire door was locked! Notwithstanding the obvious Health and Safety implications, we had a baddy to kill. And our weapon-toting, men-on-a-mission street cred had taken an embarrassing nosedive. We turned round and left the way we'd come in. Nothing to see here.

For the next five minutes we had a licence to drive like Starsky and Hutch. As we approached the armed checkpoint onto the airfield, we were accelerating through 60 mph and still weren't quite going straight, the GCAS wagon having decided that it would be easier to understeer dramatically. The Canadian guard simply didn't know what to make of it as we zipped past, Kelp shouting 'We're on a scramble!' as if it made everything OK.

This was great, and the looks on the faces of firemen, freight handlers and security told you that we weren't putting on an everyday display. Kelp, bless him, knew exactly what to do in this situation. One last mini-brief on the attack plan? One last check on the rules of engagement? Fuck no. We needed *The A-Team*. So to the sound of 1980s childhood excitement we charged down to Panther, past the aid station, C-130s and weird special mission aircraft and off to war in the skies above Afghanistan.

As we turned off the taxiway into Panther, I dropped Kelp at his aeroplane, slowing to walking pace for him to jump out. His crew, silhouetted against the southern dawn light, were waiting for him. A few sunshades later, I got to my jet, leaving the wagon behind it, still running, hazards on, A-Team just finishing up. First job: put on the LSJ. As this was a scramble, I decided that one of the two zips would do, no real need to go into battle completely dressed, the priority was to get there quickly. I quickly screwed the anti-G hose from the trousers into a receptacle on the LSJ.

'Boys, can someone move the wagon, please?' I asked.

'Aye aye, sir, no worries.' You've got to love Jack.

I took the proffered helmet and put it on. Again, I decided that there was no need to do it up just yet, all these things could be done later. Plugging in my helmet leads to the top of the LSJ, I turned to see the weapon pins in the hands of the 'bomb head', the armament specialist.

'Thanks, boys, see you later,' I managed.

I flew up the ladder and into the cockpit, and the plane captain followed me up the ladder to help with the straps, which is perfectly normal and usually a great help. Today was not normal, and I didn't need any help.

'I'll do it myself. Ladder clear, dude, and I'll start straight away!' I shouted at him.

'Roger that, sir! Good luck!' came back as he jumped off the ladder before spot turning and hauling it clear. Slamming the canopy shut, I switched on the battery master and then held the engine start switch forwards, giving the engine start signal to the maintainers as the engine kicked into life.

The Harrier's is not the quietest cockpit in the world, and with the engine running the vibration and noise of the machine give you an immediate sense of being in a position of some power. Simply the finest office in the world.

Four minutes of multi-tasking drills later, I checked in with Harrier Ops.

'Harrier Ops, Canine 51, words, please,' I called.

'Canine 51, Harrier Ops, you are scrambled in support of Axle 11, on Orange 34, 345 decimal 225, target is currently static' – before giving us the grid. I scribbled down the information as it came through the headset.

'Copied, Axle 11, Orange 34,' I read back. 'Kelp, are you up?'

'Affirm, all copied, ready in three minutes,' came the reply.

Good lad. Kelp was in a GR7, so his nav kit was a lot fiddlier than mine (I was in a GR9) and had to be treated with care. I was ready, so I got rid of the chocks, indicating outboard with both thumbs. I left the hide going south, following the marshaller's instructions. He stopped me once I was out from under the hide so I could make my seat live.[7] Confirming that my seat was live with six raised fingers, I went for the taxiway.

---

7 Making it live in the hide and suffering an accidental ejection through the roof would be 'somewhat tedious', or 'fatal' to give it its proper term.

'Kandahar Ground, scramble Canine 51 flight, flight of two scramble from Panther.' Use of the word scramble gave us total priority on the airfield. Using it twice probably didn't hurt.

Panther dispersal was very close to the end of the runway, and I looked left before turning right to head to the runway threshold. An Antonov cargo plane had stopped down the taxiway from us to let Kelp out. I was expecting to see him coming out from the other entrance to Panther, as his jet was at the other end to mine, to the south-west.

'How're you doing, mate?' I said on active.

'Just waiting on my align,' came the reply. The GR7 align couldn't be hurried, and it could be royally messed up by taking the parking brake off halfway through. Kelp had to wait.

Decision time: press as a singleton or wait for wingman? Yep, press.

'Canine 51 to Tower,' I transmitted and, without waiting for the clearance to do so, chopped to the tower frequency.

'Tower, scramble Canine 51 ready for departure, immediate.' I approached the end of the taxiway and turned left towards the threshold for runway 23, so-called because, give or take, the runway is aligned on 230 degrees.

Back came the usual laconic American voice, amusingly laid-back in the middle of our high-octane world. 'Canine 51 clear take off, contact departure, safe flight.'

There was no point hanging around. I lined up on the runway, doing my own personal 'anti-embarrassment' checks, my very own little checklist of all the things that really could make you look a prick: canopy definitely locked, seat definitely live, water armed, visors and flaps down. Everything else I could cope with later. Full power. Time to go.

I watched my ground speed as it raced towards the maximum allowed of 180 knots but used the indicated air speed as a cue to snatch the nozzles back to the STO stop to lift the aircraft off the runway with a satisfying jerk. I nozzled out gradually, staying low. With gear and flap up, I levelled off at 100 feet, accelerating to 400 knots, before pulling back on the stick, pushing back into my seat as the jet nosed into a good rate of climb. This take-off profile – fast and low before racing 'up the hill' – meant spending the minimum amount of time in no man's land: too high to be a surprise, too low to be unseen. My left hand deployed flares to prevent some cheeky tinker getting off a lucky shot with a MANPAD,[8] and I brought the nose to bear about 250 degrees. What a great feeling, on my own in this wonderful aeroplane, climbing into the clear sky with the Pegasus at combat thrust.[9] About to make a direct, personal contribution to the war effort.

And then, all of a sudden, my whole world fell in around me.

'Canine 51, Kandahar approach, be advised you have sparks leaving your aircraft!'

Oh fuck. Fuck. Fuck. Fuckeddy-Fuck! Not *now*!

---

8 Man portable air defence system.
9 Which I was allowed to use for a whole 150 seconds.

Both the aircrew manual and our Group Air Staff Orders mention the ability of the Pegasus to produce sparks. And sparks meant one thing: your engine was in terminal decline. Sparks indicated rapid, catastrophic engine failure, and both sources agreed that early ejection was the key to survival. I turned back towards the airfield, advising Kandahar that I would be for an immediate emergency recovery and called Harrier Ops.

'Harrier Ops, Canine 51, recovering with engine malfunction, sparks seen leaving the aircraft.'

'Canine, Harrier Ops copied. Getting the cards out for you.' Dave would be reading the cards that contained all the actions to take in all the possible emergencies. In this case, however, there wouldn't be a directly applicable card. The one dealing with engine failure simply said: 'If time critical – EJECT'.

Minge.

I couldn't believe this. Why today of all days? I pointed at the bit of sky to the east of Kandahar. I would have to dump fuel and probably stores to bring her back, but with an engine about to quit I didn't have time to waste. So maybe best to jettison all my load in one go. The decision was a tricky one, as if I didn't take time to dump down to a lower weight the engine, as it disintegrated, might not have enough power to let me land. It was Hobson's choice: land now and risk being under-powered for my weight and therefore crash, or take time dumping stuff and give the engine time to quit. And therefore crash.[10]

---

10 Just prior to deploying, we lost a jet at Cottesmore. The pilot, a great bloke and seasoned operator, took a very small amount of extra time

Decisions, decisions. Air traffic let me know that it was the tower controller that had reported the sparks, so I chopped to tower for my landing and asked what had happened. They told me that just as I'd started to move a shower of sparks had come out of my engine. That sounded fairly terminal.

The issue I had, however, was that I wasn't convinced. Sparks were produced by molten metal coming out of the engine. The source of the metal was the engine itself, so the sparks were actually bits of the engine being spat out by other bits of the engine. Engines that are eating themselves don't give out all that much thrust. Mine was fine. Engines that are melting overheat. Mine was fine. Engines whose fan blades are melting or flying off either dramatically accelerate or decelerate. Mine was running a constant RPM.

'Harrier Ops from Canine 51. Can you talk to the line and see if anyone else saw these sparks?' I was thinking that maybe there was another possibility, some other reason, a bit off-piste, for the sparks. Maybe a bird had got into the engine and had been spat out of the back? The sad truth, however, was that even in this case you simply had to land, as you had no idea what had happened or what damage had been caused. But then came a ray of hope.

---

to reduce his fuel load following an engine malfunction. The engine failed when he took nozzle. This crash and the subsequent discoveries about jet and engine were actually very complex and quite disturbing. The point, though, is that my friend had thought – from years of training and briefing – that he had a reasonable amount of time to get things squared. The opposite was true.

'Canine 51 from Harrier Ops, I've called the line and some of the weapons guys saw it. They think it was a BOL packet being shaken loose.' That could make sense. BOL looked like metal Risla papers stripped out into streams behind the aircraft. They were ferrous and heated up on contact with the air to the same wavelength as that of an aircraft skin, to act as a decoy against SAMs. And, unlike magnesium flares, we could carry hundreds of the things. You couldn't usually see them, but at night they looked similar to glowing embers thrown from a moving vehicle. The last packet sometimes didn't sit perfectly in the canister. My pre-take-off power checks could have shaken it out of the housing. From the tower, a fair distance away, how could they tell the difference between sparks coming from the engine and sparks coming from halfway along the wing? BOL was a more than plausible explanation.

'Kelp, are you ready yet?' I called.

'Yes, mate, just getting airborne,' he said, and as I positioned for an approach to Kandahar I saw his jet moving onto the runway. I was north of the runway, heading east, so I would descend for a landing using a wide right-hand turn to bring me back onto 230 degrees.

'Mate, did you see my aircraft and these sparks?' I asked him.

'Yeah,' came the not exactly confident reply.

'What do you think, mate? BOL or not?' I asked for more, but I was being unfair. Kelp was a relative newcomer to this game, and the chances of him having seen BOL in the half-light were nil.

'It might have been,' he offered, which wasn't helpful,

but the last thing you want is a dishonest wingman – he simply didn't know.

Right. Decision time.

Engine appears fine. Airmanship says land straight away. I could call the CAOC[11] and say sorry. There was a chance that I had time to get to a spare, but minutes are precious in this game, and the CAOC would give this mission to another unit if I landed. The boys on the ground think it's BOL. Kelp doesn't sound sure but thinks it could be. So, what does common sense say? In peacetime there wouldn't even be a discussion, I'd land and do the trip later. But this wasn't peacetime, and later may never exist again. The snake's not going to lie still for repeated attempts to behead it. It wasn't sense that was required, but an officer's decision. I decided to press.

I turned the jet towards the target and slammed to full power. As I racked the Harrier round to the west again, below me, I saw Kelp lining up on the runway. I eased off the Gs and started to climb. Pulse rate getting back to normal, but hell, I was sweating. That little bit of excitement wasn't really what I needed mid-scramble, but we were back in the fight, and the air con could do wonders for a bit of sweat in the fifteen minutes it would take to get to the target area.

'Harrier Ops, Tremors. I reckon it's BOL, the engine seems fine. See you later!'

'Your decision, mate, good flight,' came back from

---

11 Combined Air Ops Centre, the space centre in Al Udeid that ran the war.

Dave. He'd have backed me up no matter what my call had been.

I called the formation over to the C2 frequency for western Afghanistan and settled down for the cruise out to the target area at flight level 240.[12] From here on, my main concerns were the bombs and the targeting pod. From the stores page I could see that both bombs were showing as G1 – GPS guidance and quality 1, the highest of nine possible grades. Perfect. Now for the targeting pod. The Sniper pod had been bought solely for Afghanistan. It was brilliant and streets ahead of the TIALD we'd been using. The only snag was that we hadn't the cash to get the aeroplane to recognize that it was a Sniper, rather than TIALD. As a result the buttons around the screen were labelled for the wrong pod, which meant the whole thing could be quite confusing to use until you got the hang of it. The pod was arguably our most important sensor and, today, making sure its laser was set up properly was my priority as we closed on the target area at Mach .81. The weather, in its infinite wisdom, decided to loft a spanner directly into the works. There were storms in the target area. Ace.

But at least we weren't going to be operating in the crowded airspace of Helmand. There was another important difference today: we didn't want to alert the enemy to our presence, so we deliberately aimed for a point 10 miles north of the point we had been given. We checked in.

12 24,000 feet, give or take.

'Axle 11, Canine 51 with you on Orange 34.' The frequencies are all colour coded, with each of about twenty colours having forty or so frequencies. With 800 encoded frequencies you'd be disappointed to find the enemy listening in.

'Canine 51, Cobalt 62 relaying for Axle, you are loud and clear. Remain clear of the target area. We are ready for your check-in.'

'Canine 51 is two by UK Harriers, lead has two by E-Paveway 2, 1,000lb weapons, 2 has two by 540 freefall set to impact and airburst, he also carries thirty-eight rockets. We both have targeting pods, our downlink code is 4400, we are laser search capable.' I passed the well-rehearsed message to the Cobalt callsign belonging to a Predator drone flying below.

'Canine 51, this is Cobalt. Target is Hilux showing white on white-hot, currently static but all pax are now in the vehicle, how copy?' We also got the target grid.

I scribbled down the message, keeping the aeroplane in a left-hand orbit and rechecking the target coordinate. The weather was deteriorating, and that was going to make this far from straightforward. Below, the cloud layer was stormy; big weather cells were roaming around the desert, like deities out for a fight. About 5 miles across, these angry clouds were throwing rain into the desert while the wind kicked up dust. You couldn't really tell where cloud ended and dust began. Between cloud, rain and dust, these monsters were impassable, and we would simply have to live in the gaps between them, clear all the way down to the desert floor. It would be hard work, but by carefully choosing where we held and how we attacked, we could remain in the game. Kelp had done a good job of finding me in my holding pattern in a gap, and we orbited as a pair, waiting for the action to start, the aviation equivalent of staring at your feet in the changing room, wondering how much eighty minutes of rugby was going to hurt.

Cobalt reported that there was a Bone callsign above us: B-1, or B-one, hence Bone. This Cold War giant was a simply amazing aeroplane that took three times the Harrier's maximum weight in fuel every time it got to a tanker. It stayed on task for three to four hours and checked in with twenty-plus weapons. They'd even found a place on its malevolent, pointed airframe for a Sniper pod.[13] Bones didn't cock around, and if one thing was now certain, it was the fact that if we hesitated, or showed any form of weakness, or just plain fucked it up, the Bone would step in where the Harrier kids had failed and show the world how the big boys work. Our strength, however, came with our size. We were set up to deal with a small target, a target that might move, a target suited to a small single-seat fighter and his mate, not a strategic bomber.

So, there we were, a bit of an oddball team forming up in the desert to kill a single man. A pair of Harriers at medium level, a Bone at a higher level, a Cobalt down lower than us, and we were all being coordinated

---

13 If you have never seen a B-1 then you should make the effort. They are akin to a dark-grey, military Concorde with four big engines and a swing wing.

by Axle, who was using the Predator to relay all his messages.

This was a little weird. We weren't talking directly to a JTAC but to a pilotless aircraft. The operator (sorry – can't bring myself to call them pilots) was sitting in Nevada and speaking via satellite and texting the bloke in charge – Axle – who was in Bagram.

And our target decided at about this time to add a twist to proceedings. He had stopped because he couldn't see, but now the storm cell that had kept him pinned down moved off to the east. He was in the clear and he started to move, which meant we now had to find and track him before carrying out Killer's coordinated attack plan in poor weather. A point not lost on anyone else.

'Canine 51, are you able to take a moving target?'

'Canine 51 affirm,' I replied, trying to sound as upbeat about the prospect as I could. It would, of course, be hard work, but we had a plan and we weren't going to leave this one to the Bone. The worst possible scenario was that Cobalt himself – or itself – would take the target. I'd rather the fucker got away than hear a drone took a target I turned down. How could you live with yourself?

'Cobalt, Canine 51, still holding to the north of the target,' I went on. 'We need an updated grid, please.' Whether or not we could take them was largely irrelevant if we couldn't see them.

'Copied. All we are now tracking the vehicle,' came back the reply.

For the guy in the ground station to get information from his system probably takes a second or two, for him to read it takes four seconds, for me to write it down takes another two seconds, and to read it back takes four. To punch in the grid might take as many as ten seconds, and then to get the pod to look into that area another two. So from the target being at a certain grid to me getting my pod into the area could take as much as twenty-four seconds, absolute minimum. If they were racing towards Pakistan at 40 miles per hour, this was approximately 20 metres per second. So in slack hand-fuls all our information was going to be about 500 metres out. This is an awful lot for a modern targeting pod, and I couldn't find him. Nor could Kelp. Cobalt confirmed that the target was moving south-east, and this at least gave us the ability to have a look in the right direction, but to no avail. I asked for another coordinate, knowing that this would begin to look pretty amateur if we didn't pick him up quickly. Then the stakes were raised again.

'Canine 51, from War Lord, just working some legal issues, confirm that you are happy with a moving target?' War Lord was the man in charge of the entire air war. He and his staff probably had live footage from Cobalt of a 4 x 4 charging across the desert. He had a legal issue, which probably meant that someone in his legal team was holding up a red card. Only when his full, multinational team of legal advisers all gave the green card could he authorize the attack. This gave us some breathing space, but the questions were beginning to annoy me.

'Canine 51, for War Lord, affirm happy with a mover.' Not so upbeat this time, a little bit terse. 'We're coming into 8 miles for acquisition. Can you give us a laser spot?' I sensed it was time to get the game going our way. In closer and have Cobalt show our pod's electronic eyes where the target was.

'Er, negative, we cannot give you a spot, sorry,' came back from Cobalt.

Brilliant.

I think it was an equipment issue, but still disappointing. Then a new voice joined, and this guy was our guardian angel from on high.

'Canine 51, Bone 21. We are tracking the target and can give you a spot. What code do you want?'

Now we were talking.

'Bone from Canine, request laser code 342, please. We'll run in on 160.'

'Copied all, sir. Call for laser.' They had cued up their Sniper pod and would lase as soon as I called for them to do so.

I looked at my map. The last known position of the target vehicle was south-east of me at about 12 miles. If we ran in on about 160 degrees, we would shave the eastern side of a big cell and be in the clear air. There was another cell to the east, we'd be flying through a cavern of cloud and dust, but on 160 I could see the desert floor. Hauling the jet around to face 160, I settled down to work the pod. I got the pod looking into the correct bit of desert and saw some tracks. Moving the pod down the tracks, I could see from my screen that they led to the south-east. He had to be on one of them. This was looking promising.

'Laser on!' I called.

'Bone 21, laser on.'

I pushed the keys around the Sniper screen. The small crosshair in the middle of the targeting pod, a bit like a rifle sight, grew until the cross filled the screen. The kit was working, searching for the laser. I watched our range to the target. Ten miles, nothing on the pod. I recued the pod. This is about to look very bad indeed. The Brit Harriers unable to find the festering target, let alone bomb it. Six miles, I moved the pod again, taking huge chunks down towards the south-east. Recuing the laser search, I willed the screen to show me the 4 x 4. But it wouldn't. I could only see desert, and we were now far too close to the target, well inside 10 miles, and lower than planned. Fuck! Snapping into a left-hand turn, I made one of the most disappointing calls of my life.

'Canine 51, nothing seen, turning cold' – away from the target. Total disappointment. Not only were we in danger of alerting the target to the presence of his assembled nemesis, but they were now bound to hand over the target. We'd failed. Or rather *I* had failed. Kelp hadn't failed at all. Kelp was a little behind me on the right. And just as he heard my call, he saw a 4 x 4 heading south-east on his screen. Just as I had taken my oxygen mask off to shout obscenities at nothing and no one, he had found the target.

'Canine 52, contact Hilux, showing white in white hot, tracks south-east!' he called. Dear, dear Kelp, the world's finest wingman, had our baddie in his sights, and now he was ours, not the Bone's, not the Cobalt's. This target belonged to Naval Strike Wing. What a rush.

'Sweet work, mate. Talk me on, will you?' I asked as

I ran out to the north. Because I could talk to Kelp on the active radio there was no need to punch in new coordinates. He kept a constant feed coming, and I simply moved my crosshairs to the south-east. Eventually I saw what he saw: the Hilux.

'Tally target,' I called, trying not to sound too triumphant, as we'd not achieved much in the scheme of things. 'Cobalt, for Axle, Canine 51 flight both tracking Hilux heading south-east.' What I didn't realize was that we had made life very hard for ourselves.

When I had turned cold at 6 miles, I broke left away from the storm cell to our right. Kelp had pushed in closer and, by the time he saved the whole damn day by getting eyes on the target, the gap had closed, and, unable to follow, he'd turned right. Neither of us saw the other go, so engrossed were we in our screens. But we were now no longer a pair of fighters, but one to the north and one to the west.

Still, where there's a will . . .

And, luckily, I had some form when it came to the job in hand. When flying overwatch for a British takedown of a moving vehicle, I found I kept losing sight of it. Annoyed by that, I had repeatedly practised tracking vehicles with my pod, mainly using the lorries on Highway 1 as I went from task to task. The tricky bit was the mask, getting through the sixty or so degrees of turn to point back at the target at the back end of the racetrack. And I had come up with my very own technique for dealing with it. If you really flew the aircraft aggressively you could turn the corner by overbanking. And while that was a little naughty as you descended out of your height block, it came with one massive upside. By flying nearly upside down, the pod was able to see over the fuel tank slung beneath the wing. There was no mask; you never lost sight of the target. Time to put it to the test.

OK: run into 8 miles between the weather cells and turn away normally. At 12 miles, turn inbound as violently as I could, descending to 11,000 feet or so, then bring the nose up to climb, having maybe lost the target for a second or two. I simply wasn't going to lose this guy.

Then came the moment we'd been waiting for.

'Canine 51, Cobalt, here's your nine-line from Axle, although your position's going to be far more accurate than this.' And with that the man in Nevada read me out the nine details for the attack. He finished by adding, 'Just waiting on War Lord.' Which meant we weren't clear to attack just yet.

'OK, mate, let's do the checks,' I called, and Kelp read through our checklists, confirming all the systems were ready for an attack. I selected air-to-ground mode and brought the Paveway out of its hibernation, ensuring I had the correct impact angle for the weapon and that the pod was correctly set up. All I needed to do now was make the weapon live and press the pickle button on the stick. I was ready. Until I saw in my head-up display that Kelp was 7 miles away, not the half mile I expected. Oh, for the love of God, where in the name of all things that do not suck had he gone to?

'Mate, where are you?' I asked.

'West of the target by 5 miles, outbound,' came the reply.

'Er, dude, I'm north by 5 miles outbound. Are you visual?' I was clutching at straws here.

'Negative, mate, we got split up by the big storm,' said Kelp.

What to do? Join up? Delay the attack? Go in alone? What was the decision going to be? This is why you get paid as a fighter pilot, and I was helped immeasurably by the next radio call.

'Canine 51, Cobalt. War Lord clears strike as per nine-line, and you are clear all re-attacks!'

Fucking brilliant. Not only has War Lord himself just told us to attack this guy, but we're cleared all re-attacks. Our job was to kill him and kill him, then kill him some more, and then only stop when he was properly dead.

But what to do about Kelp? Stick to the plan, I told myself. I had been an air-to-air instructor in a previous life, and if there was one thing I was supposed to be able to do it was drive fighters around the sky. I turned back in towards the target, max performing the jet to run straight at him. I was at 8 miles.

'Mate, what's your distance to the target?' Too loud, I thought. Adrenaline getting the better of me.

'Eight miles,' came Kelp's immediate reply.

'Commit inbound, go to the right,' I directed. I was north, he was west. I had turned earlier than him and had deliberately gone left; he would go right, so we would run at the target, me ahead of him, with our paths converging. His jet would have a different heading to mine, but only by about sixty or so degrees. I looked at my pod. There was the vehicle, my thumb moving the switch on the throttle to keep pace with it. I moved my left thumb to the switch on top of the throttle and flicked it back, commanding the pod to 'point track'. It locked to the vehicle windscreen.

'Laser on!' I said as I pushed a small button on the inside of the throttle. In Kelp's aircraft, a small diamond displayed in the HUD settled on a point in the desert. And on his right-hand monitor he could clearly see that he was tracking the target vehicle.

'Good spot!' said Kelp, far calmer than I was.

'Canine 51 are in hot,' I told Cobalt.

'Canine 51, clear to strike and clear all re-attacks.'

I stared at my pod screen. The small tracking box never left the enemy vehicle. In the bottom left corner LAS FIRING flashed at me as I fired the laser. Above it, the laser code was correct and below it CMBT told me it was in the combat mode.

I was trying not to get too far ahead of Kelp so had my nose high and speed just above the 300 knots required to drop a bomb. Kelp was accelerating earthwards, looking for 450 knots for his weapon. His aeroplane gave him a line in the HUD; so long as he kept that line central, the aircraft would get him to the right bit of sky. Kelp flew a wonderfully smooth attack, giving his computer the best possible chance of working out all the variables. I was almost on top of the target when Kelp pressed his pickle button on his stick and held it. When a moving bar displayed on the HUD met the symbol indicating his flight path, there was a metallic clunk, and the airburst-fused 540lb bomb dropped from beneath the wing. Kelp pulled up and called 'Stores!'

As the weapon left the aircraft an electronic pulse activated the fuse, while the arming lanyard set a vane spinning in its tail. Ten seconds later, the vane having completed the requisite number of turns, the bomb armed. In its nose, the C band detector looked for the ground, waiting for a cue to tell the fuse that it was now time to detonate.

In a Hilux on the desert floor, the occupants had no idea that a bomb was inbound. It was covering 200 metres per second as gravity dragged it down towards the sand. But it had been released under steady conditions, by an aircraft cued by a laser spot that it had tracked solidly. The laser spot had been placed on the car by a pod that had never given up the track. It had been dropped by one of the world's most highly trained attack pilots, who had done absolutely everything correctly. All these things combined to produce a result that still seems a little improbable: the Hilux full of bad guys and our unguided[14] bomb were heading for the same bit of desert. And, due to the way Canine Flight had conducted the attack, they were going to get there at exactly, *exactly*, the same time.

'Reset for rockets!' I called. I was too close for a bomb myself now and began to turn outbound to the left. As the Gs mounted, I watched the 4 x 4 career across the desert. Then carnage erupted. My screen was filled with an almighty explosion. The blast of the airburst hailed fragmentation down onto the Hilux. Dust and smoke

14 This was neither GPS nor laser-guided to its target. Dumb, not smart. It was simply dropped at exactly the right time and place.

enveloped the vehicle. The weapon had gone off exactly as advertised just above the back seat of the vehicle. Then I lost it from view, everything being consumed by the boiling cloud of heat and dust that Kelp's bomb had brought to the desert.

'DH!' I shouted. Direct hit. The attack had been perfect. Despite the hard time finding the guy, despite the weather, despite the BOL incident, the Fleet Air Arm had pulled it off. Elation filled the cockpit, we'd done it. Or at least part one. Now for the *coup de grâce*. I was readying myself for the attack when Cobalt came on again.

'One squirter running west, one further pax a small distance to the south.' Bugger. Might be a job for rockets. I turned towards the target and looked for the Hilux, and damn if I couldn't see it! (Not again!)

'My pod shows only the hotspots from the bomb!' I told Cobalt. 'Where's the vehicle?'

'Go 150 metres south.'

I slewed the pod, and there it was, the vehicle had run on after the strike. I couldn't make out these squirters that they were talking about, though. I was running out of time.

'Where's the nearest squirter to the car?' I asked.

'From War Lord, hit the car!'

Change of plan. I slewed the pod over the car, firing my laser. Rocking forwards on the castle switch gave my bombs their impact point. I looked up to the HUD. The symbology told me I was already in range for the attack. I held down the pickle button and felt the weapon leave the aeroplane. I looked back at the screen and got the pod to track the static car once more. I could see movement in the back of the car, a head or arm bobbing out of the window as the Time to Impact clicked down. Then, for a second time that day, my pod picture bloomed as the desert howled under the fury of a 1,000lb weapon. And in that instant, the DT was no more. The snake lay headless in the western desert.

Now what about those squirters?

We could assume that the one close to the vehicle would not have survived the strike, which left one guy who went south and one that went west. Between the four aircraft we started a search, and Bone quickly found the guy who went south, but there was an issue: a red card at the CAOC. Someone had pointed out that if we continued, our action could be outside the law of armed conflict.

The attack must be humane and proportionate. We were on safe ground here. Our target would die, and no one else would even know about it, let alone be at risk. But the attack would also be discretionary. Our assumption was that these guys were Taliban, but we were now entering a grey area. In the post-strike dust and chaos, was that a safe assumption? Or was the guy running about a driver who had been at gunpoint in the vehicle? Law of armed conflict requires these three tests are met along with one other: necessity. Does the war effort directly benefit from what you propose to do? Was it necessary? Our mission was to remove the DT from the enemy batting order. We'd done it, so why kill anyone else?

I will be honest. In the moment, I'd have kept going. I'd have hunted every one of them over the dunes and along the tracks, over wadis until we brought them all to account. The blood was up, and the horns were out. But it wasn't up to me. The difference between us and them is that we are subject to the laws, checks and balances that ensure we know when to stop. We weren't there to blow holes in Afghanistan but to help the local population of whatever religion, of whatever tribe, make a better country and in so doing make a safer world.

It was time to go home.

The transit home was uneventful, as was the landing and taxi back to Panther. But for this sortie, and this sortie alone, I thought it appropriate to shake my wingman's hand. It somehow seemed to fit. We walked to the line with grins on our faces, cold water bottles in our hands courtesy of Jack and loads to tell the expectant throng of lads.

We were later debriefed that the strike had been a complete success, and intelligence agencies closed the case on our DT. They had gathered enough evidence from human and electronic means to be 100 per cent confident that Canine 51, with a lot of help from those other guys, had done with aplomb what everyone seemed to think we couldn't.

I wrote Kelp up for an award for his actions that day. Sadly he was not deemed worthy of one by higher authority, and it wasn't awarded, which was not uncommon.

Deploying to Afghanistan on operations with the Naval Strike Wing was a highpoint. I knew that whatever happened next it was going to take some beating, but it turned out the aviation gods had one more trick up their sleeve for me. But not, inevitably enough, without a fair amount of faffing about beforehand.

30. Going to Play with the Cat and Trap Boys and Girls

I was in Portsmouth and from memory
I was sober – although why remains a mystery.

I was in the Maritime Air Operations Centre – MAOC – when the phone rang.

My days of playing about in UK jets had come to an end in Scotland in the summer of 2010. It had been great. I had been the senior pilot of Naval Strike Wing at a time when Carrier Strike was all the rage, and that made me 'incredibly valuable'. Only it didn't. I became one of very few (possibly the first!) Joint Force Harrier senior pilots to not get a slot at staff college, and, despite some good intentions, no one seemed to know what to do with me. The MAOC felt a little half-arsed to me – an attempt by the Navy to show that, despite the job being well covered elsewhere, it could still command and control aircraft at sea. I was wasting my time.

So when the appointer rang asking for my thoughts on an Out Of Area,[1] the only correct answer was 'When do I start?'

It looked like I had wangled a way of getting back to

---

1 Out Of Area = deploy on operations as a singleton or, remarkably, in the RAF it can also mean 'Go to Cyprus'.

Afghanistan – by jumping at the chance before anyone else did.[2]

The exact details of the OOA weren't entirely clear to start with, but it sounded like: sail on the French Navy's carrier *Charles de Gaulle* for four months, go to war, miss Christmas, come home. Perfect. My job, it was explained, was to roll all three jobs the French had asked for help with into one; hence I was to be their carrier-qualified, Fixed Wing CAS expert anglophone, able to liaise on their behalf with all the units in the south-west of Afghanistan. Primarily the Brits, USMC and Aussies.

But what of the *Charles de Gaulle* experience? I found my time away enjoyable yet at times massively frustrating. The poor French boys were hamstrung by their command and their 'Decision Tree'; to get to a point where they could actually drop weapons was virtually impossible.

I was in the briefing when the pilots were told that they were prohibited from trying to find creative ways to provide the JTACs on the ground with the firepower they needed. 'Non' meant 'non'.

The French Rafale and Super Etendard crews, through no fault of their own, ran a very real risk of being seen to be timid and to be deliberately wasting people's time. People under fire in a far-off land.

I enjoyed the fighting spirit shown by some of the French, but the *Charles de Gaulle* air group dropped no

2 There are plenty of armchair quarterbacks and folk out there who take great glee in telling people like me that they 'managed to get out of that OOA' or similar. Those people are in that part of the Venn diagram marked 'not the real deal'.

weapons on that cruise. I shared their frustration. And on Christmas Eve, as we listened to the admiral speak, a French pilot told me, 'We have lost our pride and the respect of our allies. The only thing we haven't lost is our shame.' I think a lot of the French crews felt the same, given the emotion of the moment. But to be clear, they and that particular warrior will never lose respect in my eyes. Their operators and senior officers were first-class. However, their impotence in Afghanistan might explain why, when Libya kicked off a few months later, those guys were into the fight like hounds unleashed.

But this was not my abiding memory of my time with the Aeronavale. Instead, as a Harrier pilot, it was the realization that I was 'sort of part of the gang, yet sort of not'. I had never flown from a conventional Cat and Trap carrier, and while a huge amount of my experience of naval aviation remained germane, there was a fascinating amount that didn't. How did one fly the ball? What did a catapult shot feel like? Was it better to stop then land, or land then stop?

It was probably this little nugget of inquisitive doubt that kept me in the game when, halfway through the deployment, the devastating news arrived that the British Harriers and carriers were to be binned[3] in favour

3 Note to all serving personnel. If there is a defence review coming up and your capability is at risk, being on a foreign warship with limited e-mail access and a crap satellite phone is not the place to be, when all your mates are actually in the appointer's office asking what the fuck is going on. You get last dibs. In a small victory, I crashed the *Charles de Gaulle*'s internet connection downloading the CAA's airline pilot's licence guidance.

of the wheezy fat kid from Marham and Lossie. I was sad, disappointed and above all angry at being absolutely helpless (again). British Fixed Wing carrier aviation was going to be taking a ten-year time-out until the arrival of the long-promised F-35 Lightning. Stan, the boss of the Super Etendard squadrons on board *Charles de Gaulle*, called the decision 'disgusting'. Our willingness to just do without for a bit made one thing very clear: the French had become the US's key naval ally at the stroke of a British pen.

My wife was so incensed by the Harrier decision that she e-mailed 10 Downing Street and told them that not only were they binning a world-class maritime strike capability but they were taking out of service their only counter-insurgency aircraft, ostensibly to prioritize counter-insurgency – which didn't make sense. She got an e-mail back saying that the capability would be covered by our allies, and a great example of this was the fact that the *Charles de Gaulle* was currently off Pakistan, launching jets to support UK forces in Afghanistan – and that we had a UK liaison officer on board.

I wish I was lying.

I got back from *Charles de Gaulle* and went about telling just about anyone who would listen that I was 'done'. I saw no point in waiting around for the new carriers and jets – as that jam wasn't even in the same solar system, let alone this side of the horizon. As I weighed my options, I was posted to the Commander UK Task Group staff, responsible for the Navy's amphibious forces, i.e. the job of putting Royal Marines ashore. They were a really good crowd, but there was no getting round the fact that it was great job for someone with something relevant to add and something great to go back to, rather than a melancholy swansong for someone set on leaving because there were 'no fucking jets'. And so, while the people were fantastic, it would have been pointless for me personally if Libya hadn't kicked off.

The irony of the situation was hard to avoid. After going to war with a French nuclear-powered aircraft carrier operating state-of-the-art fast jets that were barely allowed to fight, I was now going to try it on a diesel-engined British amphib armed with helicopters.

The Libyan campaign was one of extreme contrasts. On the one (bad) side it was named ELLAMY, after the Greek god of fighting wars ideally suited to capabilities you've just retired. Everyone had carriers involved. The *Charles de Gaulle* and my mates from a few months earlier were operating with us. The Italian Navy deployed the *Garibaldi* and her Harriers. US Marine Corps Harriers were in town too, aboard the flat-top USS *Kearsage*. It could have been our generation's 'carrier war', but our jets were plasti-wrapped at home, *Ark Royal* had been given the chop, and our carrier was *Ocean* (half helo carrier, half building site). The maritime strike capability wasn't going to be that amazing VSTOL jet; it was the AH-46D Apache helicopter.

After a hasty work-up off Cyprus, the Apache boys and girls in the AH would go on to do some amazing stuff – I would go as far as to say that the awards granted to them after the conflict were somewhere between 'miserly' and 'an absolute disgrace'. The leadership required to keep that unit going into the threat night after night was humbling to watch. The other thing that was actually heart-warming was the way the whole ship rose to the considerable challenge of supporting them. My job was to act as the liaison between the ship and CAOC, in Italy.

I flew home from ELLAMY feeling like I had contributed, despite the obvious disappointment of waiting an entire career to deliver maritime strike, then watching the Army Air Corps heroes deliver it on the day of the races. Operating at sea, they had on occasions given almost unsettlingly efficient demonstrations of how to bring violence to the enemy. I couldn't help feeling a little put out to have finally got to a maritime strike operation only to be in a supporting role to the (magnificent but) wrong attack platform.

I was feeling magnanimous, however. Remember I mentioned that, after a bit of faffing about, the aviation gods came good? Well, that's the faffing about bit over. I was now looking forward to every naval aviator's dream – flying Super Hornets with the United States Navy.

The competition for spots had been stiff, and I am eternally grateful to those that fought my corner. From 'nothing to add, nowhere to go', I now had 'lots to add, somewhere pretty cool to go'.

31. Big Jets and Big Decks

Somewhere off San Diego. Stone-cold sober, again.[1]

One day, if all the planets align and following a series of events – both unfortunate and fortunate – you might end up taxiing to the catapult on a USN aircraft carrier. I think as a standalone event there is probably no greater thrill in aviation. The cat shot beats a Harrier VTO or VL. It doesn't have the supreme responsibility of a weapon event so is probably more enjoyable than those. The Harrier 'op launch'[2] was close – but that was because of the number of jets lined up to go at very short intervals. The cat shot is about you. The ride itself, when it comes, sits on the very edge of enjoyment and discomfort. It's like a fairground ride that has gone off the scale. It's not even at the fabled '11'[3] setting – it's more than that.

The USN deck, like any deck, is akin to a ballet. All parts working in unison. Yellow-coated marshallers directed my every move. I obeyed every signal. Full stop. No stopping and bleating about being too close to that machine, or this edge. The tempo of my heart used to increase as I got up towards the jet blast deflectors. Even

---

1 Who builds a ship with no bar? Seriously . . .
2 Line the jets up nose to tail, clear the whole lot to take off and then go at ten-second intervals.
3 Out of 10.

in the cockpit I could feel the thrust of the other jets, as my jet would thrash in their efflux. My eyes streamed as the air con delivered their exhaust gases onto my face.[4] Once it was my turn to go, I was marshalled over the jet blast deflector, which I could then see being raised again behind me. The marshaller gave me the signal to unfold my wings as he aligned me with the catapult shuttle. The yellow-coat would use hand signals above the waist for me, below the waist for everyone else. As ever, there was lots to do. While busy obeying, I was checking that the wings were locked and the big 'beer can'-sized indicator lugs were now flush with the wing, at the same time mentally rehearsing for the launch and my immediate actions thereafter. Last-chance checks abound in aviation for good reason. They save lives.

Once in the correct place, the holdback was fitted, and an extended arm from the yellow-coat, supported at the elbow by his other arm, meant 'T-Bar Down'. As the shuttle engaged the T-bar and the holdback maintained position, I felt the aircraft jolt in response. The yellow-coat then gave the signal to put the jet in tension. The oleos squatted slightly as the shuttle pulled forward and holdback stopped it going anywhere. The jet felt like a greyhound in the traps. Then came the moment that would raise the hairs on any arm or neck. The yellow-coat to the left gave me the signal of both hands beating open palm on his chest. That meant 'You're my little puppy dog now.' I just stared back, but that chest beating

4 Small trick. Hold your O2 mask just away from your face and douse your eyes in O2-rich scrubbed air. Stops them streaming.

sent shivers up and down my spine every time I saw it. Then he pointed at my aircraft and gave me the wind-up signal. Mil power.[5] Engines now joining in. Jet absolutely ready to go. Anywhere else, we'd already be in the middle or latter stages of a take-off run, but here on the cat, under tension, with power on, it was just an almighty tug of war – with a resultant of zero. Thus at full power the job was to take the stick to all four corners, to go to full deflection on the rudders – if I didn't someone watching would think that I had a problem and stop the launch. Nothing left to check. I locked my left arm to make sure the throttle didn't go anywhere. Eyeballed the yellow-coat. Saluted.[6] Right hand on towel rail. Head back. Waited . . . Waited . . . Cat shot.

The cat shot was tremendous. I'm not the smallest of pilots. Even so, it was enough to throw my mask to the side slightly. Spit I didn't know about was thrown across my cheek. My feet came off the pedals momentarily, my head forced back into the seat box, my left hand struggled to keep the throttle forward despite my arm being locked and my elbow being pressed hard against the cockpit wall. This sometimes led to over-compensation, as my left hand pushed through the detent between MIL and MAX, giving the jet a 'stroke of blower' or afterburner. If you ever get a chance to 'light the blowers', take it. There's no useful analogy, but it feels a bit like the jet has decided that laws of physics are no longer interesting and it's just going to do its own thing. Going

5 Full power, but without after-burner.
6 Or at night put your lights to STEADY BRIGHT.

off the end of the boat as the shuttle run stopped felt like flying into a wall. No more assistance, I was flying, and the first thing to do was a clearing turn – preferably as the rear wheels came off the deck.[7] Gear up, flap up. Now to fly the departure profile for the conditions. Who wouldn't have a smile on their face? Well, me, as I knew that I'd just done the easiest bit. I knew that now came the rough and tumble of the mission and then the usual challenges of getting a jet back on board.

To fly with the USN was one big, rare treat. If, as a VSTOL pilot, you get offered the chance to go and fly cat and trap, and you turn it down, I suspect St Peter would actually bar you from entering the Pearly Gates as you are clearly a bit of a twat. VSTOL has its benefits. The USN can actually learn stuff from other forces, but by and large this was a chance to come and fly with the big boys after a career of wishing for a big deck and a great aeroplane. And what an aeroplane. The Lot 33 Super Hornets that VFA-25, the 'Fist of the Fleet', flew were brand spanking new. They had everything we could want in a fighter. A simply staggering AESA radar, towed decoys, joint helmet-mounted cueing system, a jammer, AIM-9X. We even had the world's most ridiculous air-to-air load out of 'Ten Zero Two Plus': ten AMRAAM, two AIM-9X and a gun. The gun carried a manly 412 rounds of ammunition. There was no alpha limit on the aeroplane. We could run out supersonic. Yes, jets went faster. Yes, at 7.5 G some jets could pull more – but because we could sit at a very high angle of

7 No matter what you are told – looking cool is a prerequisite to winning.

attack in full after-burner we could match or beat them in a slow fight and could turn inside a rate fighter . . . and with the off boresight capability of AIM-9X that bordered on sheer lunacy – who gave a shit about rate fighters?! The best thing about the aeroplane was how it all came together. How the radar track and the Identification Friend or Foe hit were always in synch. How the air-to-surface weapons page was only a button push away and was the same for all the weapons. My opinion, at the end of a career that had spanned Sea Harrier and Harrier, was that there was simply no better Gen 4 jet in the world in which to go to war. Others will disagree, and that is their prerogative. As ever, if you've deserved your opinion, I will listen to it.

The USN guys themselves were, generally, spectacularly high-grade humans. Yes, there were knobs, except for on VFA-25, where there really weren't. As the old saying goes, 'if you can't work out who the squadron cock is – it's probably you' . . . so I guess it was me.

My CO on VFA-25 was a confident, humble, simply great person. He also kicked the shit out of me on our first hop together, and I will not forget the time I got a shot off at him later in my tour. On the first occasion, I clearly remember passing each other in air combat manoeuvring training for the first time. I went pure nose high and he went low and left. I lost sight . . . and lost. On the second, I did get that shot off – but mainly because he (wrongly) assumed that I was in good order. He was coming down the hill almost vertically, and I was going up to meet him. Because I was going up, my energy should have suited a single-circle fight – trying to turn inside his turn radius – and his a two-circle fight where he was trying to turn quicker than me. To force the fight the way I wanted it, I was always likely to 'early turn', which meant he had to counter my early turn with (you guessed it) an early turn. Unbeknownst to the skipper, though, I had completely thonged away my energy and was rapidly coming to a halt as I came up the hill towards him. So when he 'early turned' he was still out in front of me. Fox 2. I don't say this to brag. It was only my buffoonery that worked out. I was at one of those odd positions on the luck vs talent curve, and he was that good a pilot that a single cheeky Fox 2 on him was a real career highlight.

It got better.

The previous ops officer had arranged for us to go to Red Flag. We were off to Nevada.

If you ever feel that you're waning slightly, that life's marching on, get yourself in a Super Hornet and blast out of Nellis to the north-east and drink it all in. You'll feel the aggression come flooding back. You'll feel the fangs come out. You'll be back in the game.

As we turned hot for the last time in the hold and flew to the push point (the mission start point), our simply incredible APG-79s were scanning the whole of the airspace ahead of us. We could clearly see that the enemy had six different elements in the leading edge with more behind. As the AWACS gave us the picture, Fluffer summed things up brilliantly on the second radio. 'Oh my God!' came the cry. However, whilst there were a lot of jets out there, they really only represented targets. We had APG-79 and MIDS:[8] we could see everything and could tell everyone else as well. We had enough situational awareness that it was oozing from the screens – we could have bottled the stuff and sold it to passing Tornados. Swift was my leader, and he took advantage of the recently cleared 10 x AMRAAM fit to keep shooting. When it became sensible, he turned cold and positioned behind me; I then became the front fighter of our element. The aircraft displayed who you were looking at and who you were shooting on the tactical displays of the whole formation. We also had the world's finest trump card at our disposal. Behind the incredibly capable F/A-18E sat the world police – F-22 Raptor. Whenever we got a little out of synch, or there were simply too many Red Air in one particular place, the Raptor boys patted the fire out. We shattered the enemy with hammer blows, they mopped up the pieces. Where the fuck are they, I kept thinking, unable to acquire one visually – but they were there for sure! What was wonderful about the first mission was that we had Fluffer, a TOPGUN and USMC WTI grad, Taylor, an experienced leader, me and Mark. Lord knows how Mark coped – he was pretty much straight out of the box, and this was high-end stuff – but cope he did. I hadn't heard him take a shot despite the other three of us essentially using the 'Lebanese Unload'[9] technique to send the vast majority

8 Multifunction Information Distribution System or Link-16. What I could see, the whole mission could see. What my friends were attacking was all displayed simply on the tactical display in front of me.
9 Just fire everything!

of our thirty simulated AMRAAMs down range. As the battle subsided and the Red Air started going home, the Raptors started to mid-mission tank, and there was time to take stock. At about this time, Mark – who had been doing a great job of simply supporting Fluffer – at last piped up, stammering through a description of the two live Red Air he could see, the usually excellent USN comm breaking down delightfully.

'I have two contacts, cold at bullseye 280 at 60.' Then a pause. 'It's the only live group.'

'Well, shoot them, then!' came the concise but helpful advice from Fluffer.

Which he duly did. Good lad. For a first tourist to have been put into that maelstrom and to keep up with things while he heard his formation whaling away with gay abandon was excellent. To get a couple of kills in the end was great, even if he did announce things a little sheepishly! On the plus side, he didn't have many shots to QA before the debrief – we had loads!

I simply loved the furnace of a large force exercise. It finds the warrior in you, rips the vestige of malaise away and puts a smile back on the most jaded face. Particularly if you're in the world's finest self-escort strike fighter. This shit, short of war, is the business. And we were very, very good at it. In our final push, we and the Raptors rolled back the greatest threat and highest numbers Nellis could throw at us without a single loss. In the debrief, Mig 1 had stopped the tape at a certain point and said, 'At about this point I just wanted to go home – because we were getting smashed.' He was right.

Every Red aircraft died. Every regenerating aircraft died. It was a good day for Blue Air.

As I walked down the corridor, I had a wonderfully American conversation with the USAF colonel who was Commander of the Air Group (or whatever the USAF call it), who said, 'You guys are killers, man. Evil mother-fuckers. What you just did was so beautiful I was crying watching it!'

We'll take that.

Things appeared to be going swimmingly until two things happened in quick succession. Of the eight commanders in the Royal Navy with Fixed Wing experience, two left at once. I got promoted to commander at about the same time. That left the Navy with a manning problem and me with a career problem. It was time to return home. At about this point I sensed that the system no longer supported me in promotion and appointment decisions, judging that there were more worthy cases stacking up behind me. In the end, the answer was actually very simple. If I couldn't drive the fight, it was time to leave. Far better to walk off with a full dit cauldron and many happy memories than stay an hour too long and tarnish the whole experience.

I was done.

32. Reflection

Raising a glass to the single-seat
maritime fighter pilots, particularly those in
marshal, out there somewhere, right now.

Above all else, a fighter pilot must possess the ability to be highly, but realistically, self-critical. To that I would add confident, decisive and preferably humble. Plenty of my forebears could not manage confident without arrogance; humility is a far more becoming characteristic. If you're good enough, you don't need to tell anyone how good you are. Anyone that purports to be 'the best' is likely a complete turkey. Another critical attribute for a fighter pilot is judgement. He or she needs to know what's important and what isn't, and to know the important stuff inside out.

I've been critical and even scathing of both my own and others' performances. Consider this, though. RAF Valley trains the UK's fighter pilots. In my day, RAF Valley seemed to continually fail to reach its target of producing sixty fighter pilots in any given year. So this was then reduced to an aspiration to produce forty – some of whom would fail before making it to the frontline. Even at the higher target, Valley would only churn out 240 fighter pilots every four years – approximately 10 per cent of whom didn't make it to a frontline squadron. That would leave 216. At the more realistic, but still aspirational, forty per year mark this is only 144 – less than half the number of athletes we send to the summer Olympics. That's the sort of performance benchmark we're talking about, and the context in which I would like my criticisms and observations to be taken. In the UK, about 700,000 people are born each year, from which we produce about thirty-five frontline fast jet pilots: one in 20,000 people.

Of those progressing through flying training in my day, just one in ten or thereabouts went through 899 Naval Air Squadron to become Sea Harrier pilots.

You never know what your standing is in a community. It's not something you can reach out and touch. It's what people say about you when you're not there. It's how the junior guys discuss you when they're playing 'best fantasy fourship'. Your standing is what feeds your formation's confidence as you plan for a tricky mission. It's what causes the jets to snuggle up in the crap weather. It takes a career to build and can be completely gone in a single second. Shattered at a single stroke of buffoonery or dishonesty. It's a blend of credibility, character, manner, skill and experience. No living fighter pilot knows what their standing is or was, but most have an idea. An inkling. I'd like to think mine's OK. I hope so. But you'll have to ask someone else.

Despite no end of frustrations, I had a great time in the Royal Navy. The good always vastly outweighed the bad. I was fortunate enough to fly three truly great aircraft types – with truly great people. I always saw myself as an operator as opposed to an aviator, because operating the jets was what mattered. Slipping the surly bonds was fun, but it really didn't.

Through a combination of hard work and a sprinkling of good luck I took both VSTOL and conventional jets to the deck by day and night, over four frontline tours, served as an instructor and delivered some pain onto Her Majesty's foes. This all seemed pretty average at the time, but the more I think about it, it was only by dint of having a skewed idea of what average was. I picked up a gallantry award – entry level, and very much due to the circumstances. I did only what any Harrier pilot would have done, but I'd rather have it than not.

It's hard to be categorical about my best moment in the RN. My first trap in a T-45 is definitely up there; my first ever deck landing in the FA2, my first live drop in Now Zad, the time F3[1] took me to my children's school in a Lynx and my short conversation at Timmy Horton's with the bloke who thought that we'd saved him[2] would also all be in the running. However, tying for first place is that moment in a dusty valley somewhere near Qalat when the firing had stopped and the JTACs could speak with normal tones and breathing rate – which meant that Simon and I had done our duty. Sharing the top spot: my final handling test at 899 NAS, on the very short taxi from Charlie Pad to the 899 dispersal, when I found out I was a Sea Harrier pilot.

---

1 The cruel, inaccurate and grammatically woeful abbreviation for Fat Fucker Phil.
2 Still not 100 per cent convinced that it was Simon and me, but it was one of our bunch and nice nonetheless.

Postscript

I could do with a drink.

As I pen these last few words, the Taliban are now back in control of Kabul. The situation is pretty much exactly the same as it was before we, the Coalition, went to war in Afghanistan. As I sit here now, some years later, having watched recent events unfold, I am aghast that the Taliban have swept once more across Afghanistan, baffled at the speed of collapse of the Afghan forces but also at the unseemly rush of the West to be rid of the problem.

The chaos at Kabul and the foreboding news blackout from the rest of the country engendered reactions of sadness for the Afghans, anger and disappointment. If ever there was a physical frontline we ought to man, or a fight we ought to commit to, then a stand against an enemy practising medieval cruelty would seem to offer a perfect opportunity. If you do have a £40 billion defence budget, how evil, and where, does someone have to be for you to fight them? If you had to pick one group to stand in front of and say, 'Sorry, but you will not pass,' surely the Taliban come near the top of the list? And let's be clear, a leopard doesn't change its spots. This bunch are the same sadistic despots as their forebears.

I wrote home from KAF, and indeed noted earlier in this book, that I thought the military presence in Afghanistan should only have been a facet of a broader campaign. I still think that, and I think that's the reason

347

we eventually failed. We brought security, but pain. Cash, but corruption. I addressed a small assembly of folk near Cottesmore once and said that one of the reasons I enjoyed my time in Afghanistan was the sense of it being a great undertaking. As it turns out, well within the military's compass at a tactical level but far too great an undertaking for politicians and some military leaders.

The truly ridiculous part of the story is that the US has decided to end the so-called 'Forever Wars', and its doctrine is now firmly set on state versus state conflict and sub-threshold contest. We're copying them. The threat is Russia and China. Russia and China have filled the void in Afghanistan. They have dialogue with the Taliban and have emissaries in the country. The US and her allies have lost the first round of the new age of state-on-state conflict. Hands down. These allies of the US cannot act on their own, of course, which is another hard truth.

There will be countless tomes written on our failure in Afghanistan and the humiliating end of our presence there. Some will prefer a positive view – that a ten-year glimpse of freedom was better than none at all and that while we failed strategically we can look back fondly on tactical success. I don't share that view. For my part, I would simply say that I thought it was the right fight to be in. However, there's not much you can do as a military practitioner if a myriad other factors are not looked after by others. Personally, I don't think that the tariff to endure was too high. Particularly when you consider what the US and her allies will now spend to rebalance the strategic shock of their opponents being pivotal in central Asia.

As far as an egress goes, you can talk it up as an air mobility triumph as much as you want. I think that we acted at, or after, the eleventh hour and we will undoubtedly have left many behind who deserved far, far better and are now faced with unspeakable horrors. It sure feels like total defeat.

Following some purely selfish introspection, I have found that I had assumed that our operations in Afghanistan were going to be something upon which we would look back with pride, well into our twilight years. Much as the veterans of the Falklands War are, despite the horrors of conflict and harrowing memories, hopefully able to think back on a job well done. I feel that we simply didn't stand up for what was right when it mattered. I think back to why I joined up in the first place. To stand up for others and to stand against those that could do such cruel things. We've decided not to when it was absolutely within our ability to do so.

When you consider that we are back where we started, the only sensible conclusion to draw is that *our* war, in Afghanistan, was a complete waste of life, blood, tears and time.

Acknowledgements

If this book was to be dedicated to anyone, it would be to four groups of people. Those we lost along the way, those who did jobs I could never do, the high-performing community I was a part of and those who supported us doing it.

I fondly remember the superb people we lost when two 849 Naval Air Squadron Sea Kings collided in Gulf War 2; Simon the Army Air Corps pilot who died in a helicopter crash on his way back to Middle Wallop from a school visit, inspiring the next generation; Jenny and Rod of Richmond Flight.

Jak London – a Sea Harrier pilot and therefore one of our own who died at RAF Wittering – was a deity to us young pups on 800 NAS. He was once told by Wings[1] to 'have a very stern word' with me after I overshot the carrier on an awfully ill-judged approach and ended up hovering in front of it. He decided that instead of a stern word I should get a smile and a wink. A great man.

We also lost my best friend Kris and a super bloke called Candles many years later.

As single-seat Fixed Wing aircrew, you tend to go through life in the knowledge that you could do the jobs of most people you meet, given the right amount

---

1 Commander (Air), head of the aviation department on board an aircraft carrier.

of preparation and training. This is not true of Special Forces, Bomb Disposal, the Parachute Regiment and the Royal Marines. To them I humbly doff my cap.

The team I was part of – the maritime single-seaters who are able to operate on their own, to and from aircraft carriers by day and night – are a special bunch. It was a privilege and a pleasure to be part of that community. Without a host of other folk, however, the maintainers, survival equipment team, the aircraft handlers, ship's company, air traffic controllers, fighter controllers and many I will forget, for which I apologize, they would amount to nothing. It's a team game.

Lastly, to those who waited at home, sometimes with an inkling of what we were up to, sometimes without a clue. They really do have the hardest job in the fleet.

Glossary

ACM	Air combat manoeuvring – visual fighting against other aeroplanes; largely the same as ACT and BFM
ACT	Air combat training
AD	Air defence – sport of kings
AMRAAM	AIM-120 advanced medium-range air-to-air missile; never go to an air-to-air fight without one
AO	Area of operations
ARH	Aircraft recovery heading – the aircraft's heading when landing on a ship that's going in the wrong direction
ASW	Anti-submarine warfare – tedium that drives its victims to window licking
AWACS	Airborne warning and control system
AWC	Air Warfare Centre
AWI	Air warfare instructor – warlord and king of all airborne combatants
BDA	Battle damage assessment
BFM	Basic fighter manoeuvres – by dint of being in a fighter, not actually that basic
BITS	Back in the saddle – rude awakening as one knocked the rust off
BOL	Saab-built infra-red countermeasure
BRA	Bearing range altitude – used to direct a single fighter onto a single enemy

BRNC	Britannia Royal Naval College
C2	Command and control
CAOC	Combined Air Ops Centre
CAP	Combat air patrol – flying at a prescribed point, waiting for the action
CAS	Close air support – weapons provided close to ground troops where close coordination is necessary and mandatory
CFI	Chief flying instructor
COMAO	Composite air operations – unruly mob of aeroplanes
Comm-out	Without radio communication – using standard procedures, hand signals or the force
CSAR	Combat search and rescue – brave, brave boys and girls tasked with recovery of isolated personnel
CVN	Nuclear aircraft carrier
CVS	Invincible class aircraft carrier – small bath tub with a tarmac roof
DACT	Dissimilar air combat training – visual fighting against someone else
DBFM	Defensive basic fighter manoeuvres – what to do when you're being killed
DFC	Designated flying course – which way Mum would be pointing for launch and recovery
DT	Dynamic target – one the CAOC hadn't planned for
EOD	Explosive Ordnance Disposal – heroes
EMCON	Emission control

FC	Fighter controller – purveyor of situational awareness
FTAP	Fuel tank air pressurization
GASO	Group Air Staff Orders
GCAS	Ground close air support – sitting at alert like a coiled spring
GCI	Ground controlled intercept – what some air forces call FCs
HE	High explosive
HUD	Head-up display
Humvee	High-mobility multipurpose wheeled vehicle
IED	Improvised explosive device
IGV	Inlet guide vanes – guide airflow into a jet engine's compressor
IMD	Intake momentum drag – in most jets no big deal, deadly in the Harrier
IN	Inertial navigation
IR	Infra-red – in weapon terms a heat-seeking weapon or 'heater'
JEFTS	Joint Elementary Flying Training School
JFH	Joint Force Harrier – a bit like an air warfare Dojo, but in Rutland
JTAC	Joint terminal attack controller
KAF	Kandahar airfield
Late Arm	The master armament switch in the Harrier; it needed to be live for stores to be released
LGB	Laser-guided bomb
LOFT	The weapons mode that allowed one to loft or throw a bomb at a target ahead
LSJ	Lifesaving jacket

MADGE	Microwave aircraft digital guidance equipment – most probably a contrived acronym but a great capability that allowed a pilot to recover in poor-weather comm-out
MAOC	Maritime Air Operations Centre – small office at back of ship with delusions of grandeur
MPC	Missile practice camp
MPCD	Multi-purpose crystal display – TV in cockpit showing whatever one selected
Mud-mover	Attack aircraft – those that move mud, usually scurrying around at low level
NAS	Naval Air Squadron – dens of iniquity, courage and brilliance
Nine-line	The nine pieces of information that a JTAC gave you prior to an attack, usually reduced to the four absolutely mandatory ones – essentially what and where the target is
OBFM	Offensive basic fighter manoeuvres – what to do when you're in control
OFT	Operational Flying Training – the grinder that was 899 NAS
OOW	Officer of the watch – sub-species able to navigate up to walking speed
PAN	A radio call announcing that one is experiencing an emergency. A watered-down Mayday.
Pickle	*Noun*: the weapon release switch; *verb*: to press this switch
PID	Positive identification – not the 100 per cent science that some assume it to be
PKM	A Russian belt-fed machine gun
QA	Quality assurance

QCVS	Queen's Commendation for Valuable Service
QFI	Qualified flying instructor – one a little too preoccupied with being airborne as opposed to what to do once airborne
QNH	The pressure setting on an altimeter such that it reads in altitude above mean sea level
QRA	Quick reaction alert – usually tasked with homeland defence
QWI	Qualified weapon instructor – the slightly less cool cousin of the AWI
Race track	A flight path that from above would look like an athletics track
RADALT	Radio altimeter – a high-fidelity method of measuring actual height above terrain
RPM	Revolutions per minute
R/T	Radio telephony – at some point someone decided that 'Are Tee' was better than simply 'radio'
RWR	Radar warning receiver – the bit of kit which told a pilot which threat systems were looking at them
SA	Situational awareness – the life blood of airborne combat
SAM	Surface-to-air missile
SHAR	Sea Harrier – arguably, after the Spitfire, the most iconic British aircraft of all time
SP	Senior pilot
STOVL	Short take-off vertical landing – very similar to V/STOL but someone with time on their hands considered it more physically correct

Symbology	The green writing, shapes and symbols projected onto the HUD
TACAN	Tactical air navigation system – which produces a range and bearing to a beacon
Tac Lead	Leader of a tactical formation; not necessarily the person who was leading at launch
TIALD	Thermal Imaging and Laser Designation – a British targeting pod
TIC	Troops in contact
TLT	Tactical leadership training
Trap	An arrested deck landing using a tailhook and wire
USAF	United States Air Force – the biggest of all the big dogs
USMC	US Marine Corps – heroes who insist on wearing camouflage cloth helmet covers
USN	United States Navy – the masters of maritime aviation. Full stop
VIFF	Vector in forward flight – complicated way of gaining a small advantage or instigating complete disaster
V/STOL	Vertical/short take-off and landing
VTO	Vertical take-off. Nozzles down. Slam
VL	Vertical landing – the back end of the 'stop then land' manoeuvre